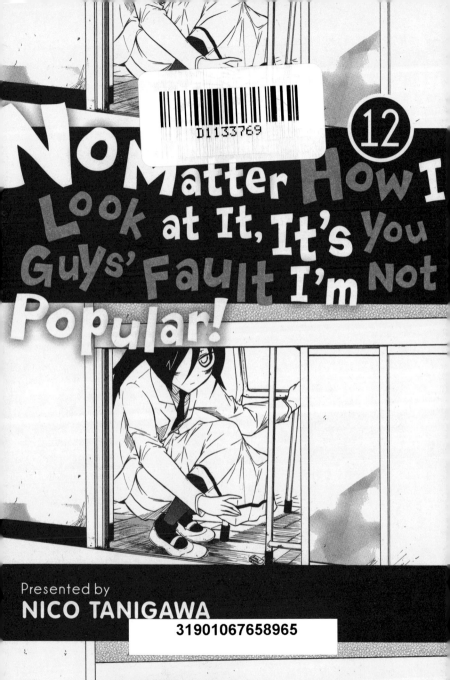

NO Matter How I Look at It, It's You Guys' Fault I'm Not Popular!

12

Presented by
NICO TANIGAWA

...AWW, IF I'D BEEN A WORM, I WOULD'VE HAD A MAN FROM THE GET-GO AND DEFINITELY HAVE HAD S●X, NOT TO MENTION KIDS...

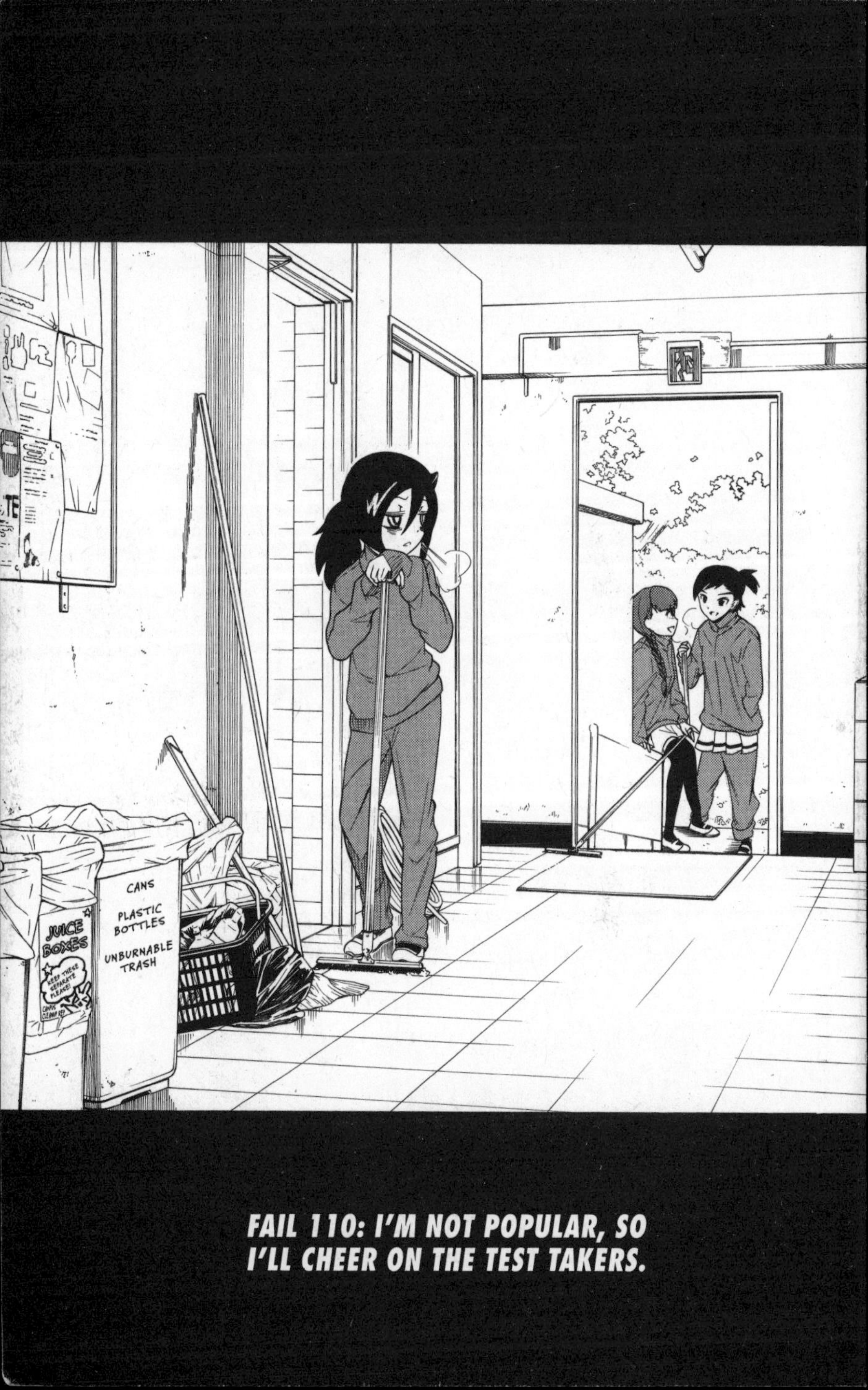
CANS
PLASTIC BOTTLES
UNBURNABLE TRASH
JUICE BOXES

FAIL 110: I'M NOT POPULAR, SO I'LL CHEER ON THE TEST TAKERS.

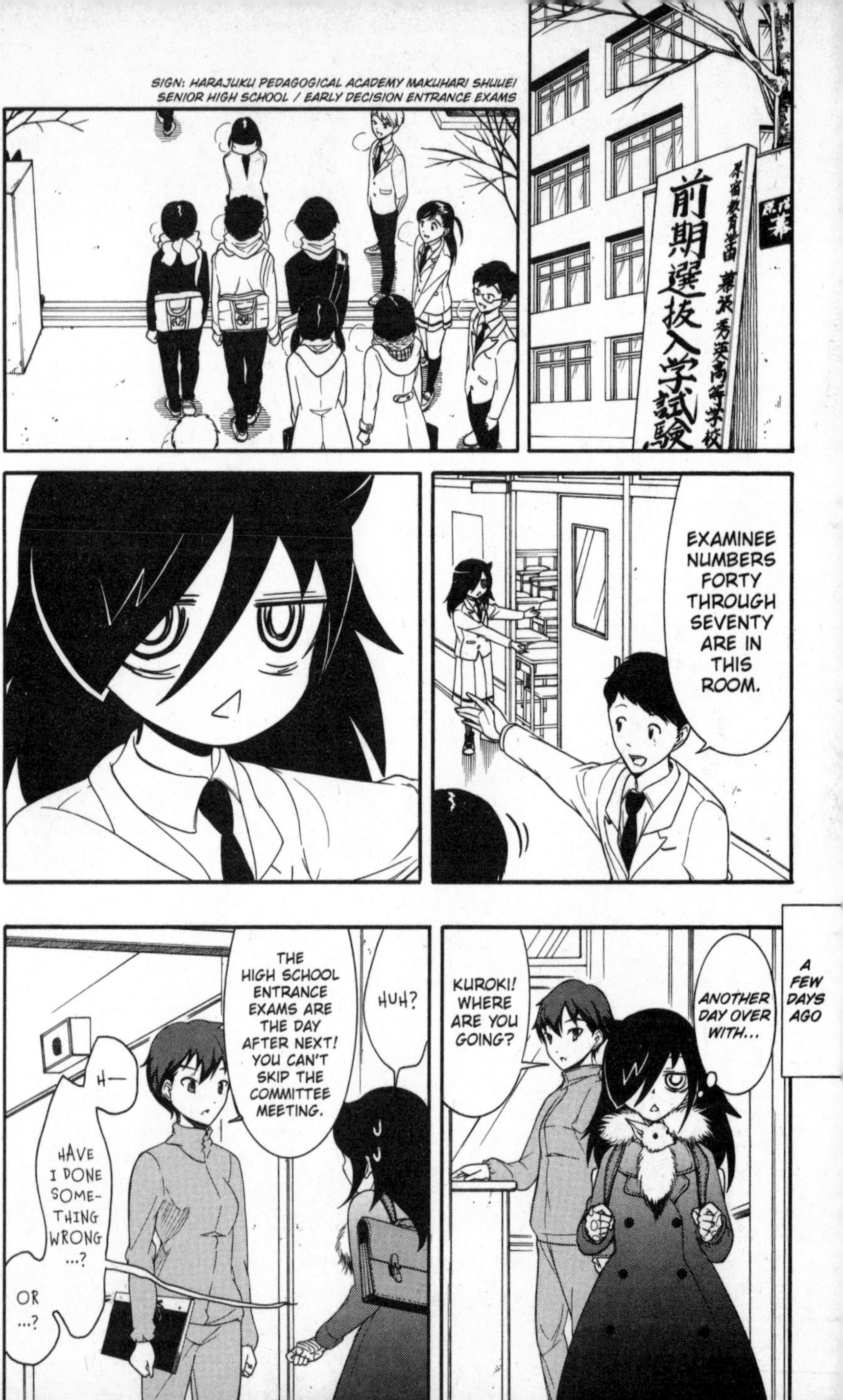

前期選抜入学試験
SIGN: HARAJUKU PEDAGOGICAL ACADEMY MAKUHARI SHUUEI SENIOR HIGH SCHOOL / EARLY DECISION ENTRANCE EXAMS
EXAMINEE NUMBERS FORTY THROUGH SEVENTY ARE IN THIS ROOM.
A FEW DAYS AGO
ANOTHER DAY OVER WITH...
KUROKI! WHERE ARE YOU GOING?
HUH?
THE HIGH SCHOOL ENTRANCE EXAMS ARE THE DAY AFTER NEXT! YOU CAN'T SKIP THE COMMITTEE MEETING.
H—
HAVE I DONE SOME-THING WRONG ...?
OR ...?

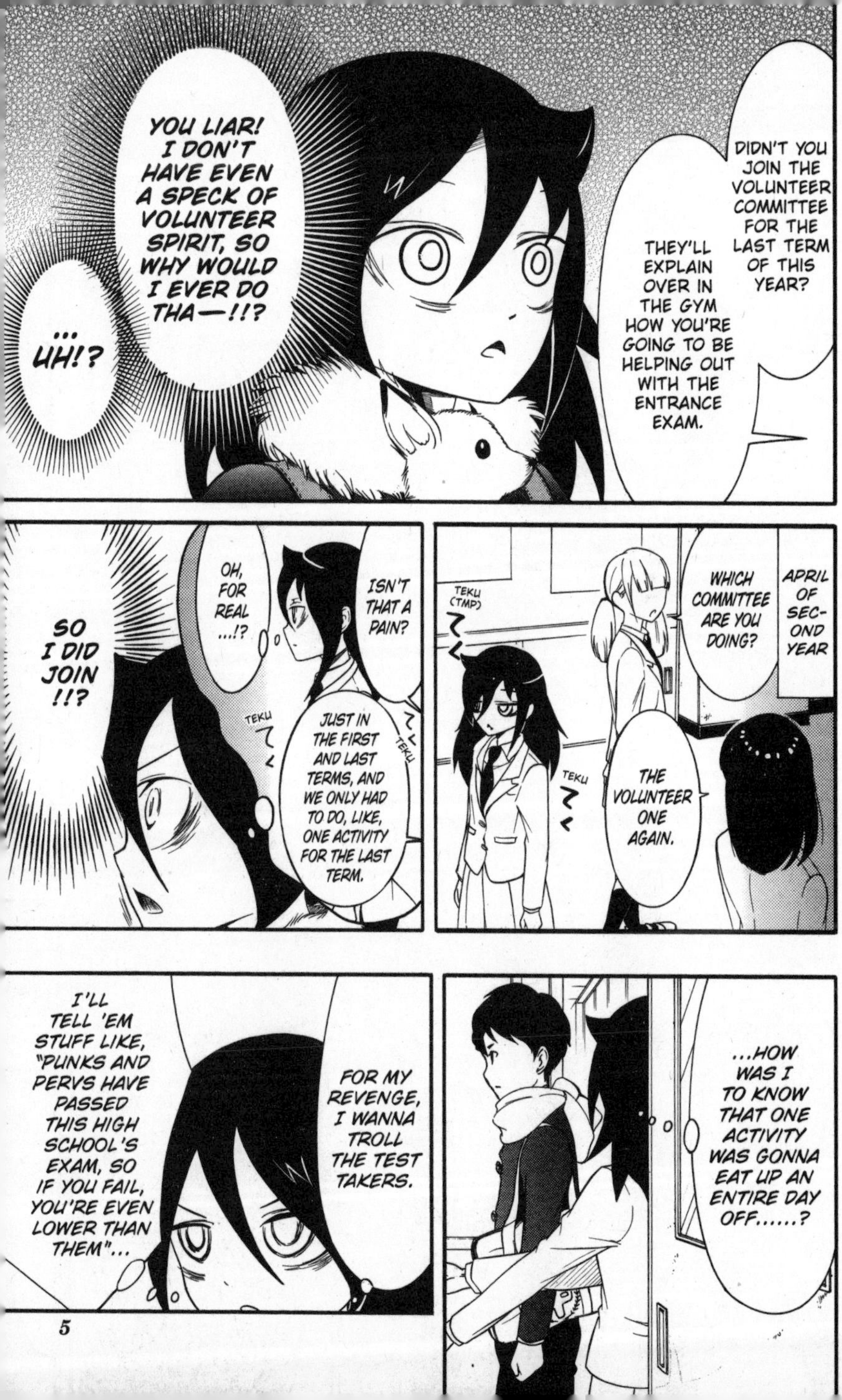
DIDN'T YOU JOIN THE VOLUNTEER COMMITTEE FOR THE LAST TERM OF THIS YEAR?
THEY'LL EXPLAIN OVER IN THE GYM HOW YOU'RE GOING TO BE HELPING OUT WITH THE ENTRANCE EXAM.
YOU LIAR! I DON'T HAVE EVEN A SPECK OF VOLUNTEER SPIRIT, SO WHY WOULD I EVER DO THA—!!?
...UH!?
APRIL OF SEC-OND YEAR
WHICH COMMITTEE ARE YOU DOING?
TEKU (TMP)
THE VOLUNTEER ONE AGAIN.
TEKU
ISN'T THAT A PAIN?
OH, FOR REAL ...!?
JUST IN THE FIRST AND LAST TERMS, AND WE ONLY HAD TO DO, LIKE, ONE ACTIVITY FOR THE LAST TERM.
TEKU
TEKU
SO I DID JOIN !!?
...HOW WAS I TO KNOW THAT ONE ACTIVITY WAS GONNA EAT UP AN ENTIRE DAY OFF......?
FOR MY REVENGE, I WANNA TROLL THE TEST TAKERS.
I'LL TELL 'EM STUFF LIKE, "PUNKS AND PERVS HAVE PASSED THIS HIGH SCHOOL'S EXAM, SO IF YOU FAIL, YOU'RE EVEN LOWER THAN THEM"...

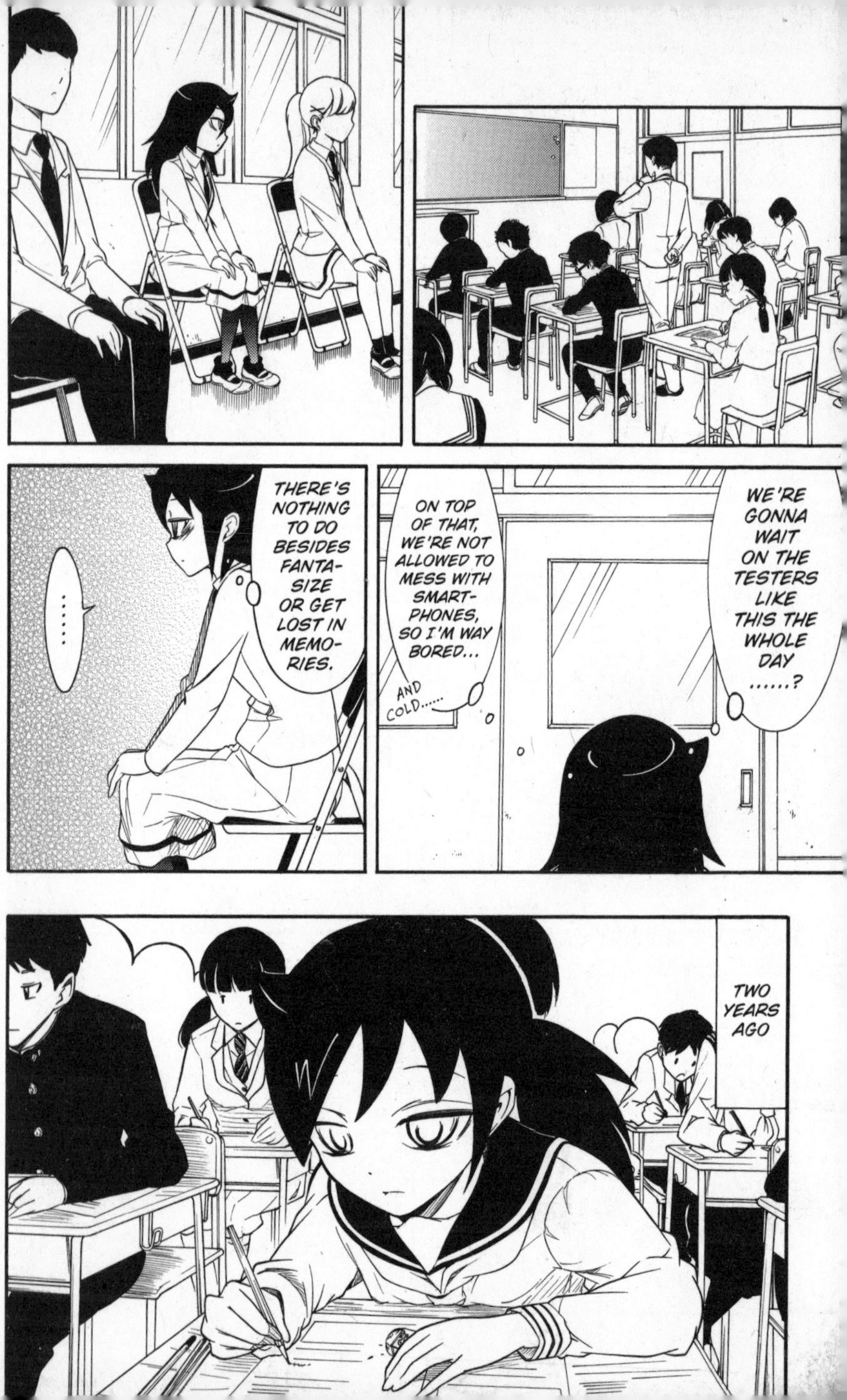
WE'RE GONNA WAIT ON THE TESTERS LIKE THIS THE WHOLE DAY ......?
ON TOP OF THAT, WE'RE NOT ALLOWED TO MESS WITH SMART-PHONES, SO I'M WAY BORED...
AND COLD......
THERE'S NOTHING TO DO BESIDES FANTA-SIZE OR GET LOST IN MEMO-RIES.
......
TWO YEARS AGO

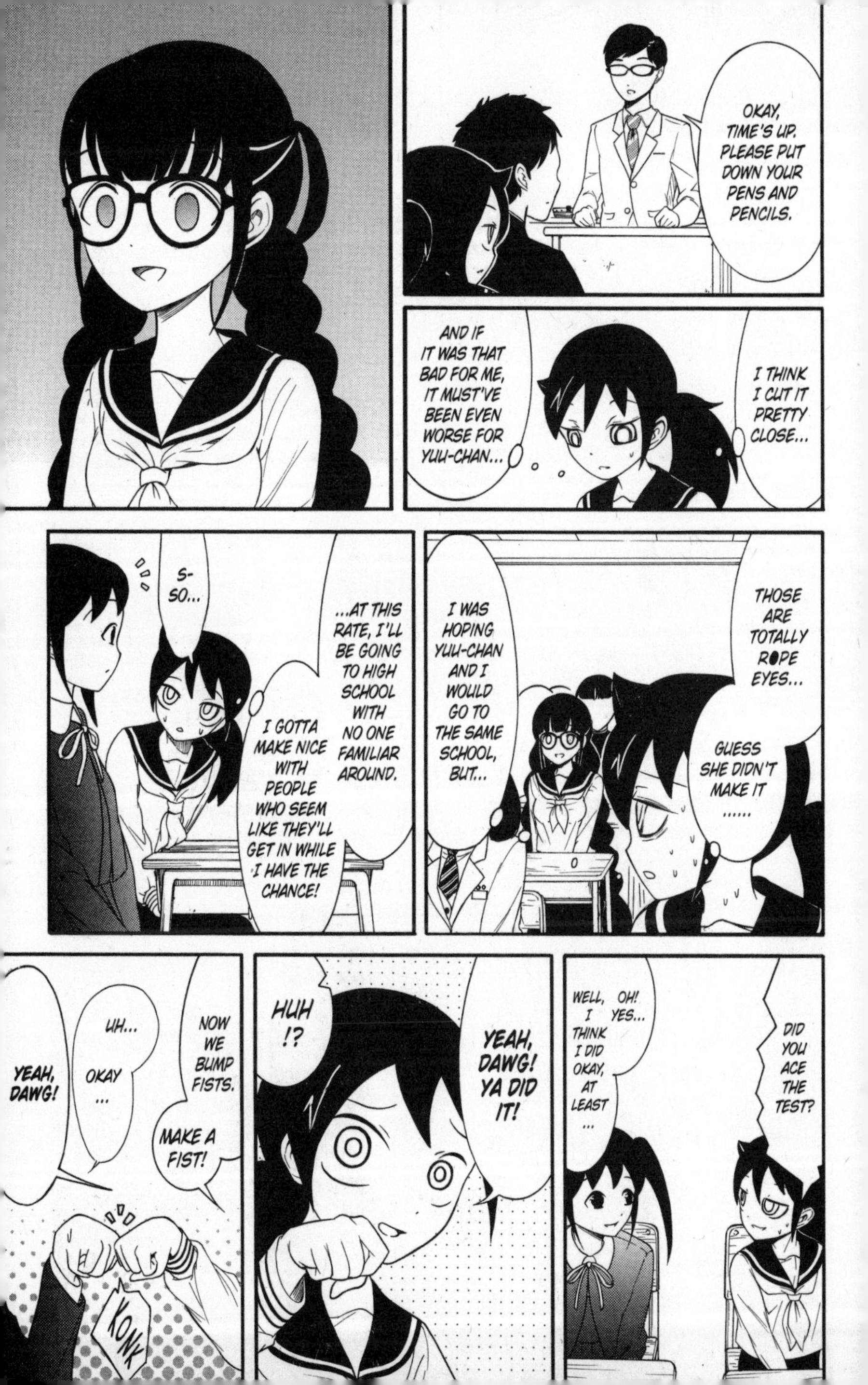
OKAY, TIME'S UP. PLEASE PUT DOWN YOUR PENS AND PENCILS.
I THINK I CUT IT PRETTY CLOSE...
AND IF IT WAS THAT BAD FOR ME, IT MUST'VE BEEN EVEN WORSE FOR YUU-CHAN...
THOSE ARE TOTALLY ROPE EYES...
GUESS SHE DIDN'T MAKE IT ......
I WAS HOPING YUU-CHAN AND I WOULD GO TO THE SAME SCHOOL, BUT...
...AT THIS RATE, I'LL BE GOING TO HIGH SCHOOL WITH NO ONE FAMILIAR AROUND.
I GOTTA MAKE NICE WITH PEOPLE WHO SEEM LIKE THEY'LL GET IN WHILE I HAVE THE CHANCE!
S-SO...
DID YOU ACE THE TEST?
OH! YES...
WELL, I THINK I DID OKAY, AT LEAST...
YEAH, DAWG! YA DID IT!
HUH!?
NOW WE BUMP FISTS.
MAKE A FIST!
UH...
OKAY...
YEAH, DAWG!
KONK

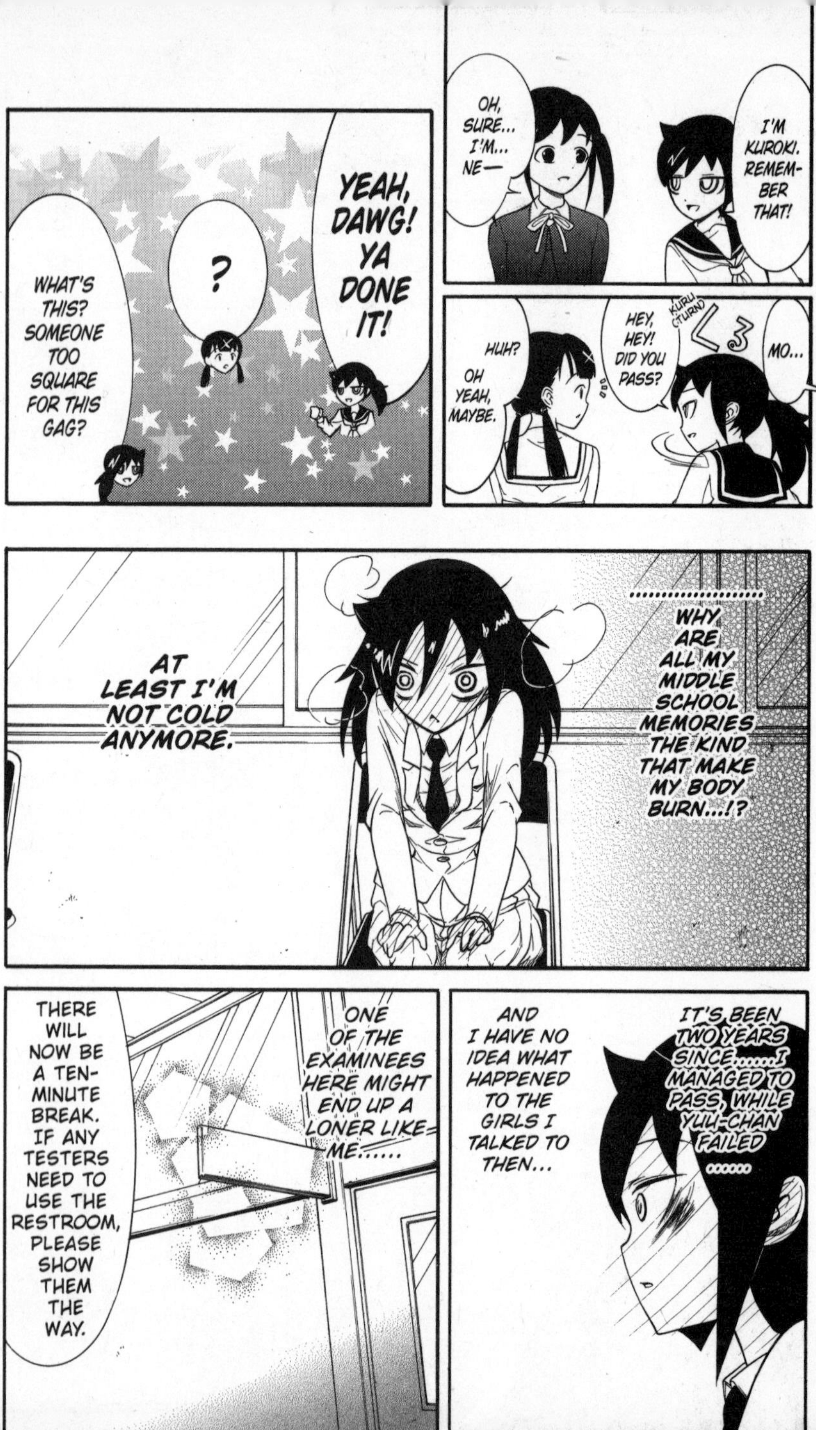
I'M KUROKI. REMEMBER THAT!
OH, SURE... I'M... NE—
MO...
KURU (TURN)
HEY, HEY! DID YOU PASS?
HUH? OH YEAH, MAYBE.
YEAH, DAWG! YA DONE IT!
?
WHAT'S THIS? SOMEONE TOO SQUARE FOR THIS GAG?
....
WHY ARE ALL MY MIDDLE SCHOOL MEMORIES THE KIND THAT MAKE MY BODY BURN...!?
AT LEAST I'M NOT COLD ANYMORE.
IT'S BEEN TWO YEARS SINCE......I MANAGED TO PASS, WHILE YUU-CHAN FAILED ......
AND I HAVE NO IDEA WHAT HAPPENED TO THE GIRLS I TALKED TO THEN...
ONE OF THE EXAMINEES HERE MIGHT END UP A LONER LIKE ME......
THERE WILL NOW BE A TEN-MINUTE BREAK. IF ANY TESTERS NEED TO USE THE RESTROOM, PLEASE SHOW THEM THE WAY.

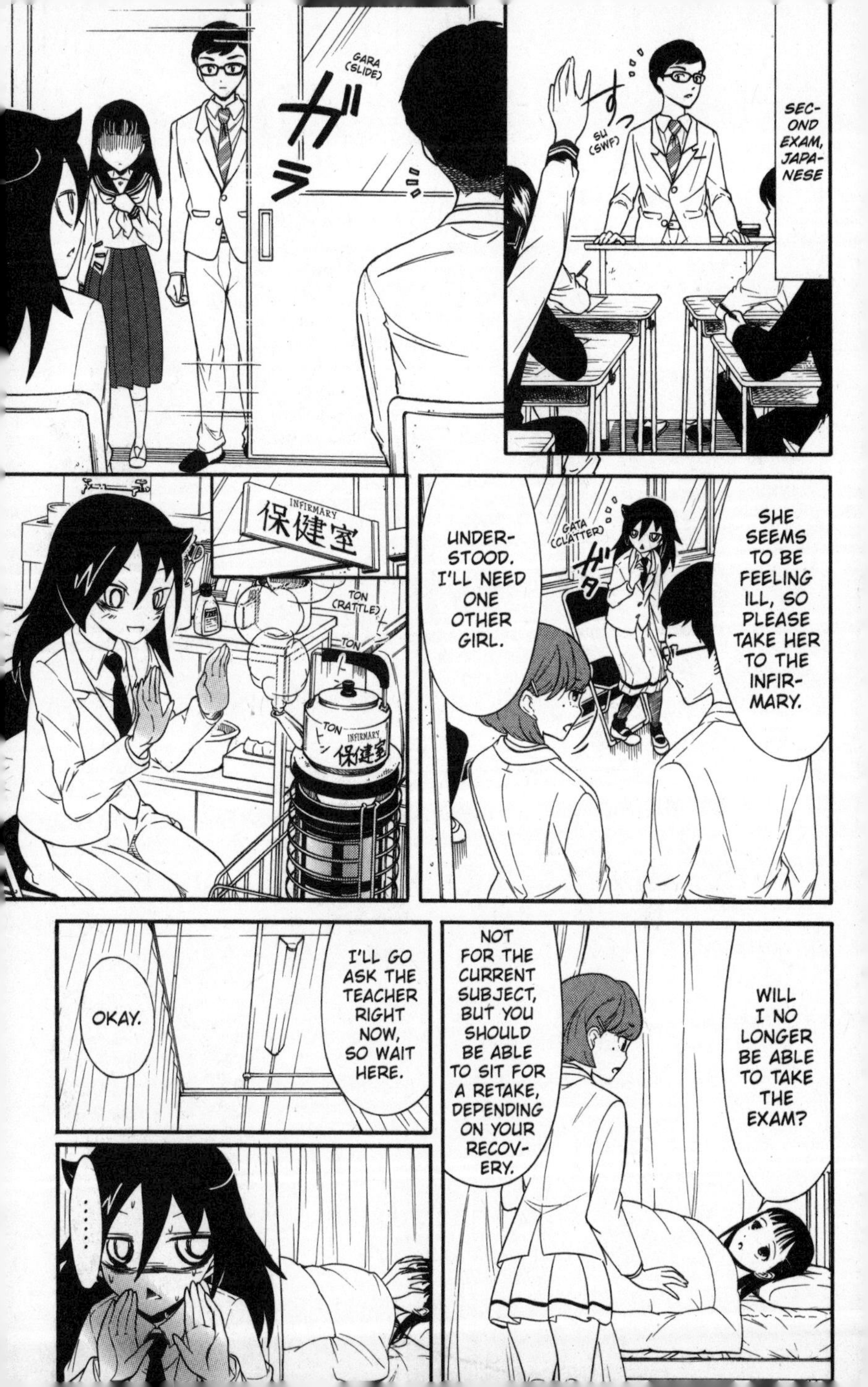
SECOND EXAM, JAPANESE
SU (SWF)
GARA (SLIDE)
SHE SEEMS TO BE FEELING ILL, SO PLEASE TAKE HER TO THE INFIRMARY.
GATA (CLATTER)
UNDERSTOOD. I'LL NEED ONE OTHER GIRL.
INFIRMARY
保健室
TON (RATTLE)
TON
TON
INFIRMARY
保健室
WILL I NO LONGER BE ABLE TO TAKE THE EXAM?
NOT FOR THE CURRENT SUBJECT, BUT YOU SHOULD BE ABLE TO SIT FOR A RETAKE, DEPENDING ON YOUR RECOVERY.
I'LL GO ASK THE TEACHER RIGHT NOW, SO WAIT HERE.
OKAY.
......

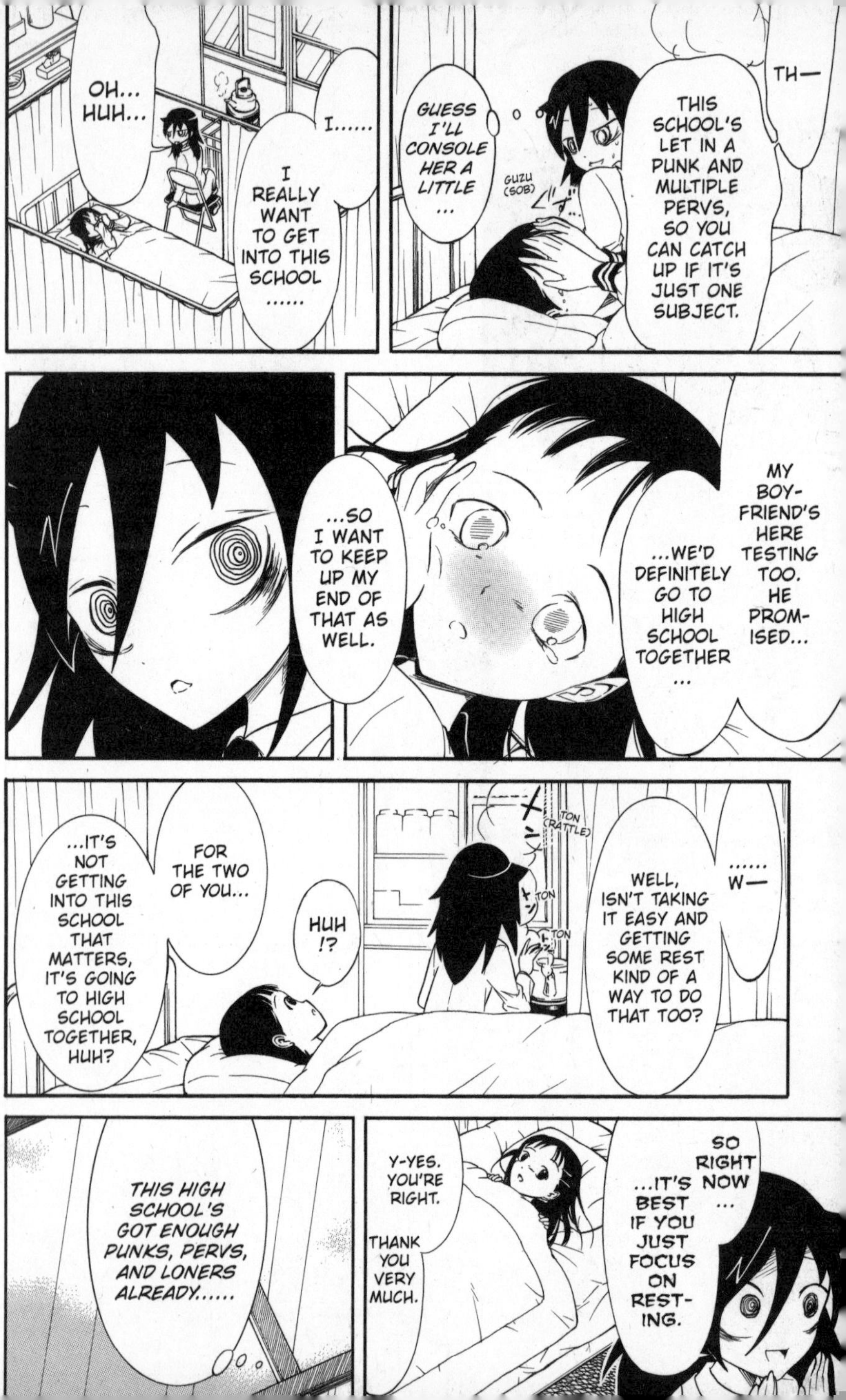

TH—
THIS SCHOOL'S LET IN A PUNK AND MULTIPLE PERVS, SO YOU CAN CATCH UP IF IT'S JUST ONE SUBJECT.
GUZU (SOB)
GUESS I'LL CONSOLE HER A LITTLE ...
I......
I REALLY WANT TO GET INTO THIS SCHOOL ......
OH... HUH...
MY BOY-FRIEND'S HERE TESTING TOO. HE PROM-ISED...
...WE'D DEFINITELY GO TO HIGH SCHOOL TOGETHER ...
...SO I WANT TO KEEP UP MY END OF THAT AS WELL.
......W—
WELL, ISN'T TAKING IT EASY AND GETTING SOME REST KIND OF A WAY TO DO THAT TOO?
TON (RATTLE)
TON
TON
HUH !?
FOR THE TWO OF YOU...
...IT'S NOT GETTING INTO THIS SCHOOL THAT MATTERS, IT'S GOING TO HIGH SCHOOL TOGETHER, HUH?
SO RIGHT NOW ...
...IT'S BEST IF YOU JUST FOCUS ON REST-ING.
Y-YES. YOU'RE RIGHT.
THANK YOU VERY MUCH.
THIS HIGH SCHOOL'S GOT ENOUGH PUNKS, PERVS, AND LONERS ALREADY......

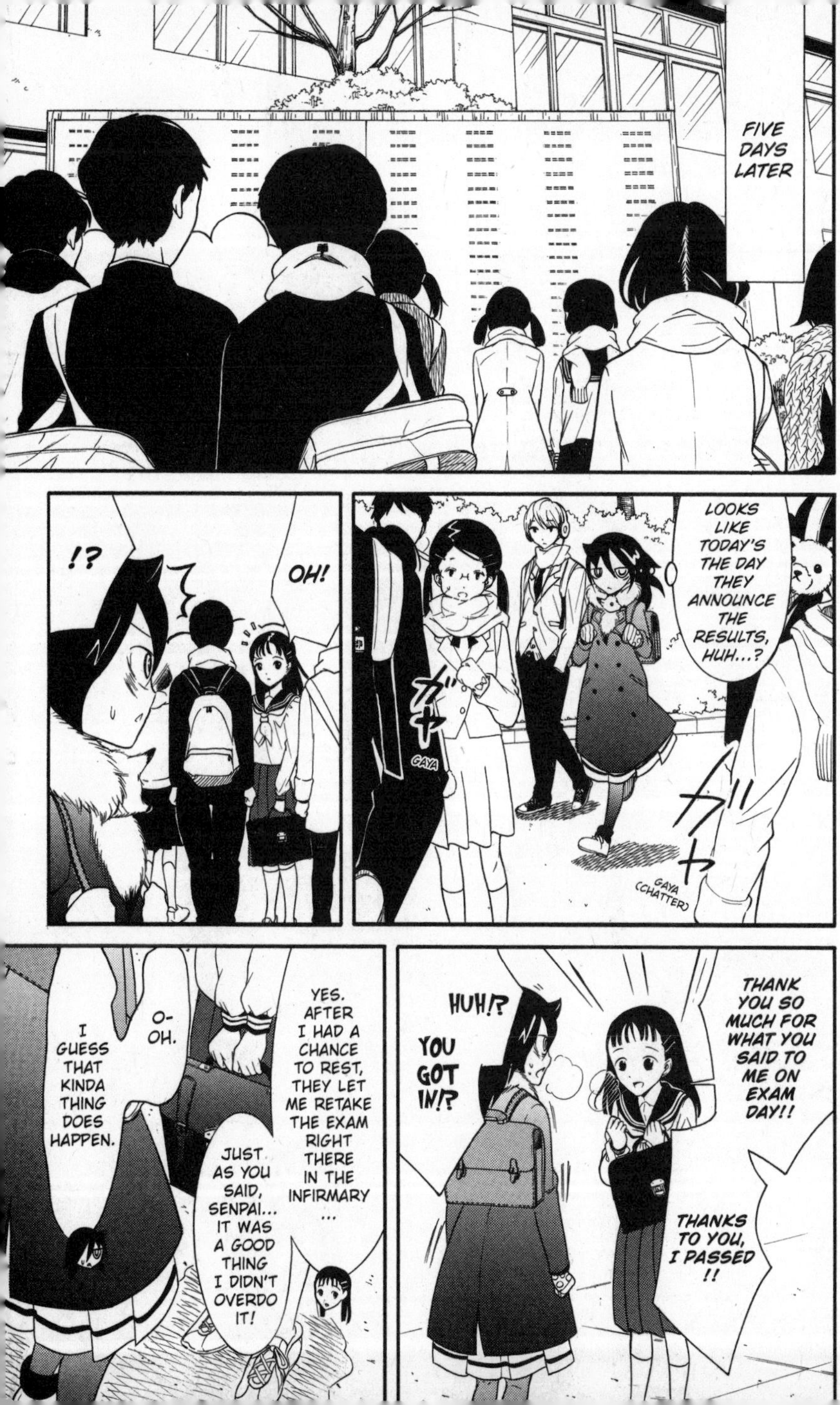

FIVE DAYS LATER
LOOKS LIKE TODAY'S THE DAY THEY ANNOUNCE THE RESULTS, HUH...?
GAYA (CHATTER)
GAYA
OH!
!?
THANK YOU SO MUCH FOR WHAT YOU SAID TO ME ON EXAM DAY!!
HUH!?
YOU GOT IN!?
THANKS TO YOU, I PASSED!!
YES. AFTER I HAD A CHANCE TO REST, THEY LET ME RETAKE THE EXAM RIGHT THERE IN THE INFIRMARY...
O-OH.
JUST AS YOU SAID, SENPAI... IT WAS A GOOD THING I DIDN'T OVERDO IT!
I GUESS THAT KINDA THING DOES HAPPEN.

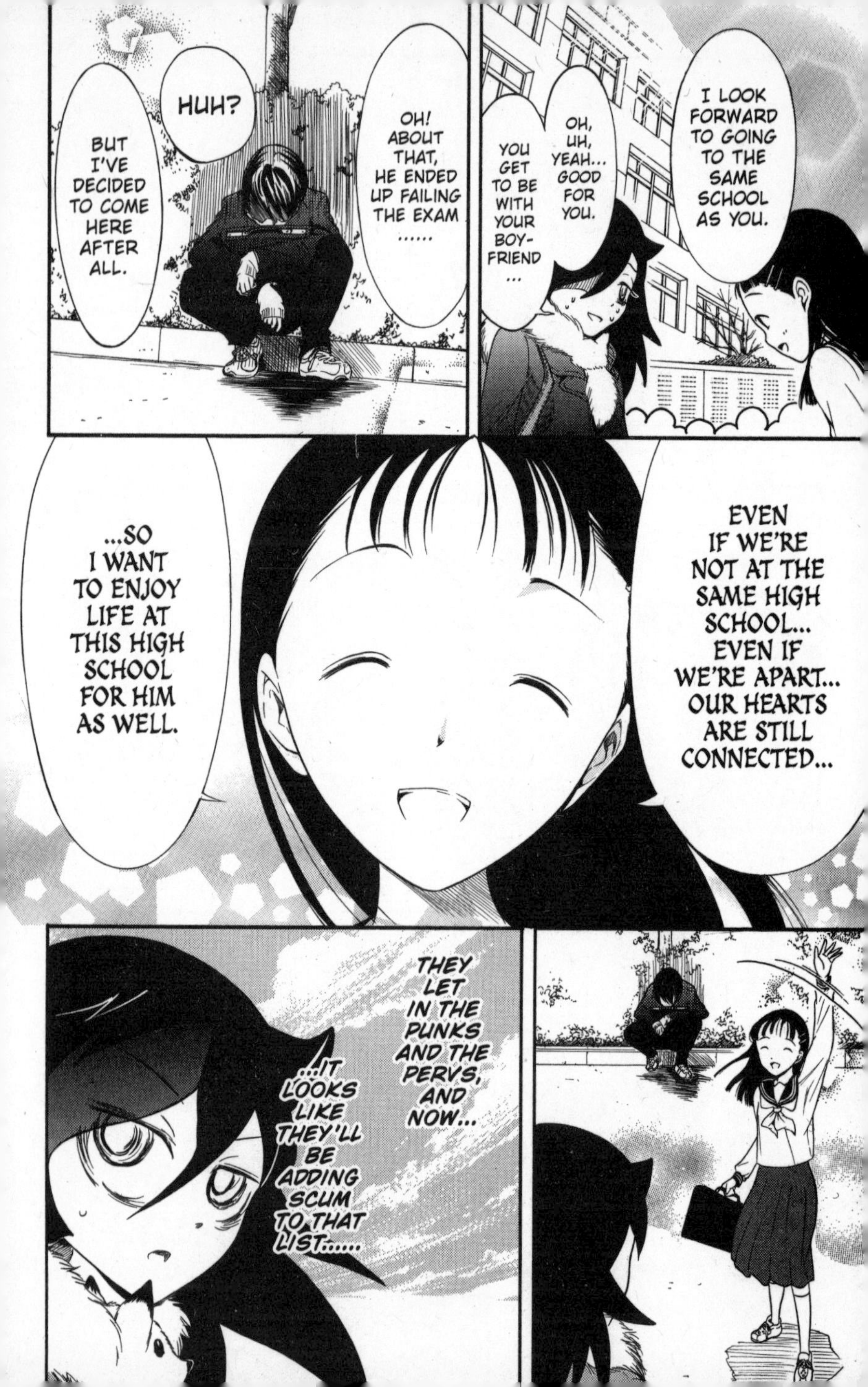
I LOOK FORWARD TO GOING TO THE SAME SCHOOL AS YOU.
OH, UH, YEAH... GOOD FOR YOU.
YOU GET TO BE WITH YOUR BOY-FRIEND...
OH! ABOUT THAT, HE ENDED UP FAILING THE EXAM ......
HUH?
BUT I'VE DECIDED TO COME HERE AFTER ALL.
EVEN IF WE'RE NOT AT THE SAME HIGH SCHOOL... EVEN IF WE'RE APART... OUR HEARTS ARE STILL CONNECTED...
...SO I WANT TO ENJOY LIFE AT THIS HIGH SCHOOL FOR HIM AS WELL.
THEY LET IN THE PUNKS AND THE PERVS, AND NOW...
...IT LOOKS LIKE THEY'LL BE ADDING SCUM TO THAT LIST......

NO Matter How I Look at It, It's You Guys' Fault I'm Not Popular!

FAIL 111: I'M NOT POPULAR, SO I'LL DO A REPLAY.

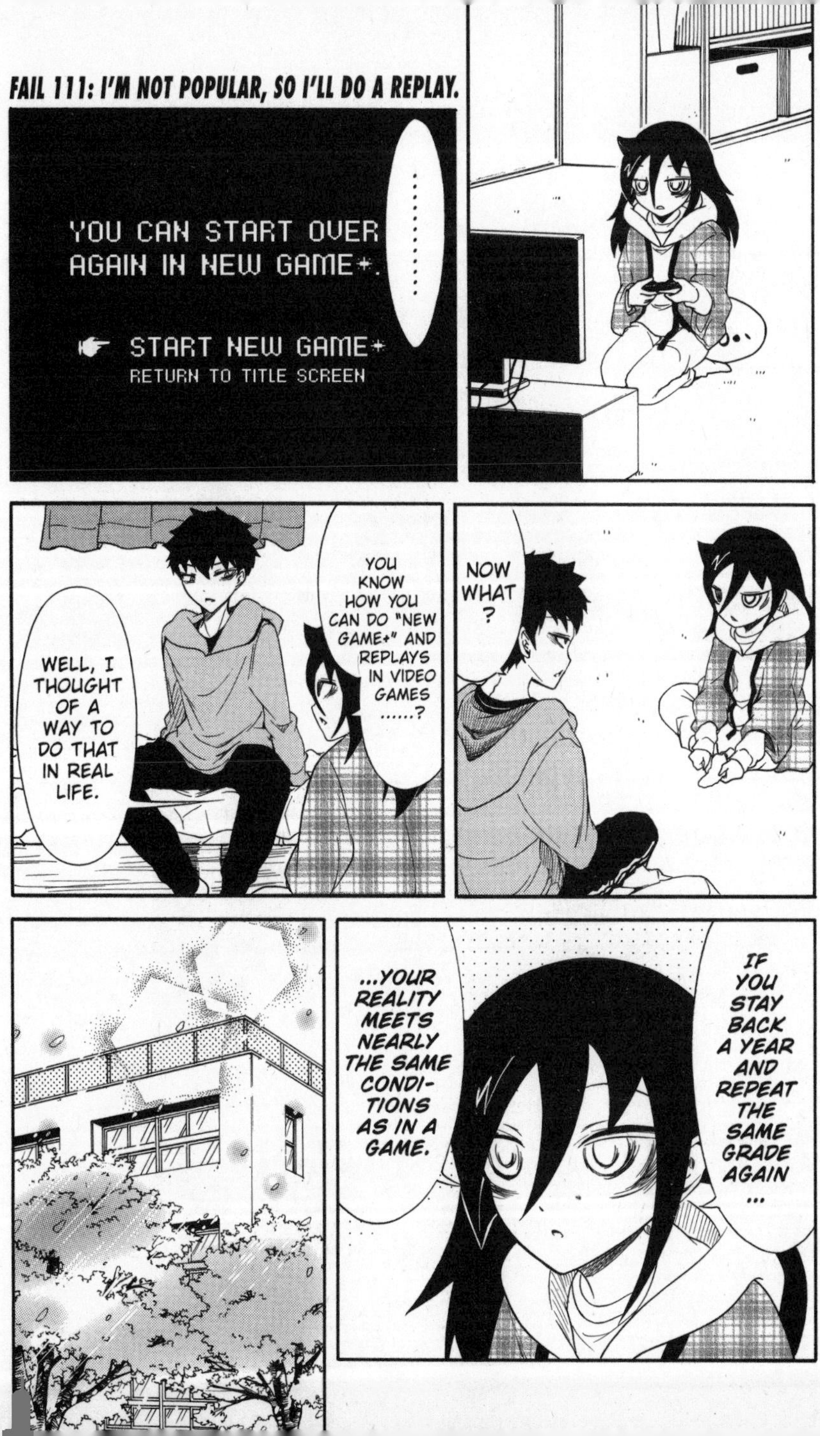
......
YOU CAN START OVER AGAIN IN NEW GAME+.
START NEW GAME+
RETURN TO TITLE SCREEN
NOW WHAT?
YOU KNOW HOW YOU CAN DO "NEW GAME+" AND REPLAYS IN VIDEO GAMES ......?
WELL, I THOUGHT OF A WAY TO DO THAT IN REAL LIFE.
IF YOU STAY BACK A YEAR AND REPEAT THE SAME GRADE AGAIN ...
...YOUR REALITY MEETS NEARLY THE SAME CONDITIONS AS IN A GAME.

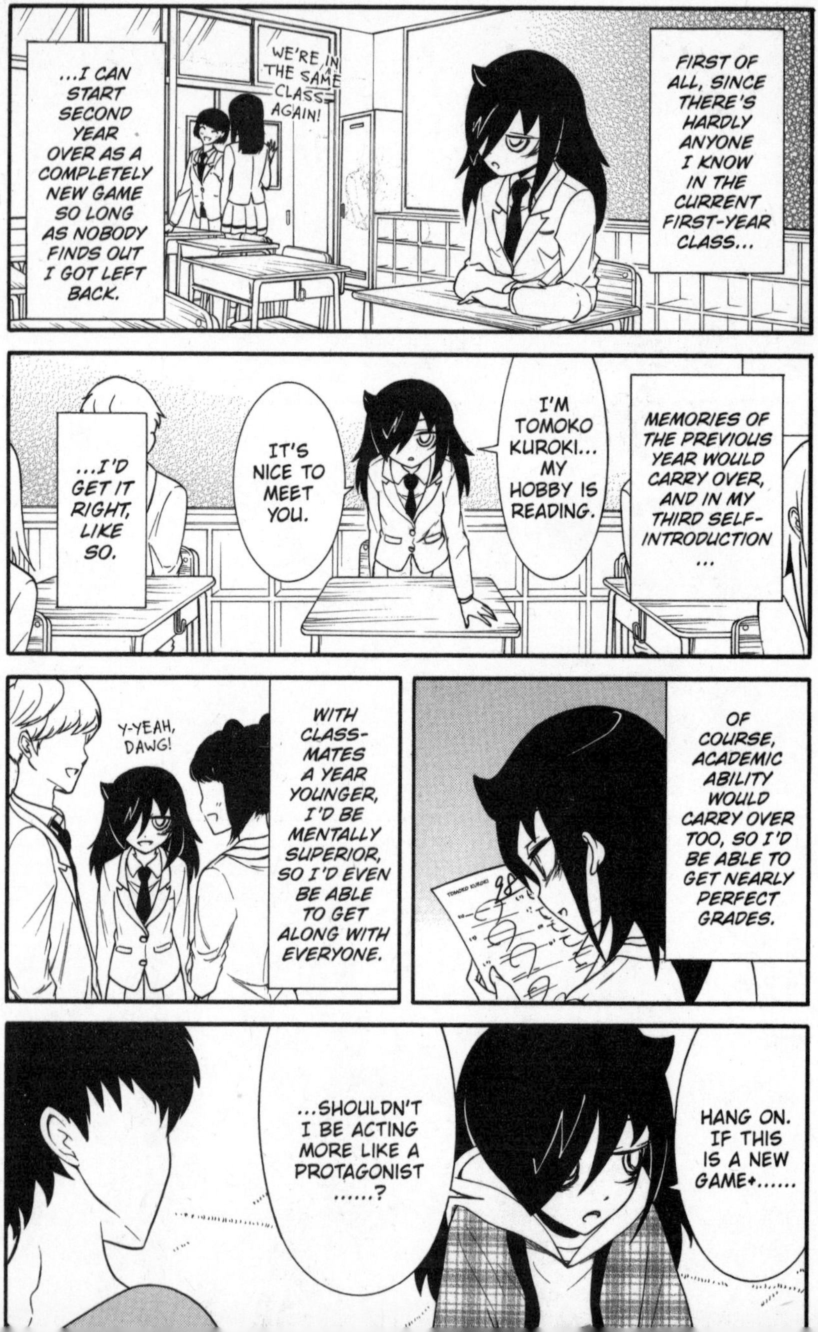
FIRST OF ALL, SINCE THERE'S HARDLY ANYONE I KNOW IN THE CURRENT FIRST-YEAR CLASS...
WE'RE IN THE SAME CLASS AGAIN!
...I CAN START SECOND YEAR OVER AS A COMPLETELY NEW GAME SO LONG AS NOBODY FINDS OUT I GOT LEFT BACK.
MEMORIES OF THE PREVIOUS YEAR WOULD CARRY OVER, AND IN MY THIRD SELF-INTRODUCTION ...
I'M TOMOKO KUROKI... MY HOBBY IS READING.
IT'S NICE TO MEET YOU.
...I'D GET IT RIGHT, LIKE SO.
OF COURSE, ACADEMIC ABILITY WOULD CARRY OVER TOO, SO I'D BE ABLE TO GET NEARLY PERFECT GRADES.
WITH CLASSMATES A YEAR YOUNGER, I'D BE MENTALLY SUPERIOR, SO I'D EVEN BE ABLE TO GET ALONG WITH EVERYONE.
Y-YEAH, DAWG!
HANG ON. IF THIS IS A NEW GAME+......
...SHOULDN'T I BE ACTING MORE LIKE A PROTAGONIST ......?

HOLD IT, TOMOKO KUROKI!!

ZAWA! | ZAWA (MURMUR)

3	2	1
MAKI SAKAI	TOMOKO KUROKI	
486	492	

How come her grades are so good?

HISO HISO (WHISPER) Kuroki-san's always sleeping in class...

OH, GOOD GRIEF...

YOU TOOK THE TOP SPOT IN OUR GRADE, AND YOU BEAT ME, SO LOOK HAPPIER THAN THAT!!

WHO CARES? I'LL BEAT HER NEXT TIME FOR SURE!

GOOD GRIEF... GOOD GRIEF... OH...

STILL, JUST WHO IS THAT GIRL ANYWAY...?

SHE SHOWS NO SIGN OF MAKING AN EFFORT, YET SHE'S ALWAYS TOPS IN OUR GRADE.

SHUT UP! NUMBER THREE IN OUR YEAR DOESN'T GET A SAY!

HEY! STOP IT, SAKAI. DON'T RAG ON KUROKI.

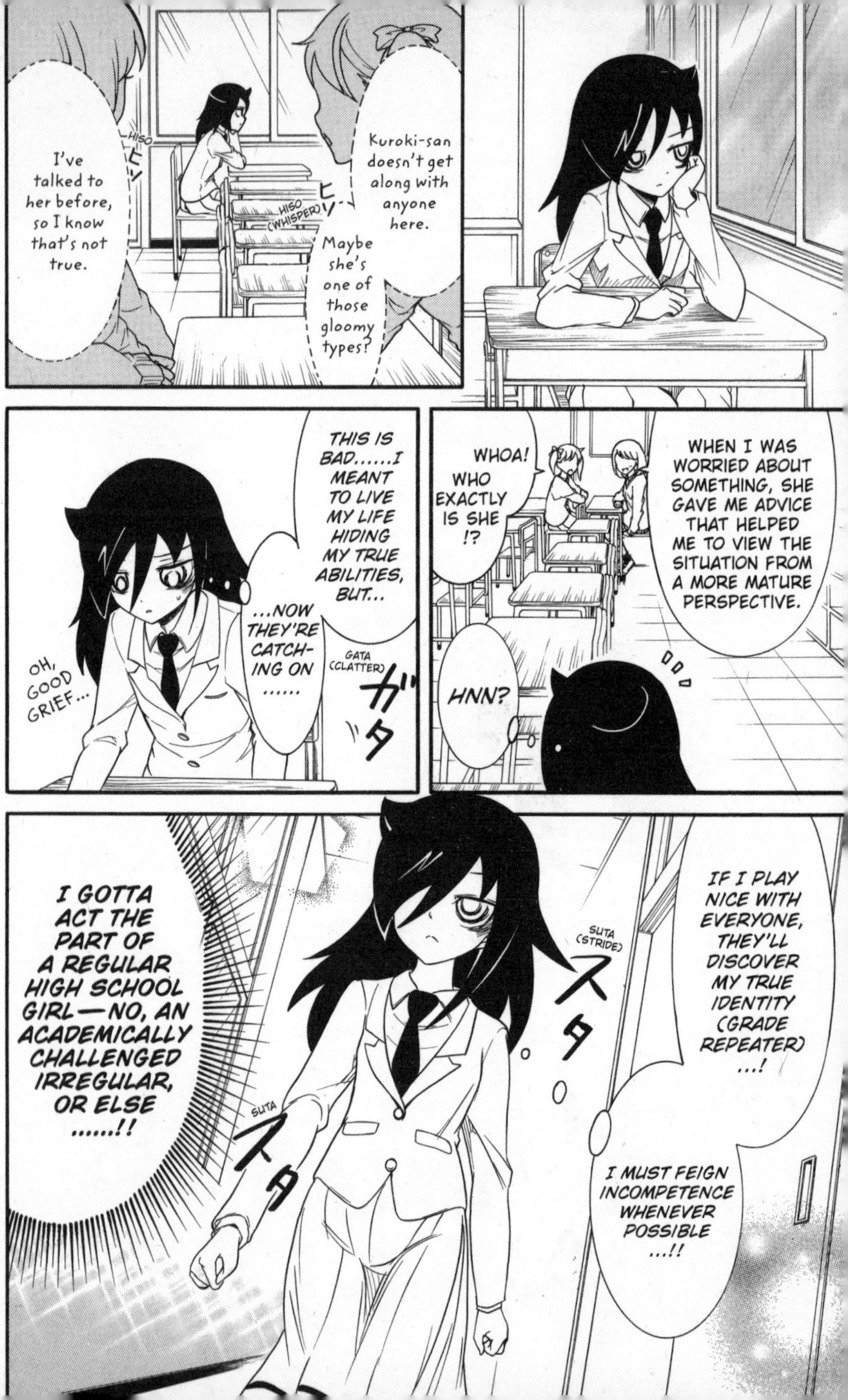
Kuroki-san doesn't get along with anyone here.
Maybe she's one of those gloomy types?
HISO (WHISPER)
HISO
I've talked to her before, so I know that's not true.
WHEN I WAS WORRIED ABOUT SOMETHING, SHE GAVE ME ADVICE THAT HELPED ME TO VIEW THE SITUATION FROM A MORE MATURE PERSPECTIVE.
WHOA!
WHO EXACTLY IS SHE !?
HNN?
THIS IS BAD......I MEANT TO LIVE MY LIFE HIDING MY TRUE ABILITIES, BUT...
...NOW THEY'RE CATCHING ON ......
GATA (CLATTER)
OH, GOOD GRIEF...
IF I PLAY NICE WITH EVERYONE, THEY'LL DISCOVER MY TRUE IDENTITY (GRADE REPEATER) ...!
I MUST FEIGN INCOMPETENCE WHENEVER POSSIBLE ...!!
SUTA (STRIDE)
SUTA
I GOTTA ACT THE PART OF A REGULAR HIGH SCHOOL GIRL—NO, AN ACADEMICALLY CHALLENGED IRREGULAR, OR ELSE ......!!

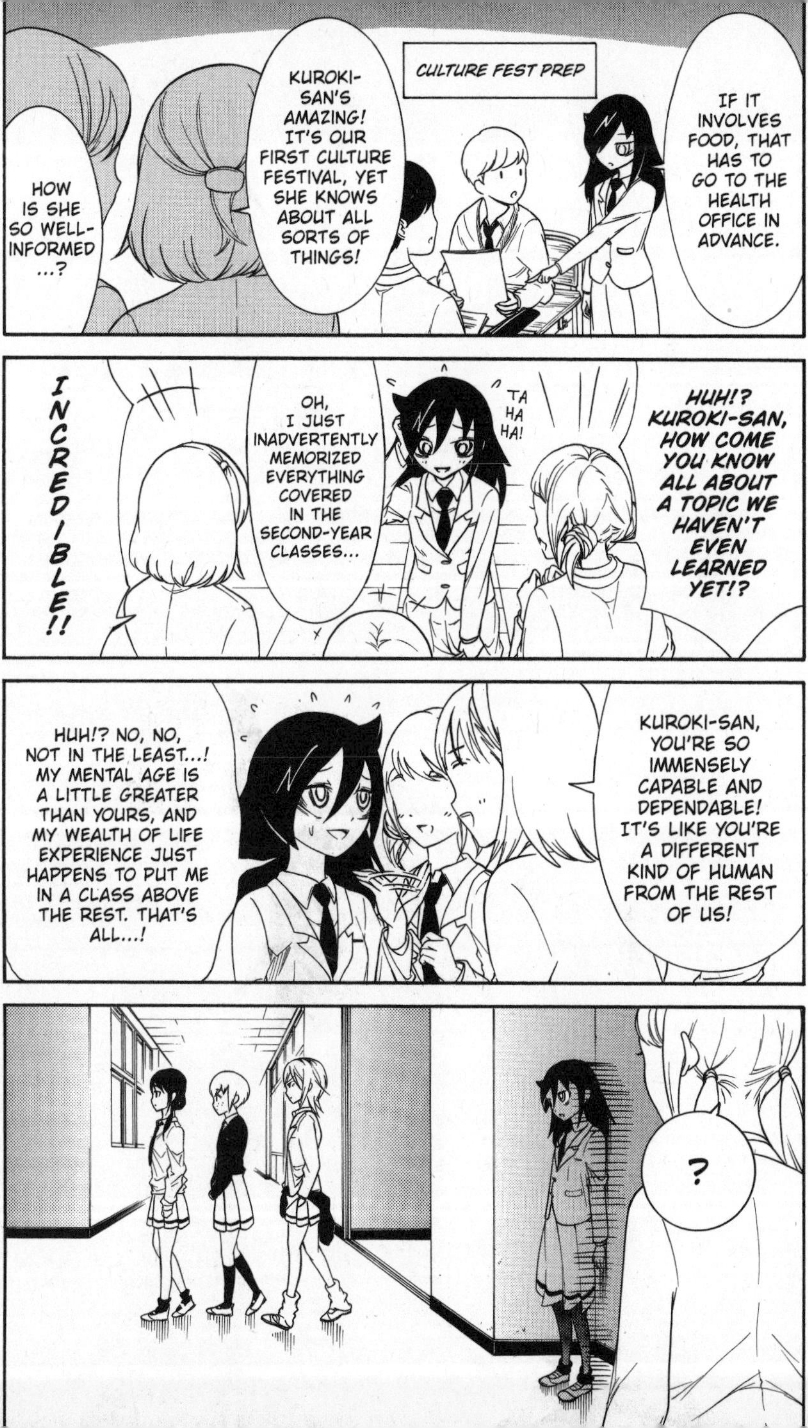
CULTURE FEST PREP
IF IT INVOLVES FOOD, THAT HAS TO GO TO THE HEALTH OFFICE IN ADVANCE.
KUROKI-SAN'S AMAZING! IT'S OUR FIRST CULTURE FESTIVAL, YET SHE KNOWS ABOUT ALL SORTS OF THINGS!
HOW IS SHE SO WELL-INFORMED ...?
HUH!? KUROKI-SAN, HOW COME YOU KNOW ALL ABOUT A TOPIC WE HAVEN'T EVEN LEARNED YET!?
TA HA HA!
OH, I JUST INADVERTENTLY MEMORIZED EVERYTHING COVERED IN THE SECOND-YEAR CLASSES...
INCREDIBLE!!
KUROKI-SAN, YOU'RE SO IMMENSELY CAPABLE AND DEPENDABLE! IT'S LIKE YOU'RE A DIFFERENT KIND OF HUMAN FROM THE REST OF US!
HUH!? NO, NO, NOT IN THE LEAST...! MY MENTAL AGE IS A LITTLE GREATER THAN YOURS, AND MY WEALTH OF LIFE EXPERIENCE JUST HAPPENS TO PUT ME IN A CLASS ABOVE THE REST. THAT'S ALL...!
?

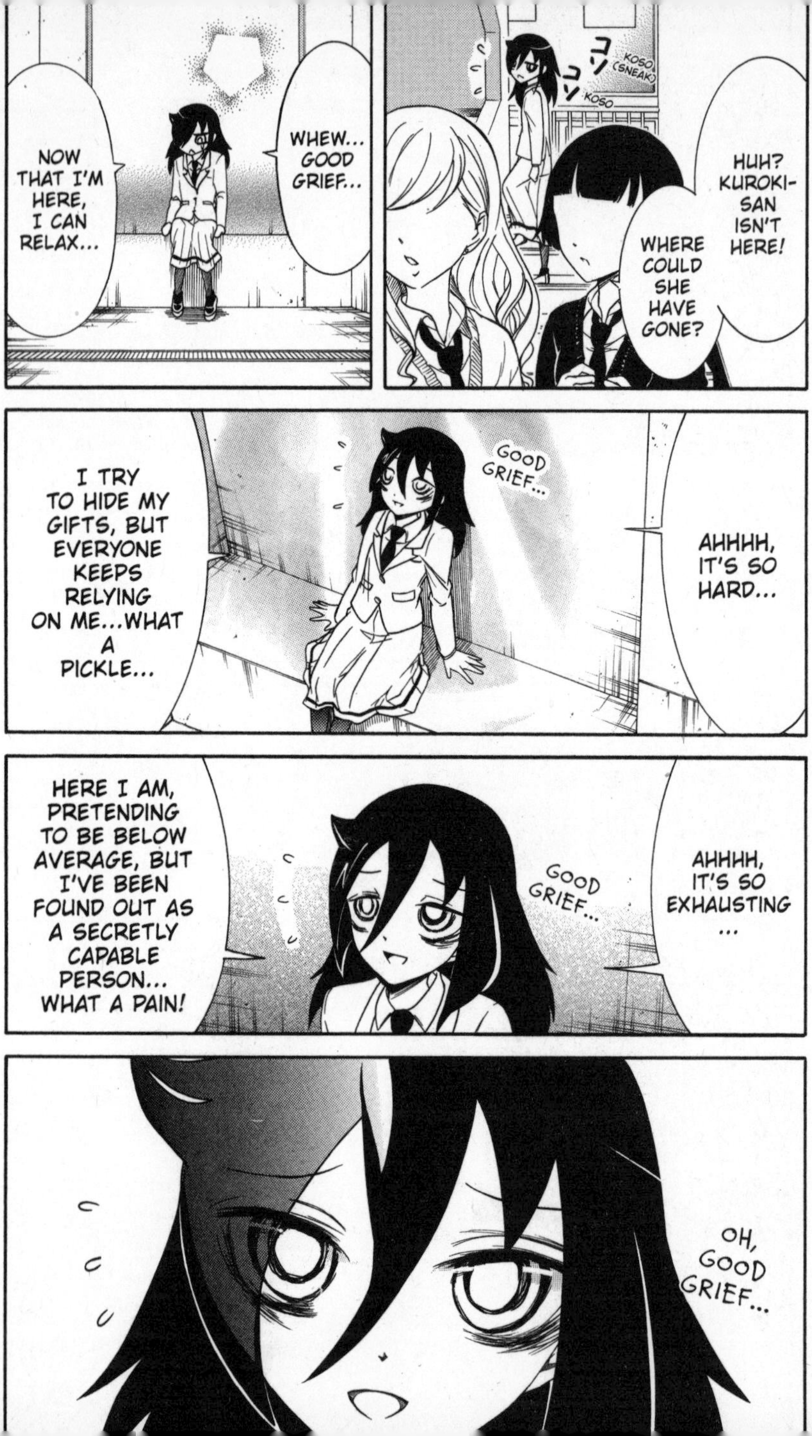
HUH? KUROKI-SAN ISN'T HERE!
WHERE COULD SHE HAVE GONE?
コソ
KOSO (SNEAK)
コソ
KOSO
WHEW... GOOD GRIEF...
NOW THAT I'M HERE, I CAN RELAX...
AHHHH, IT'S SO HARD...
GOOD GRIEF...
I TRY TO HIDE MY GIFTS, BUT EVERYONE KEEPS RELYING ON ME...WHAT A PICKLE...
AHHHH, IT'S SO EXHAUSTING...
GOOD GRIEF...
HERE I AM, PRETENDING TO BE BELOW AVERAGE, BUT I'VE BEEN FOUND OUT AS A SECRETLY CAPABLE PERSON... WHAT A PAIN!
OH, GOOD GRIEF...

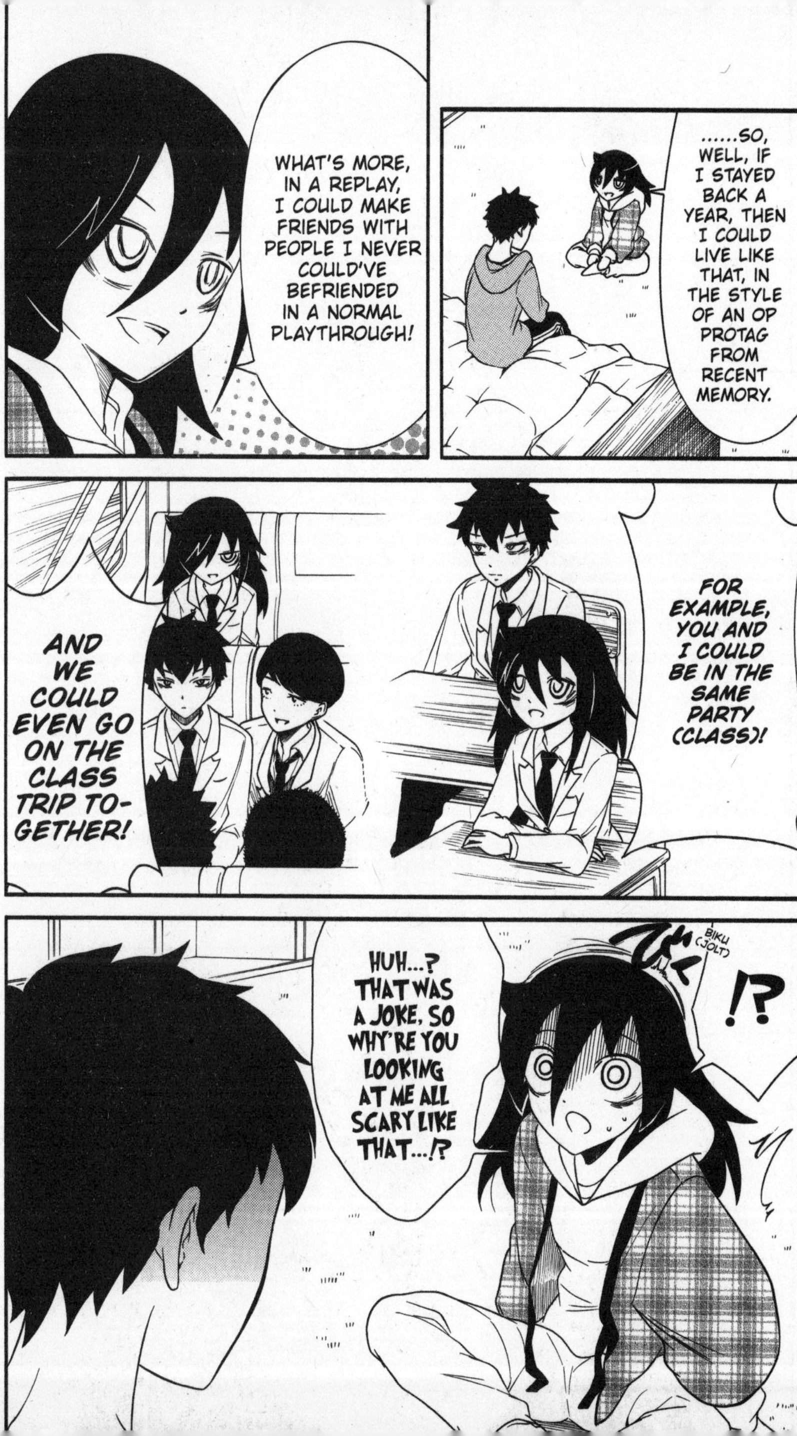
......SO, WELL, IF I STAYED BACK A YEAR, THEN I COULD LIVE LIKE THAT, IN THE STYLE OF AN OP PROTAG FROM RECENT MEMORY.
WHAT'S MORE, IN A REPLAY, I COULD MAKE FRIENDS WITH PEOPLE I NEVER COULD'VE BEFRIENDED IN A NORMAL PLAYTHROUGH!
FOR EXAMPLE, YOU AND I COULD BE IN THE SAME PARTY (CLASS)!
AND WE COULD EVEN GO ON THE CLASS TRIP TOGETHER!
BIKU (JOLT)
!?
HUH...? THAT WAS A JOKE, SO WHY'RE YOU LOOKING AT ME ALL SCARY LIKE THAT...!?

No Matter How I Look at It, It's You Guys' Fault I'm Not Popular!

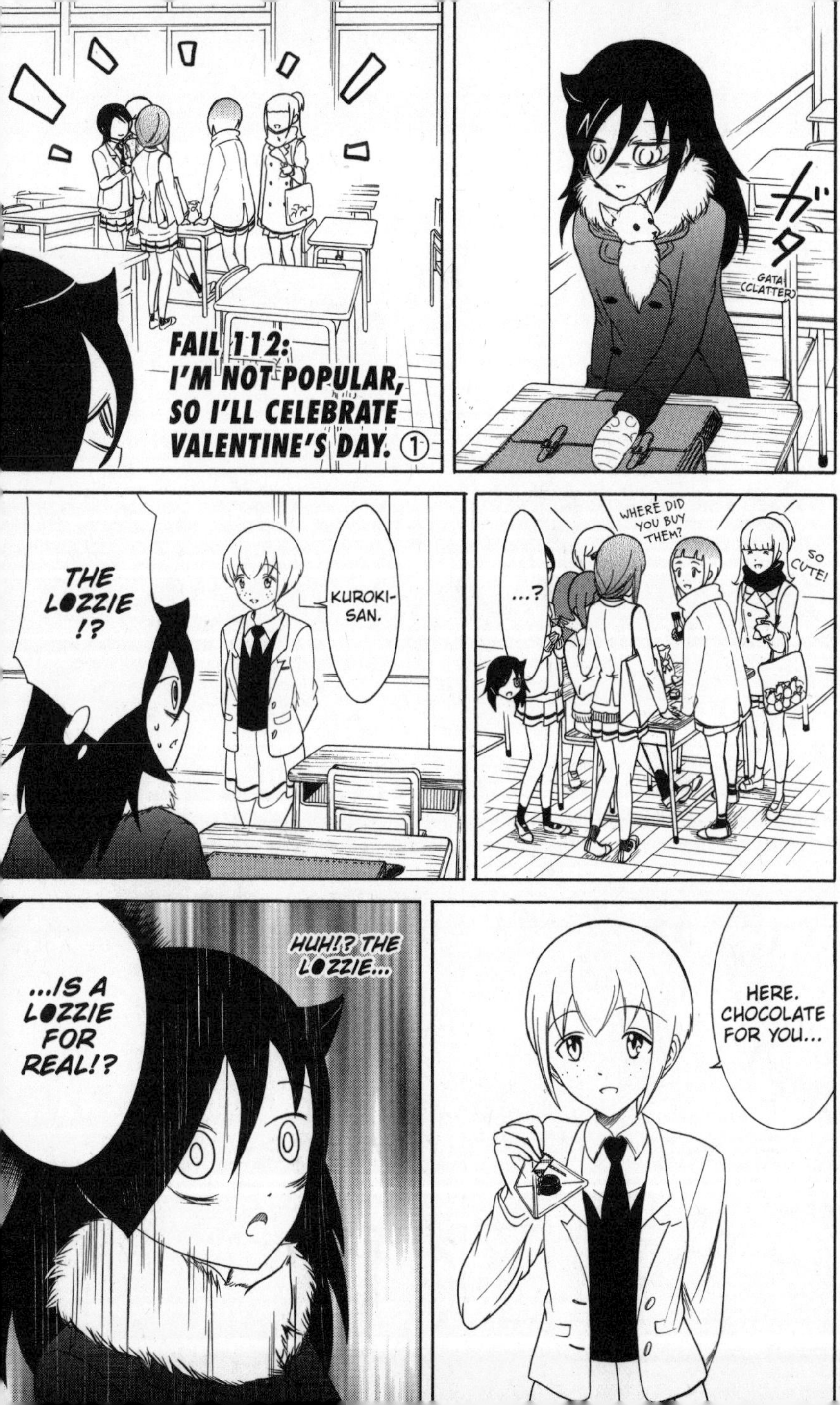
ガタ
GATA (CLATTER)
FAIL 112: I'M NOT POPULAR, SO I'LL CELEBRATE VALENTINE'S DAY. ①
WHERE DID YOU BUY THEM?
SO CUTE!
...?
KUROKI-SAN.
THE LOZZIE!?
HERE. CHOCOLATE FOR YOU...
HUH!? THE LOZZIE...
...IS A LOZZIE FOR REAL!?

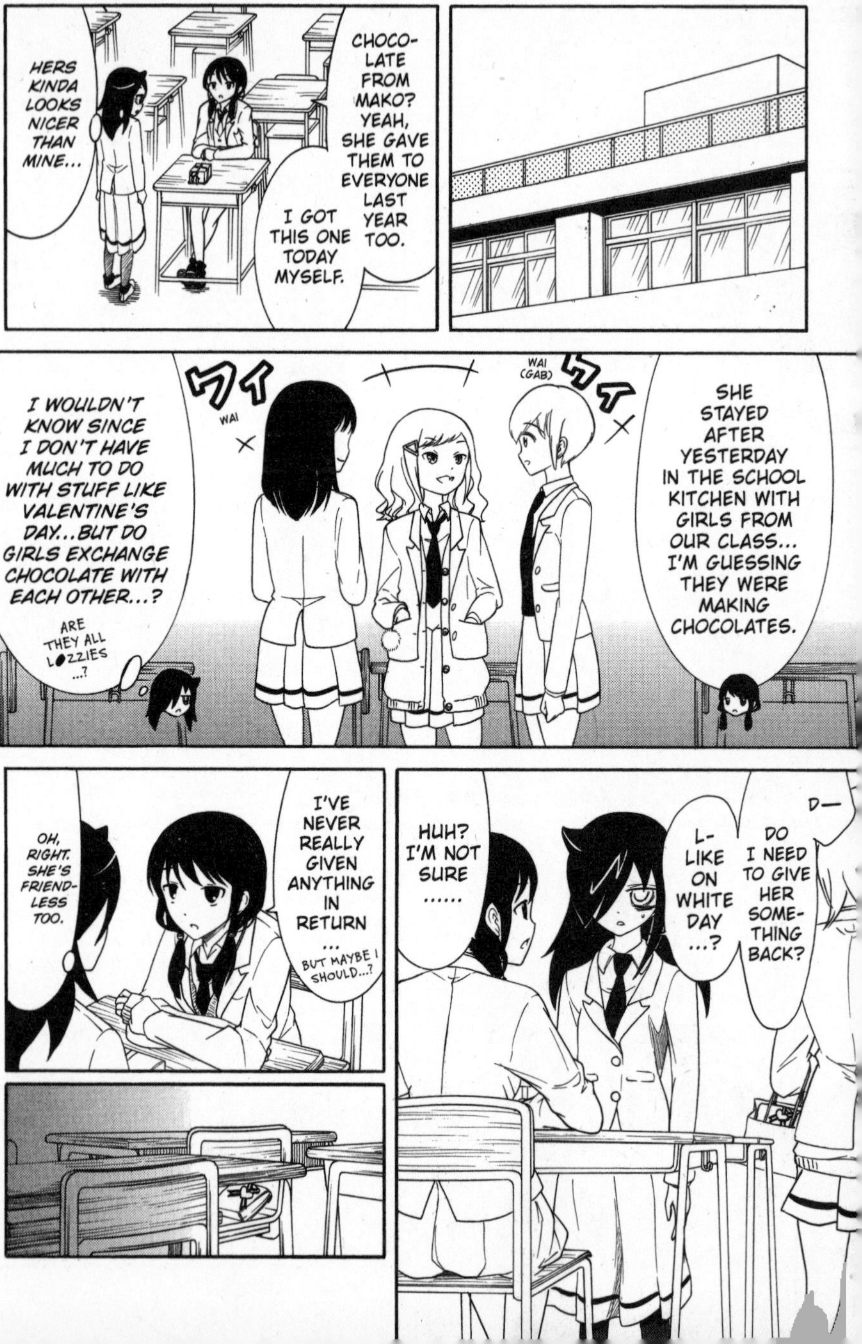
CHOCO-LATE FROM MAKO? YEAH, SHE GAVE THEM TO EVERYONE LAST YEAR TOO.
I GOT THIS ONE TODAY MYSELF.
HERS KINDA LOOKS NICER THAN MINE...
SHE STAYED AFTER YESTERDAY IN THE SCHOOL KITCHEN WITH GIRLS FROM OUR CLASS... I'M GUESSING THEY WERE MAKING CHOCOLATES.
ワイ
WAI (GAB)
ワイ
WAI
I WOULDN'T KNOW SINCE I DON'T HAVE MUCH TO DO WITH STUFF LIKE VALENTINE'S DAY...BUT DO GIRLS EXCHANGE CHOCOLATE WITH EACH OTHER...?
ARE THEY ALL L●ZZIES ...?
D—
DO I NEED TO GIVE HER SOME-THING BACK?
L-LIKE ON WHITE DAY ...?
HUH? I'M NOT SURE ......
I'VE NEVER REALLY GIVEN ANYTHING IN RETURN ...
BUT MAYBE I SHOULD...?
OH, RIGHT. SHE'S FRIEND-LESS TOO.

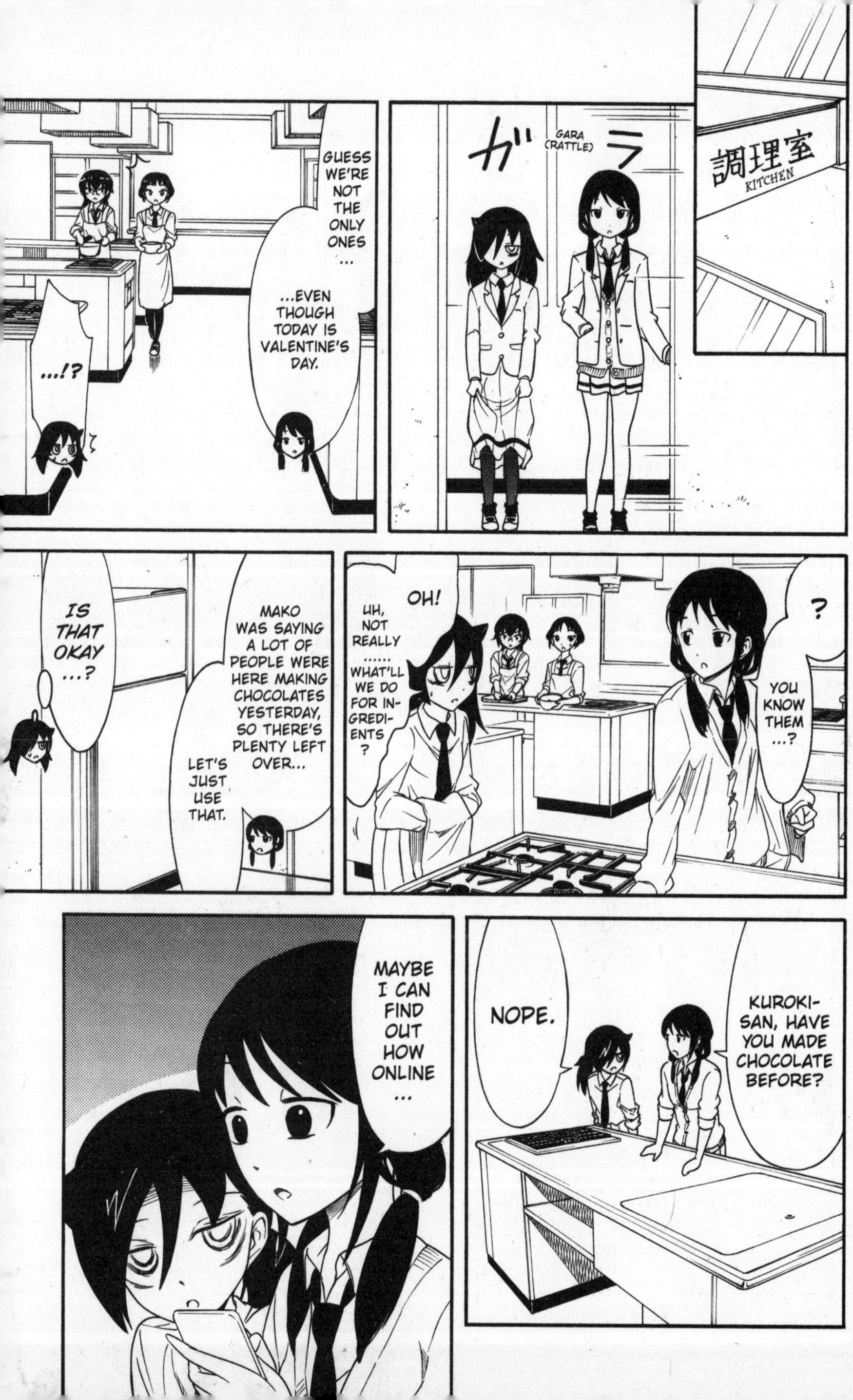
調理室
KITCHEN
ガラ
GARA (RATTLE)
GUESS WE'RE NOT THE ONLY ONES...
...EVEN THOUGH TODAY IS VALENTINE'S DAY.
...!?
?
YOU KNOW THEM...?
OH!
UH, NOT REALLY...... WHAT'LL WE DO FOR INGREDIENTS?
MAKO WAS SAYING A LOT OF PEOPLE WERE HERE MAKING CHOCOLATES YESTERDAY, SO THERE'S PLENTY LEFT OVER...
LET'S JUST USE THAT.
IS THAT OKAY...?
KUROKI-SAN, HAVE YOU MADE CHOCOLATE BEFORE?
NOPE.
MAYBE I CAN FIND OUT HOW ONLINE...

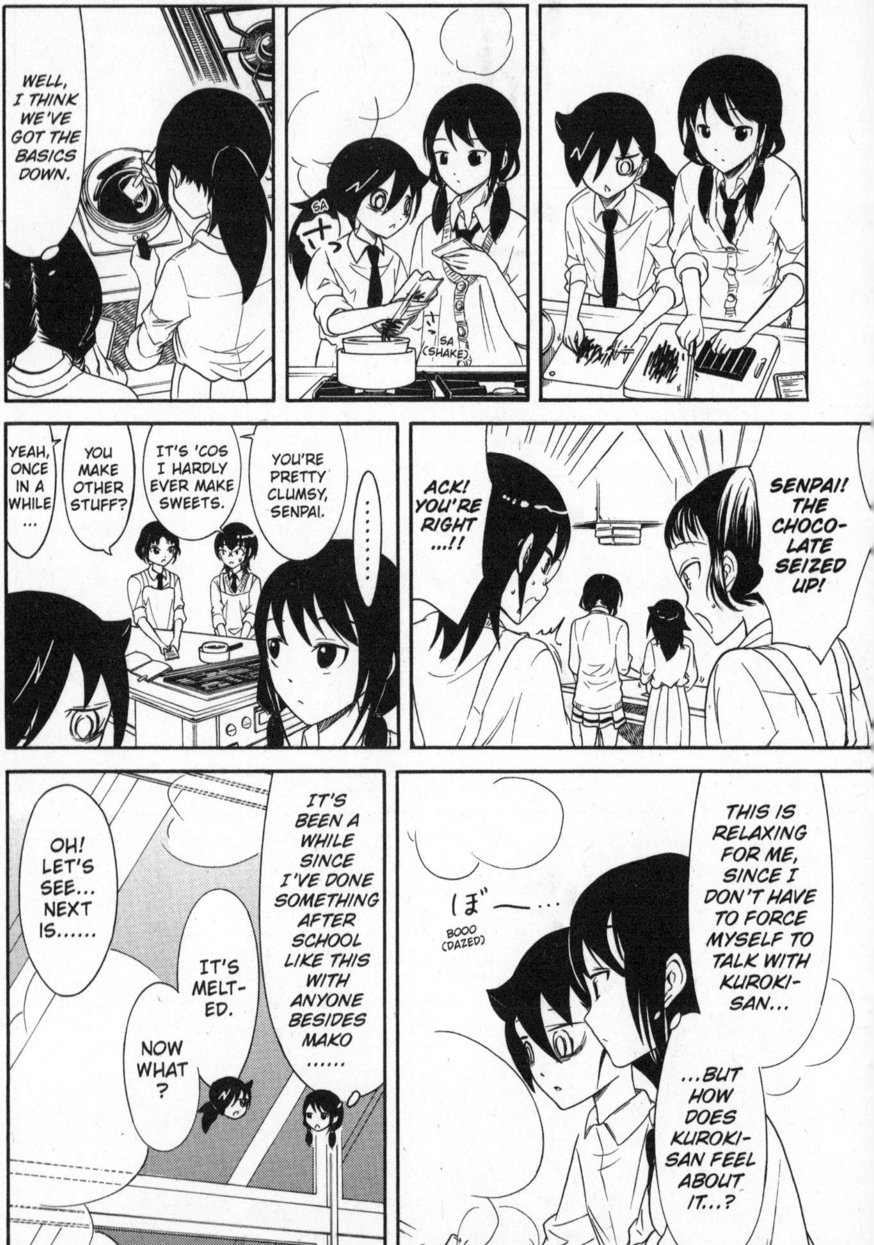
さっ
SA
SA (SHAKE)
WELL, I THINK WE'VE GOT THE BASICS DOWN.
SENPAI! THE CHOCOLATE SEIZED UP!
ACK! YOU'RE RIGHT ...!!
......
YOU'RE PRETTY CLUMSY, SENPAI.
IT'S 'COS I HARDLY EVER MAKE SWEETS.
YOU MAKE OTHER STUFF?
YEAH, ONCE IN A WHILE ...
THIS IS RELAXING FOR ME, SINCE I DON'T HAVE TO FORCE MYSELF TO TALK WITH KUROKI-SAN...
ぼー…
BOOO (DAZED)
...BUT HOW DOES KUROKI-SAN FEEL ABOUT IT...?
IT'S BEEN A WHILE SINCE I'VE DONE SOMETHING AFTER SCHOOL LIKE THIS WITH ANYONE BESIDES MAKO ......
OH! LET'S SEE... NEXT IS......
IT'S MELT-ED.
NOW WHAT ?

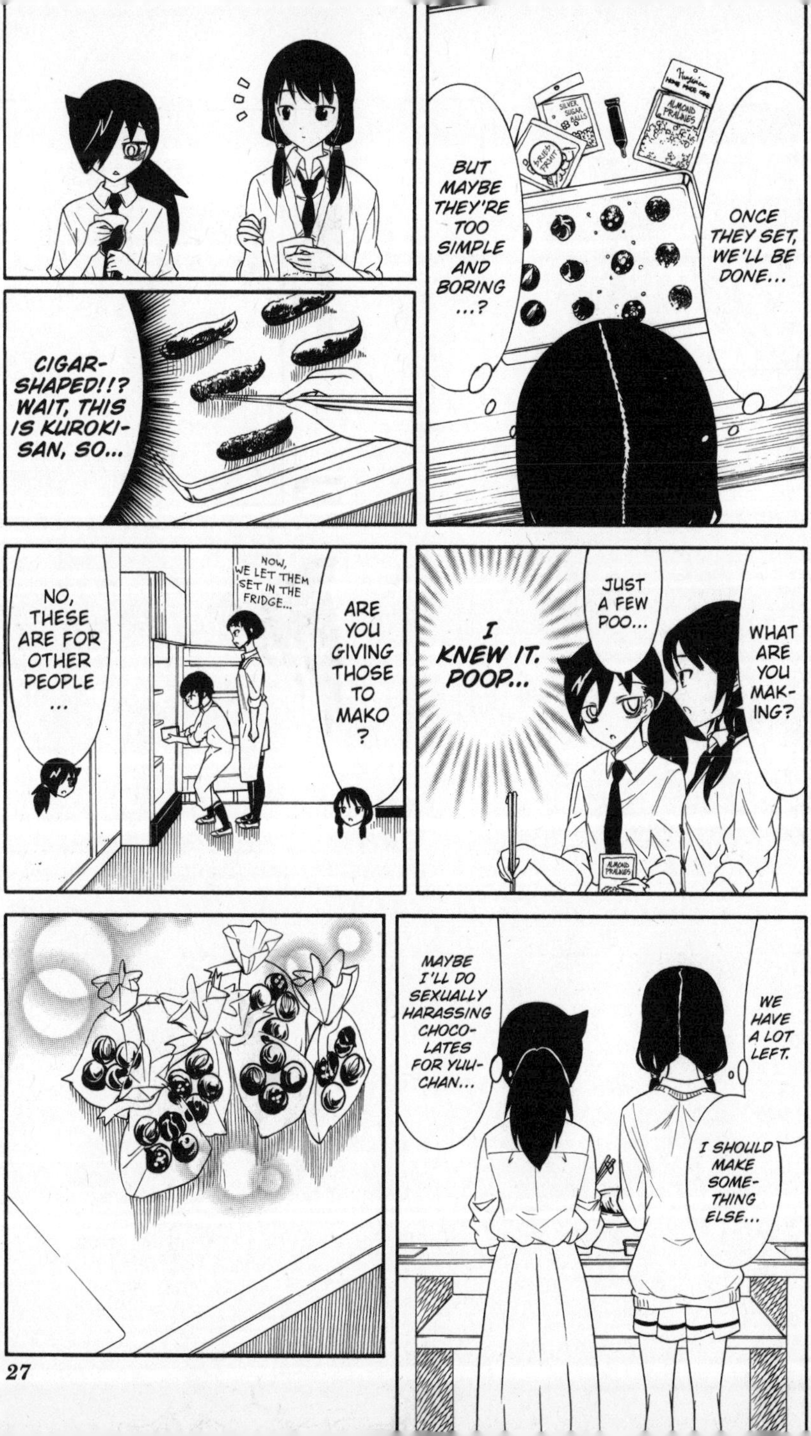
ONCE THEY SET, WE'LL BE DONE...
BUT MAYBE THEY'RE TOO SIMPLE AND BORING ...?
SILVER SUGAR BALLS
ALMOND PRALINES
CIGAR-SHAPED!!? WAIT, THIS IS KUROKI-SAN, SO...
WHAT ARE YOU MAKING?
JUST A FEW POO...
I KNEW IT. POOP...
ALMOND PRALINES
ARE YOU GIVING THOSE TO MAKO?
NOW, WE LET THEM SET IN THE FRIDGE...
NO, THESE ARE FOR OTHER PEOPLE ...
WE HAVE A LOT LEFT.
I SHOULD MAKE SOMETHING ELSE...
MAYBE I'LL DO SEXUALLY HARASSING CHOCOLATES FOR YUU-CHAN...

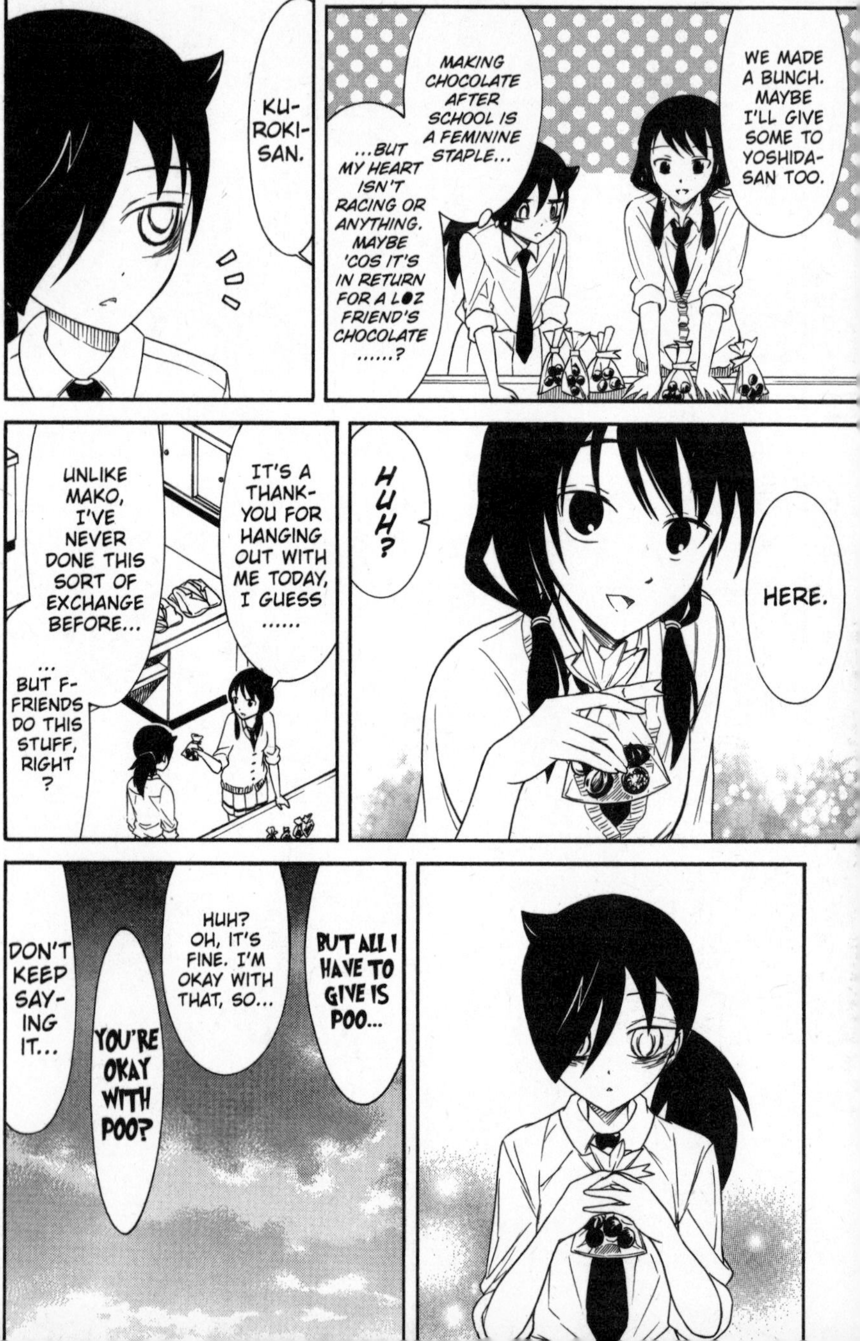
WE MADE A BUNCH. MAYBE I'LL GIVE SOME TO YOSHIDA-SAN TOO.
MAKING CHOCOLATE AFTER SCHOOL IS A FEMININE STAPLE...
...BUT MY HEART ISN'T RACING OR ANYTHING. MAYBE 'COS IT'S IN RETURN FOR A L●Z FRIEND'S CHOCOLATE ......?
KU-ROKI-SAN.
HERE.
HUH?
IT'S A THANK-YOU FOR HANGING OUT WITH ME TODAY, I GUESS ......
UNLIKE MAKO, I'VE NEVER DONE THIS SORT OF EXCHANGE BEFORE...
...BUT F-FRIENDS DO THIS STUFF, RIGHT?
BUT ALL I HAVE TO GIVE IS POO...
HUH? OH, IT'S FINE. I'M OKAY WITH THAT, SO...
YOU'RE OKAY WITH POO?
DON'T KEEP SAYING IT...

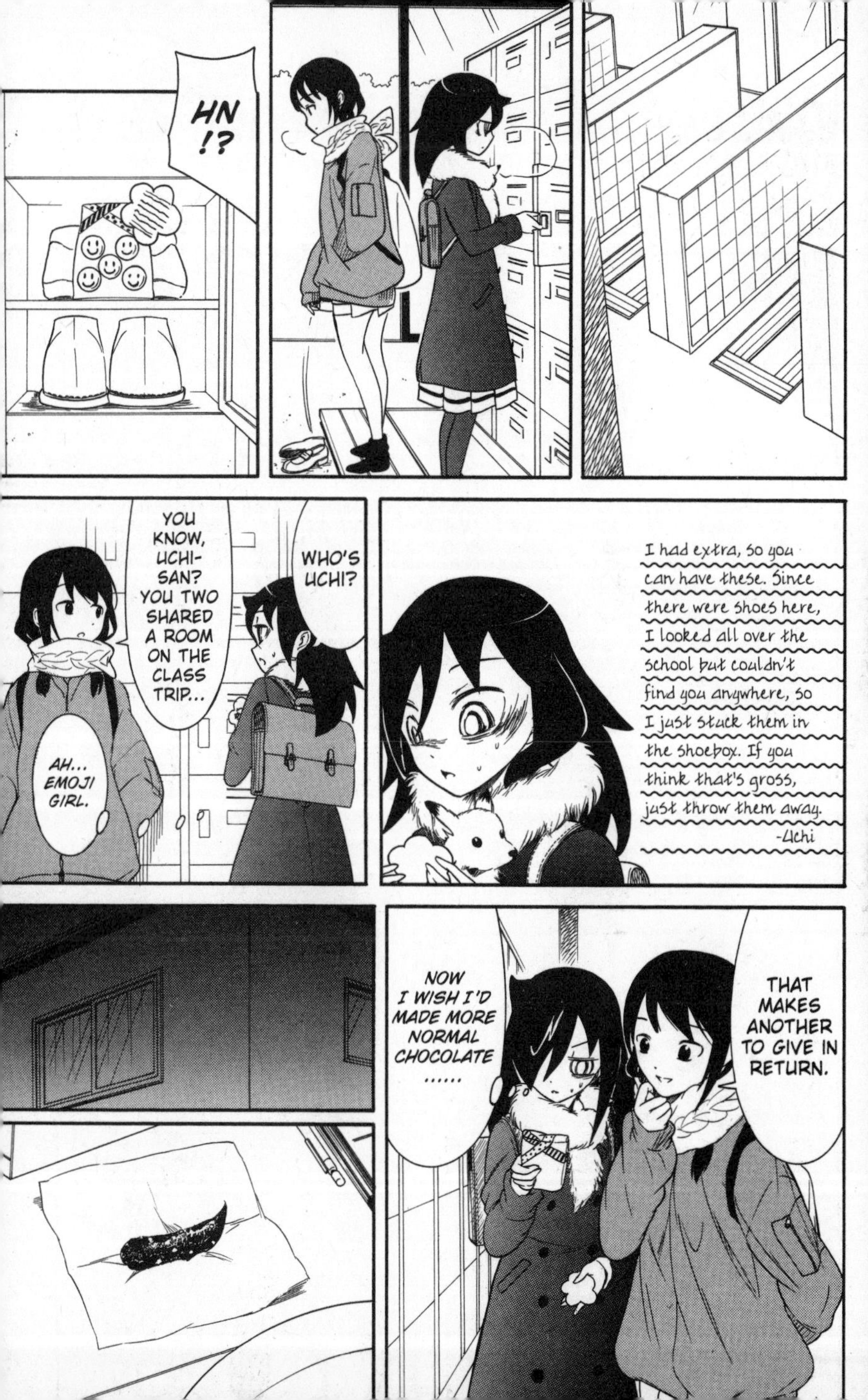
HN !?
I had extra, so you can have these. Since there were shoes here, I looked all over the school but couldn't find you anywhere, so I just stuck them in the shoebox. If you think that's gross, just throw them away.
-Uchi
WHO'S UCHI?
YOU KNOW, UCHI-SAN? YOU TWO SHARED A ROOM ON THE CLASS TRIP...
AH... EMOJI GIRL.
THAT MAKES ANOTHER TO GIVE IN RETURN.
NOW I WISH I'D MADE MORE NORMAL CHOCOLATE ......

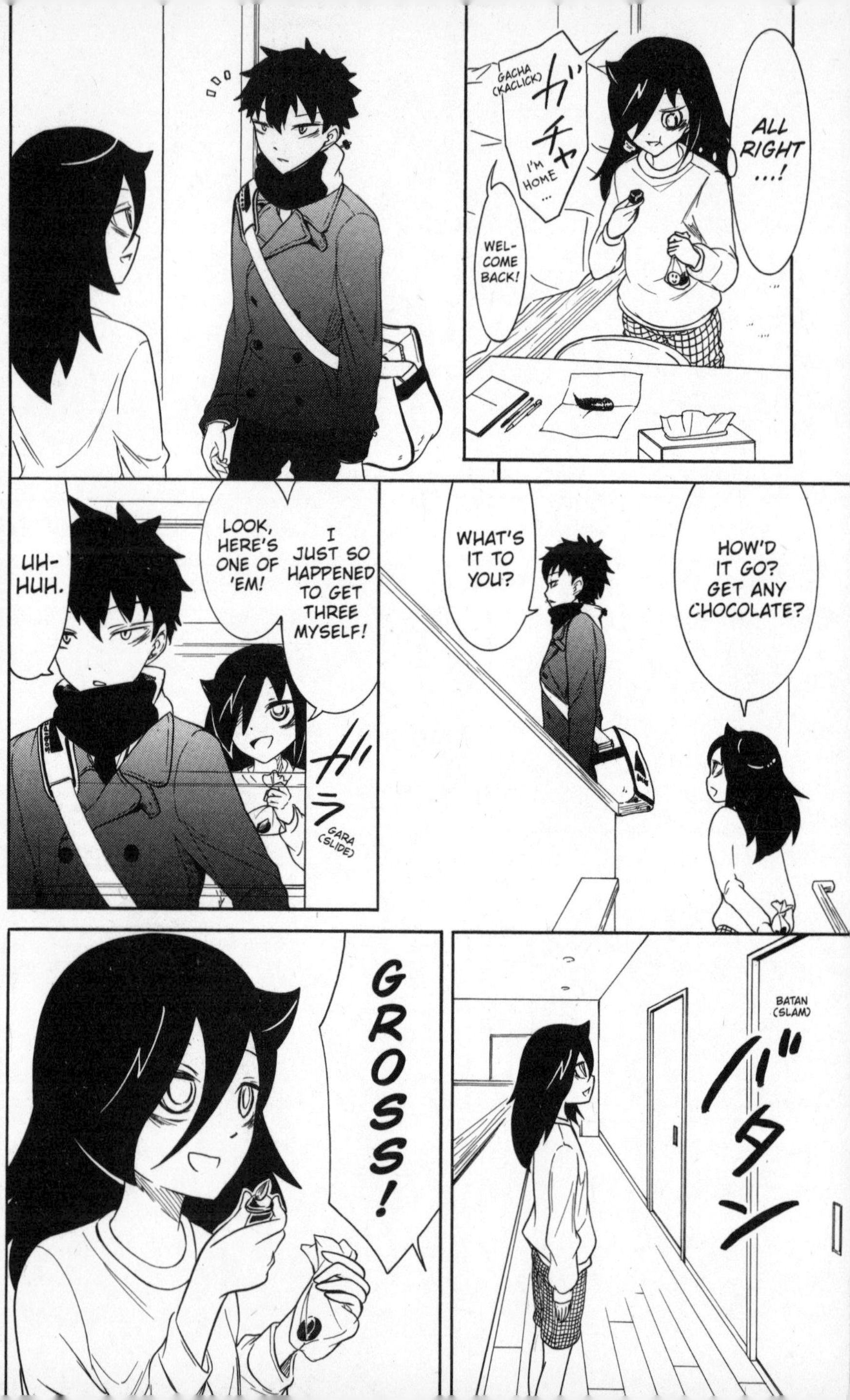
ALL RIGHT ...!
...
...
ガチャ
GACHA (KACLICK)
I'M HOME ...
WEL-COME BACK!
HOW'D IT GO? GET ANY CHOCOLATE?
WHAT'S IT TO YOU?
I JUST SO HAPPENED TO GET THREE MYSELF!
LOOK, HERE'S ONE OF 'EM!
ガラ
GARA (SLIDE)
UH-HUH.
バタン
BATAN (SLAM)
GROSS!

No Matter How I Look at It, It's You Guys' Fault I'm Not Popular!

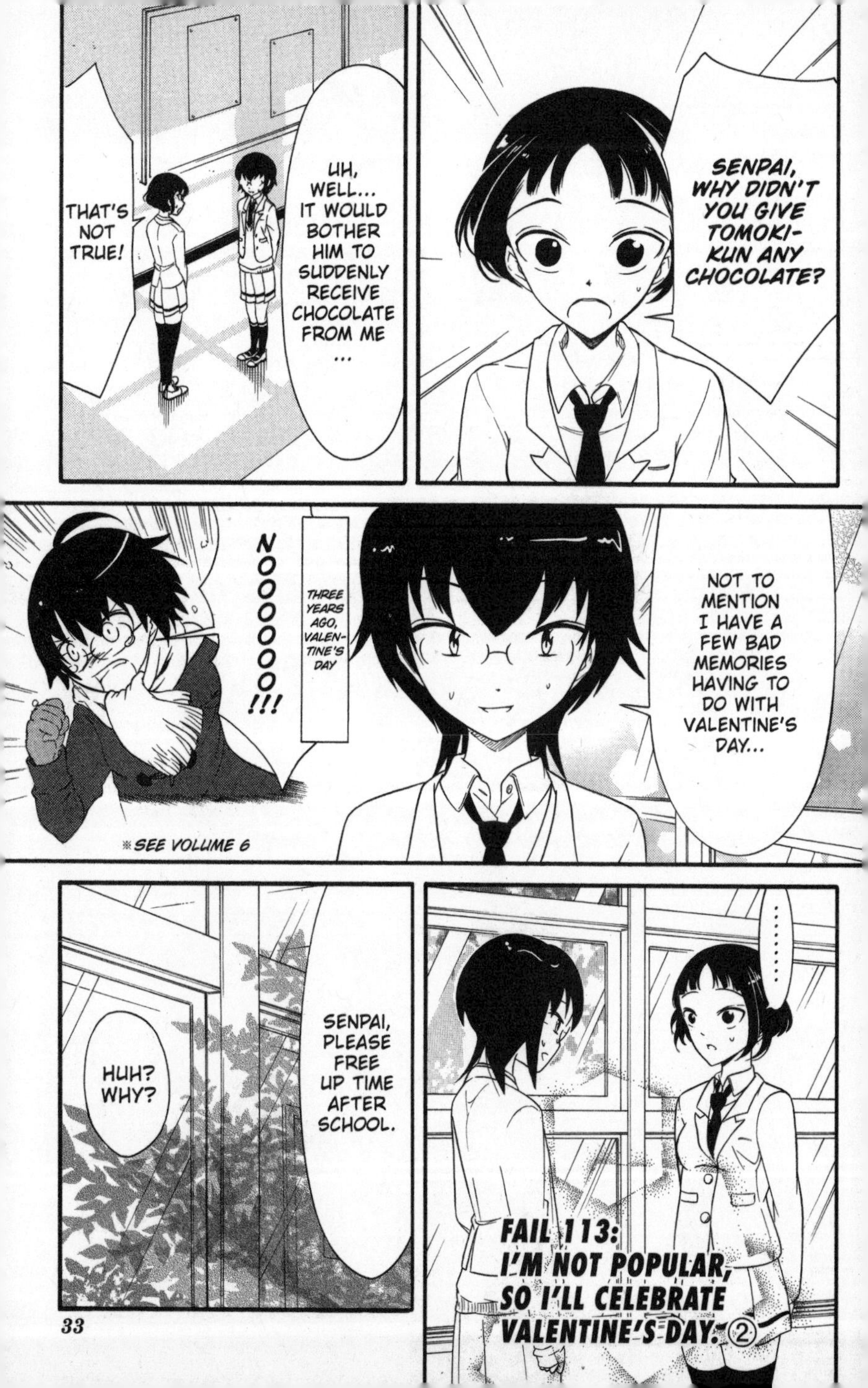
SENPAI, WHY DIDN'T YOU GIVE TOMOKI-KUN ANY CHOCOLATE?
UH, WELL... IT WOULD BOTHER HIM TO SUDDENLY RECEIVE CHOCOLATE FROM ME ...
THAT'S NOT TRUE!
NOT TO MENTION I HAVE A FEW BAD MEMORIES HAVING TO DO WITH VALENTINE'S DAY...
THREE YEARS AGO, VALENTINE'S DAY
NOOOOOOO!!!
※SEE VOLUME 6
......
FAIL 113: I'M NOT POPULAR, SO I'LL CELEBRATE VALENTINE'S DAY. ②
SENPAI, PLEASE FREE UP TIME AFTER SCHOOL.
HUH? WHY?

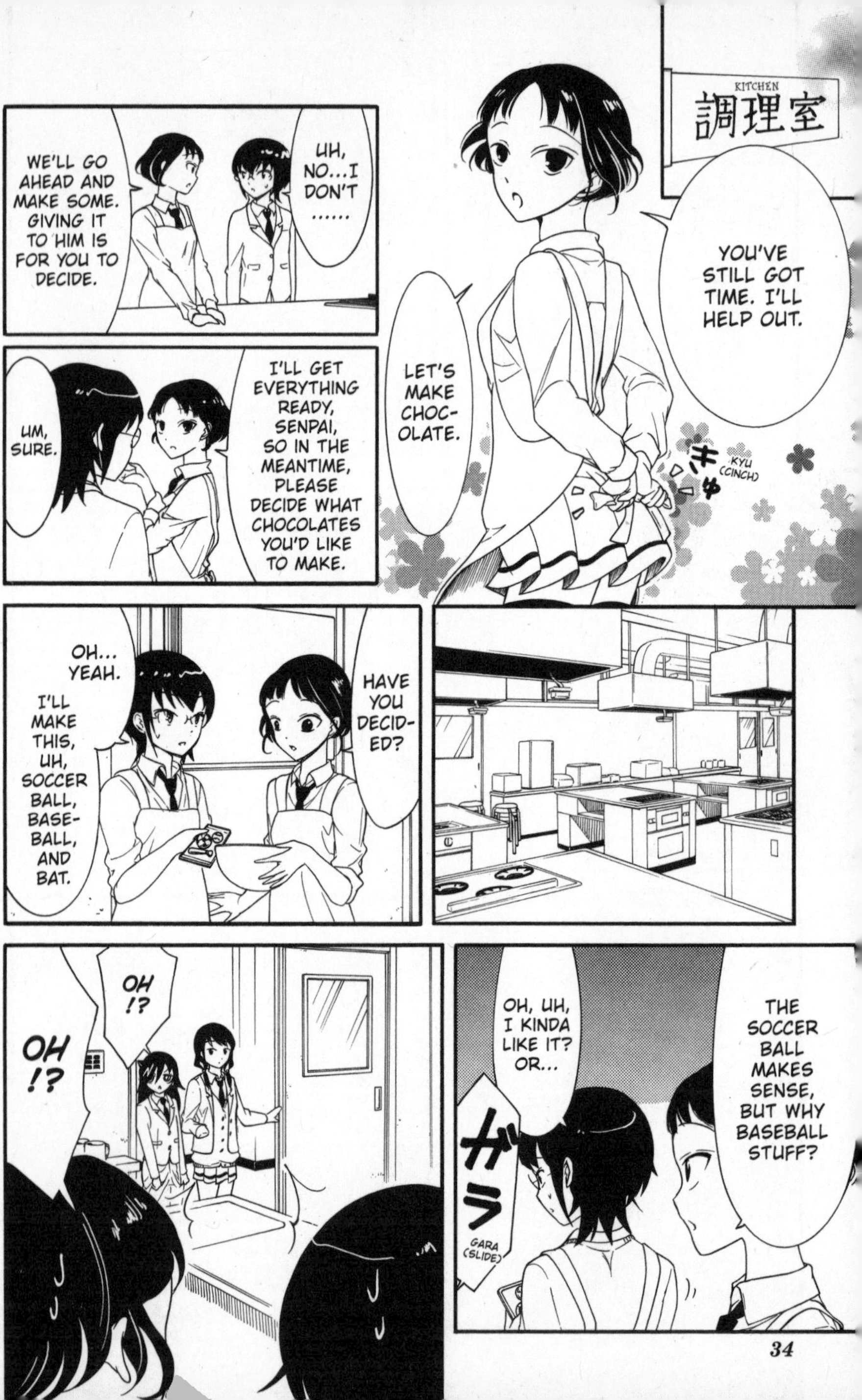
KITCHEN
調理室
YOU'VE STILL GOT TIME. I'LL HELP OUT.
LET'S MAKE CHOCOLATE.
キュ
KYU (CINCH)
UH, NO...I DON'T ......
WE'LL GO AHEAD AND MAKE SOME. GIVING IT TO HIM IS FOR YOU TO DECIDE.
I'LL GET EVERYTHING READY, SENPAI, SO IN THE MEANTIME, PLEASE DECIDE WHAT CHOCOLATES YOU'D LIKE TO MAKE.
UM, SURE.
HAVE YOU DECID-ED?
OH... YEAH.
I'LL MAKE THIS, UH, SOCCER BALL, BASE-BALL, AND BAT.
THE SOCCER BALL MAKES SENSE, BUT WHY BASEBALL STUFF?
OH, UH, I KINDA LIKE IT? OR...
ガラ
GARA (SLIDE)
OH !?
OH !?

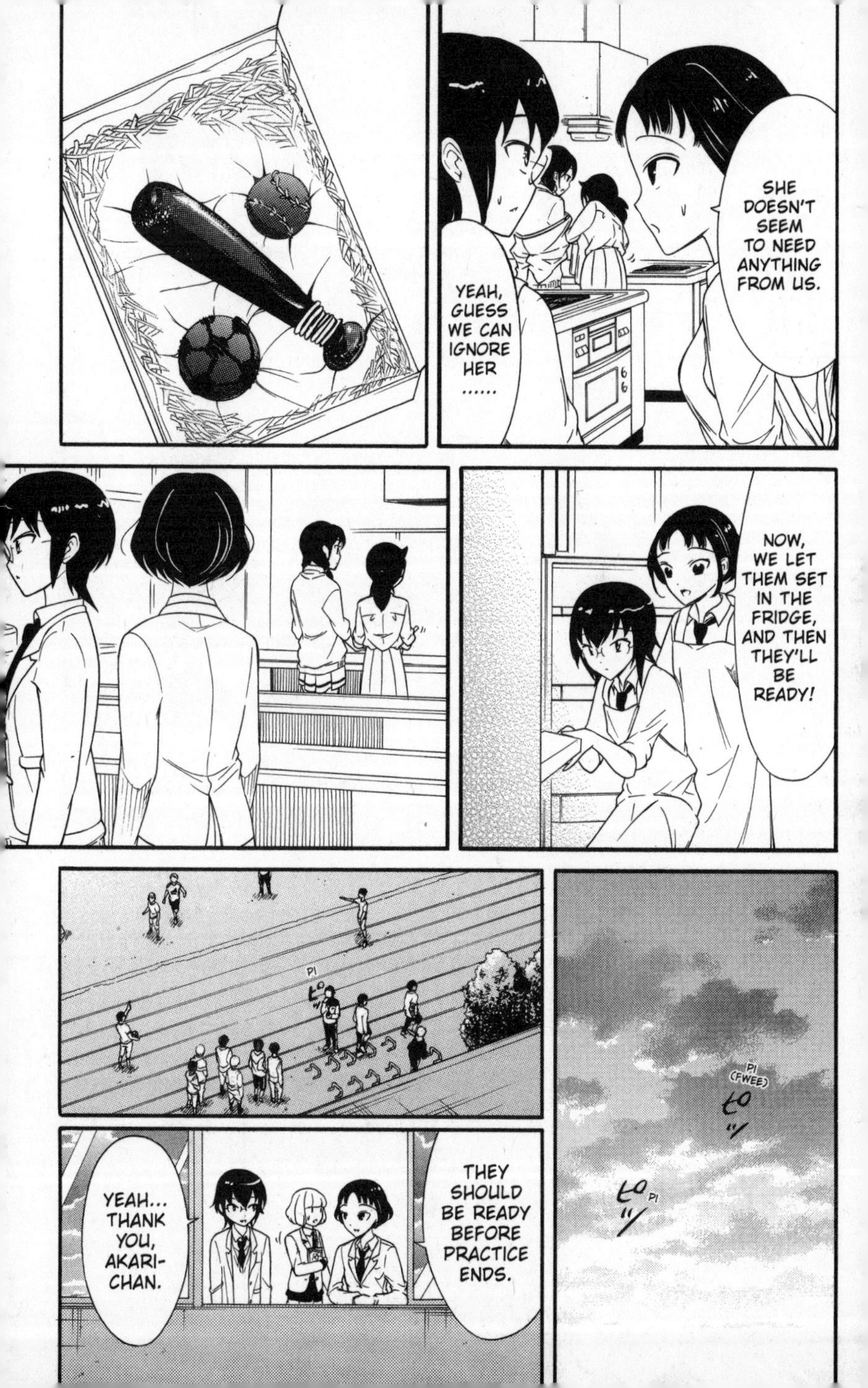
SHE DOESN'T SEEM TO NEED ANYTHING FROM US.
YEAH, GUESS WE CAN IGNORE HER ......
NOW, WE LET THEM SET IN THE FRIDGE, AND THEN THEY'LL BE READY!
PI (FWEE)
ピッ
ピッ
PI
PI
ピッ
THEY SHOULD BE READY BEFORE PRACTICE ENDS.
YEAH... THANK YOU, AKARI-CHAN.

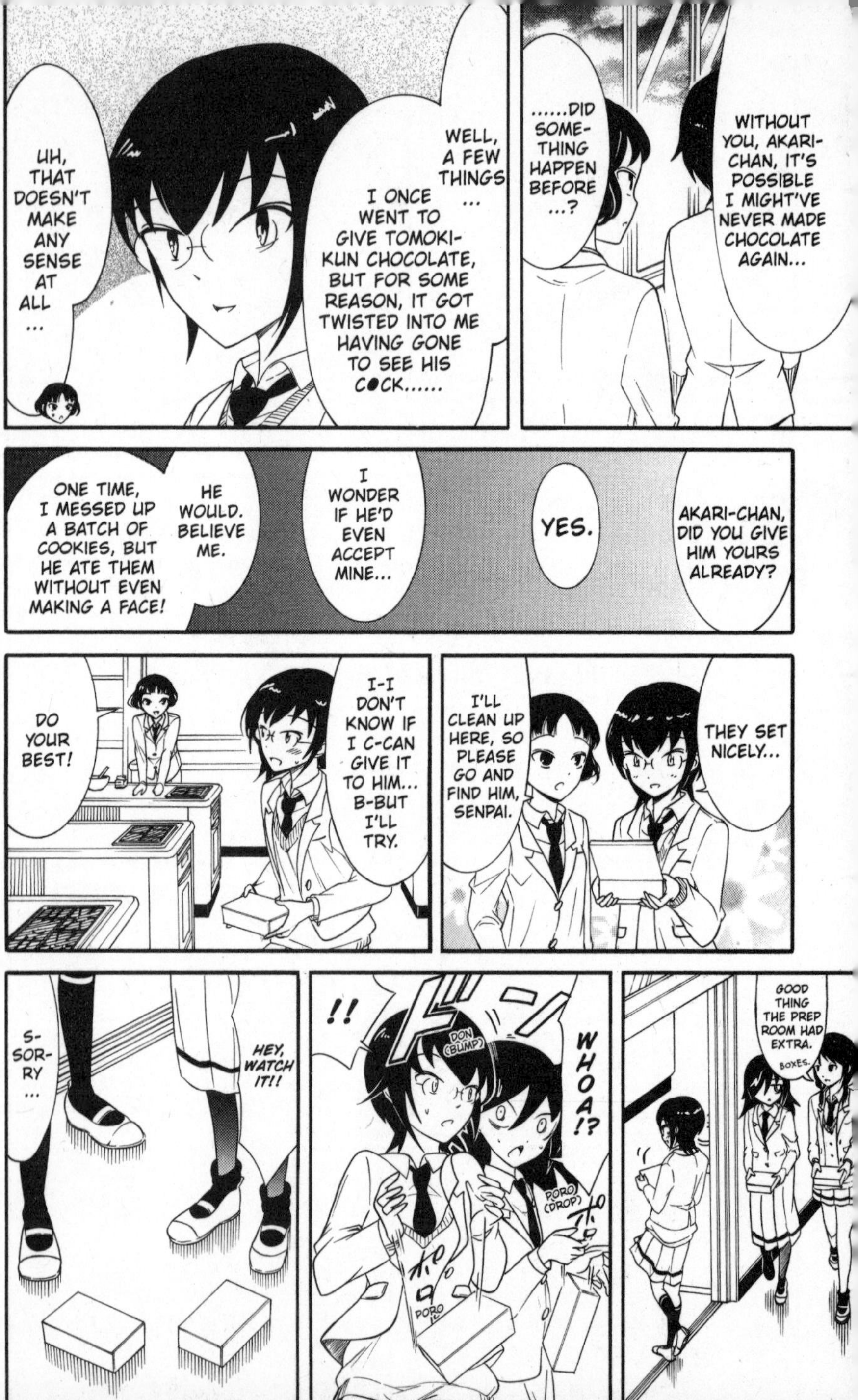
WITHOUT YOU, AKARI-CHAN, IT'S POSSIBLE I MIGHT'VE NEVER MADE CHOCOLATE AGAIN...
......DID SOMETHING HAPPEN BEFORE ...?
WELL, A FEW THINGS ...
I ONCE WENT TO GIVE TOMOKI-KUN CHOCOLATE, BUT FOR SOME REASON, IT GOT TWISTED INTO ME HAVING GONE TO SEE HIS C●CK......
UH, THAT DOESN'T MAKE ANY SENSE AT ALL ...
AKARI-CHAN, DID YOU GIVE HIM YOURS ALREADY?
YES.
I WONDER IF HE'D EVEN ACCEPT MINE...
HE WOULD. BELIEVE ME.
ONE TIME, I MESSED UP A BATCH OF COOKIES, BUT HE ATE THEM WITHOUT EVEN MAKING A FACE!
THEY SET NICELY...
I'LL CLEAN UP HERE, SO PLEASE GO AND FIND HIM, SENPAI.
I-I DON'T KNOW IF I C-CAN GIVE IT TO HIM... B-BUT I'LL TRY.
DO YOUR BEST!
GOOD THING THE PREP ROOM HAD EXTRA.
BOXES.
!!
DON (BUMP)
WHOA!?
PORO (DROP)
PORO
HEY, WATCH IT!!
S-SORRY ...

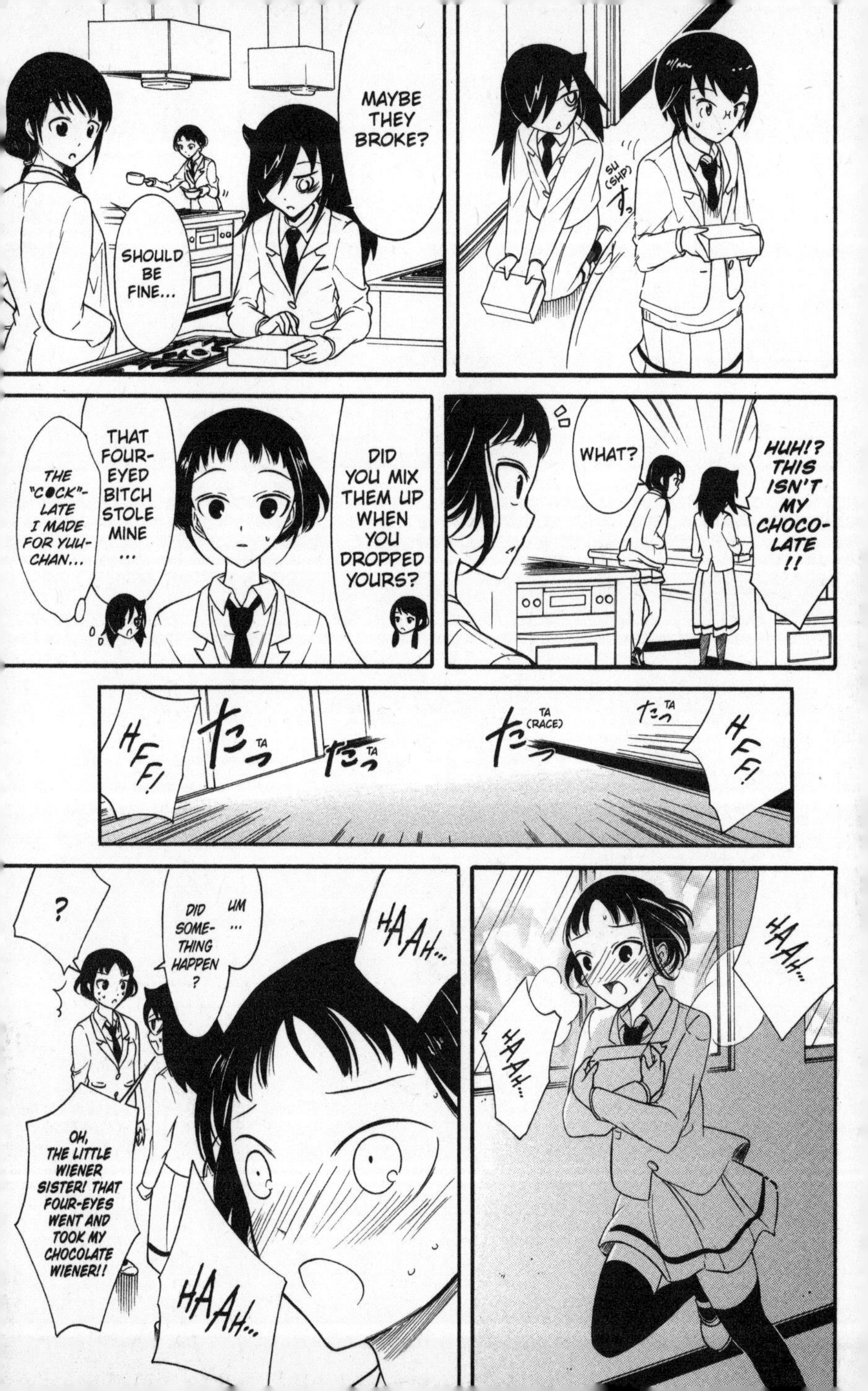
SU (SHP)
すっ
MAYBE THEY BROKE?
SHOULD BE FINE...
HUH!? THIS ISN'T MY CHOCOLATE!!
WHAT?
DID YOU MIX THEM UP WHEN YOU DROPPED YOURS?
THAT FOUR-EYED BITCH STOLE MINE...
THE "C●CK"-LATE I MADE FOR YUU-CHAN...
HFF!
たっ TA
たっ TA (RACE)
たっ TA
たっ TA
HFF!
HAAH...
HAAH...
HAAH...
UM...
DID SOMETHING HAPPEN?
?
OH, THE LITTLE WIENER SISTER! THAT FOUR-EYES WENT AND TOOK MY CHOCOLATE WIENER!!
HAAH...

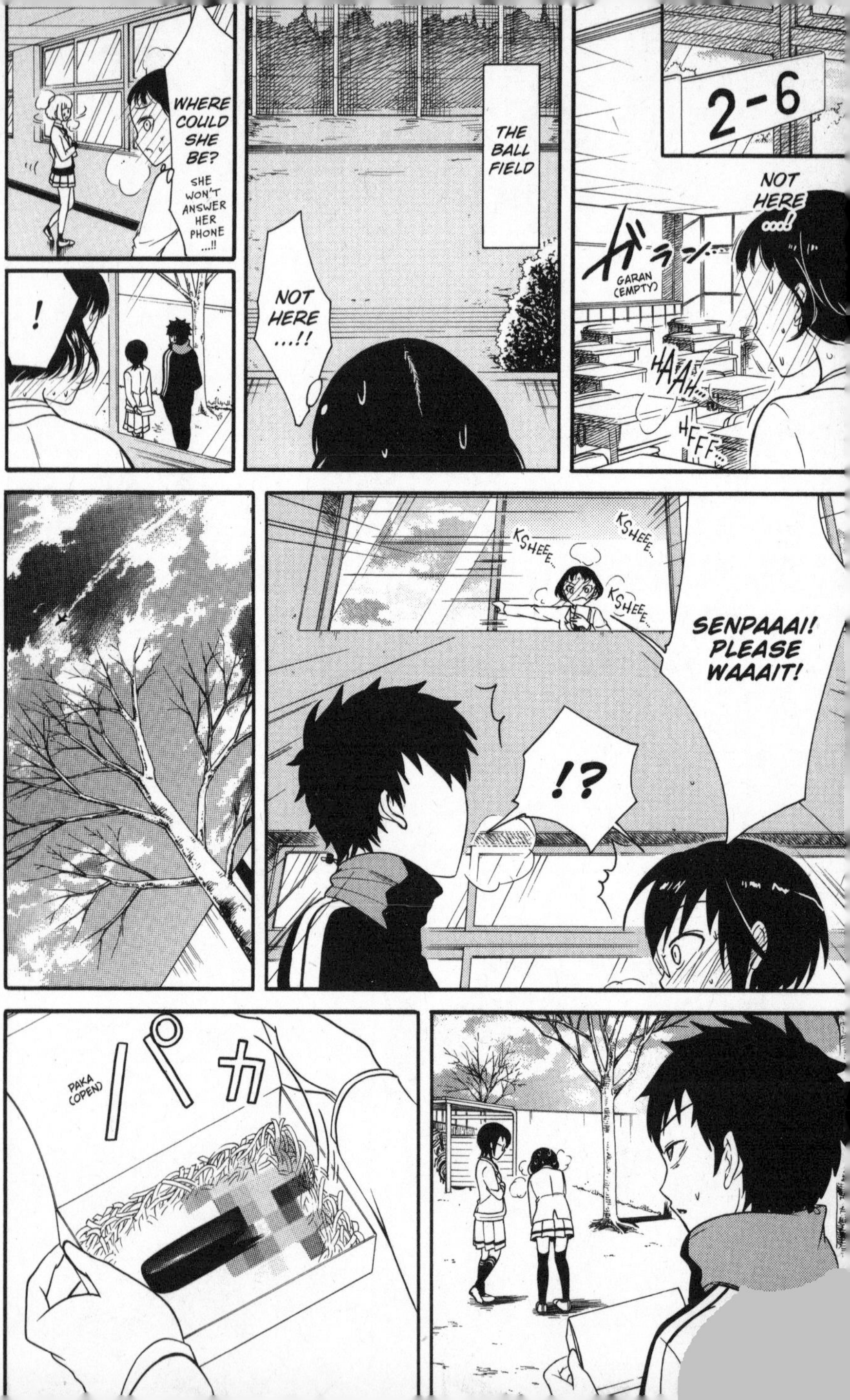
2-6
NOT HERE...!
ガラン
GARAN (EMPTY)
HAAH...
HFFF...
THE BALL FIELD
NOT HERE...!!
WHERE COULD SHE BE?
SHE WON'T ANSWER HER PHONE...!!
!
KSHEEE...
KSHEEE...
KSHEEE...
SENPAAAI! PLEASE WAAAIT!
!?
パカ
PAKA (OPEN)

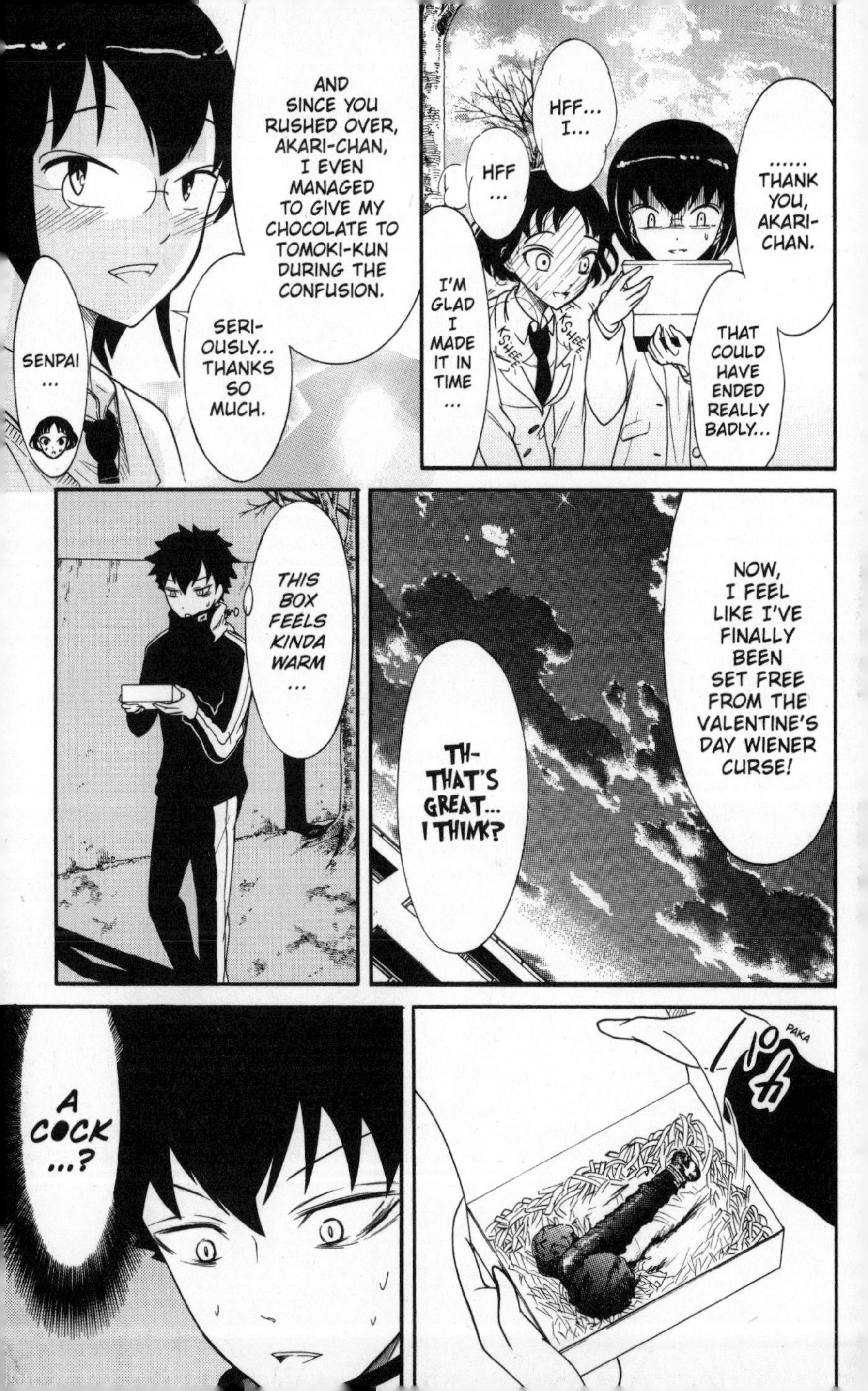
......THANK YOU, AKARI-CHAN.
HFF... I...
HFF...
THAT COULD HAVE ENDED REALLY BADLY...
KSHEE
KSHEE
I'M GLAD I MADE IT IN TIME...
AND SINCE YOU RUSHED OVER, AKARI-CHAN, I EVEN MANAGED TO GIVE MY CHOCOLATE TO TOMOKI-KUN DURING THE CONFUSION.
SERI-OUSLY... THANKS SO MUCH.
SENPAI...
NOW, I FEEL LIKE I'VE FINALLY BEEN SET FREE FROM THE VALENTINE'S DAY WIENER CURSE!
TH-THAT'S GREAT... I THINK?
THIS BOX FEELS KINDA WARM...
PAKA
A COCK...?

No Matter How I Look at It, It's You Guys' Fault I'm Not Popular!

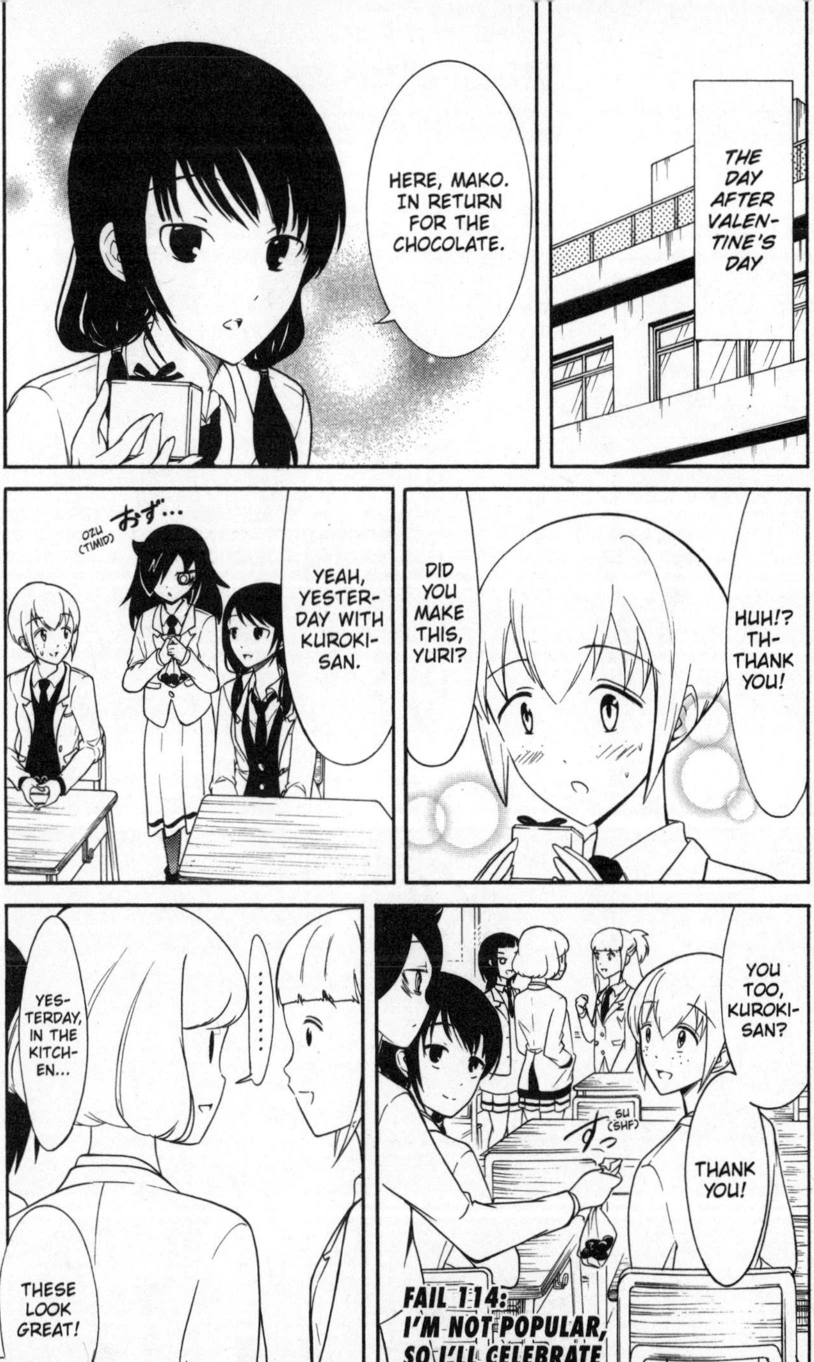
THE DAY AFTER VALENTINE'S DAY
HERE, MAKO. IN RETURN FOR THE CHOCOLATE.
HUH!? TH-THANK YOU!
DID YOU MAKE THIS, YURI?
YEAH, YESTERDAY WITH KUROKI-SAN.
おず… OZU (TIMID)
YOU TOO, KUROKI-SAN?
すっ SU (SHF)
THANK YOU!
FAIL 114: I'M NOT POPULAR, SO I'LL CELEBRATE VALENTINE'S DAY. ③
......
YESTERDAY, IN THE KITCHEN...
THESE LOOK GREAT!

STEALTH CHOCOLATE ①

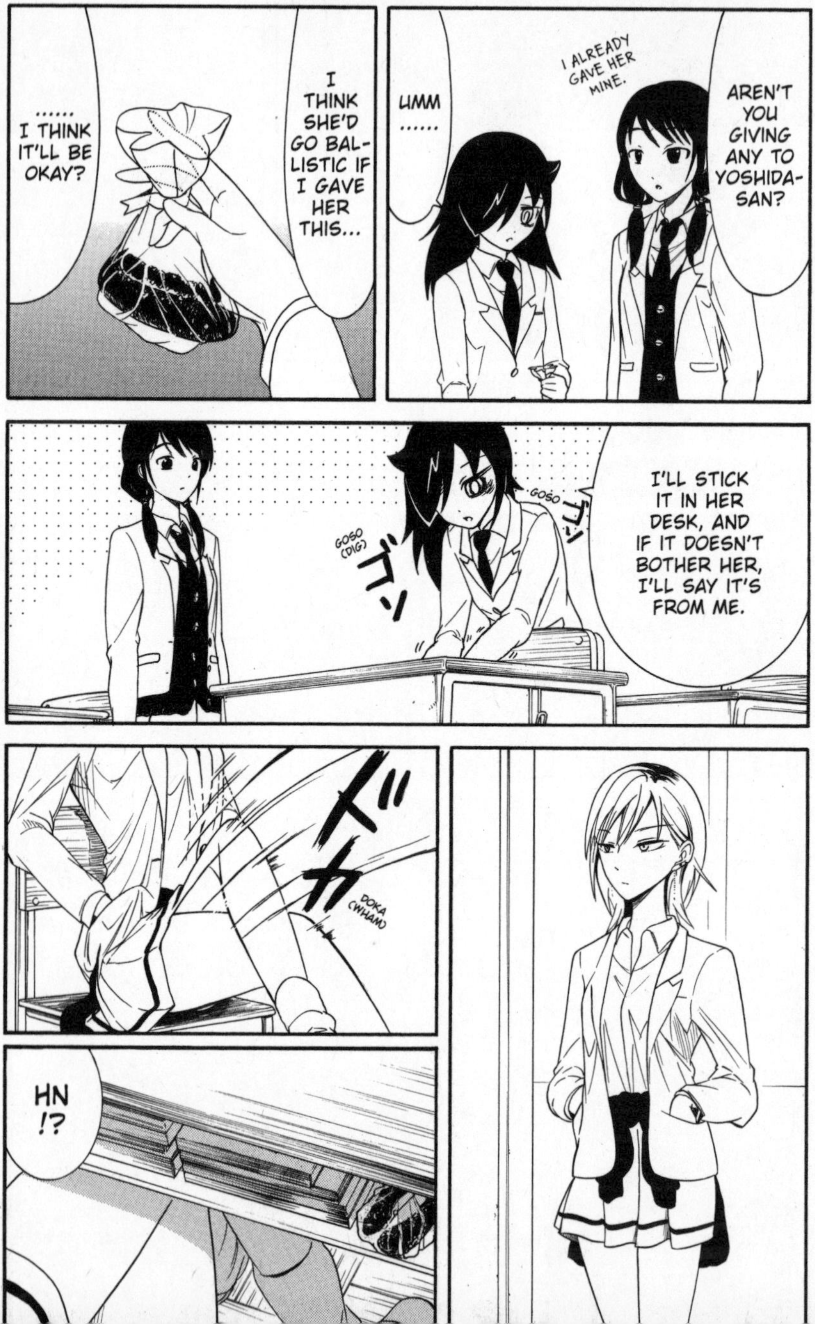
AREN'T YOU GIVING ANY TO YOSHIDA-SAN?
I ALREADY GAVE HER MINE.
UMM ......
I THINK SHE'D GO BAL-LISTIC IF I GAVE HER THIS...
...... I THINK IT'LL BE OKAY?
I'LL STICK IT IN HER DESK, AND IF IT DOESN'T BOTHER HER, I'LL SAY IT'S FROM ME.
GOSO
GOSO (DIG)
DOKA (WHAM)
HN !?

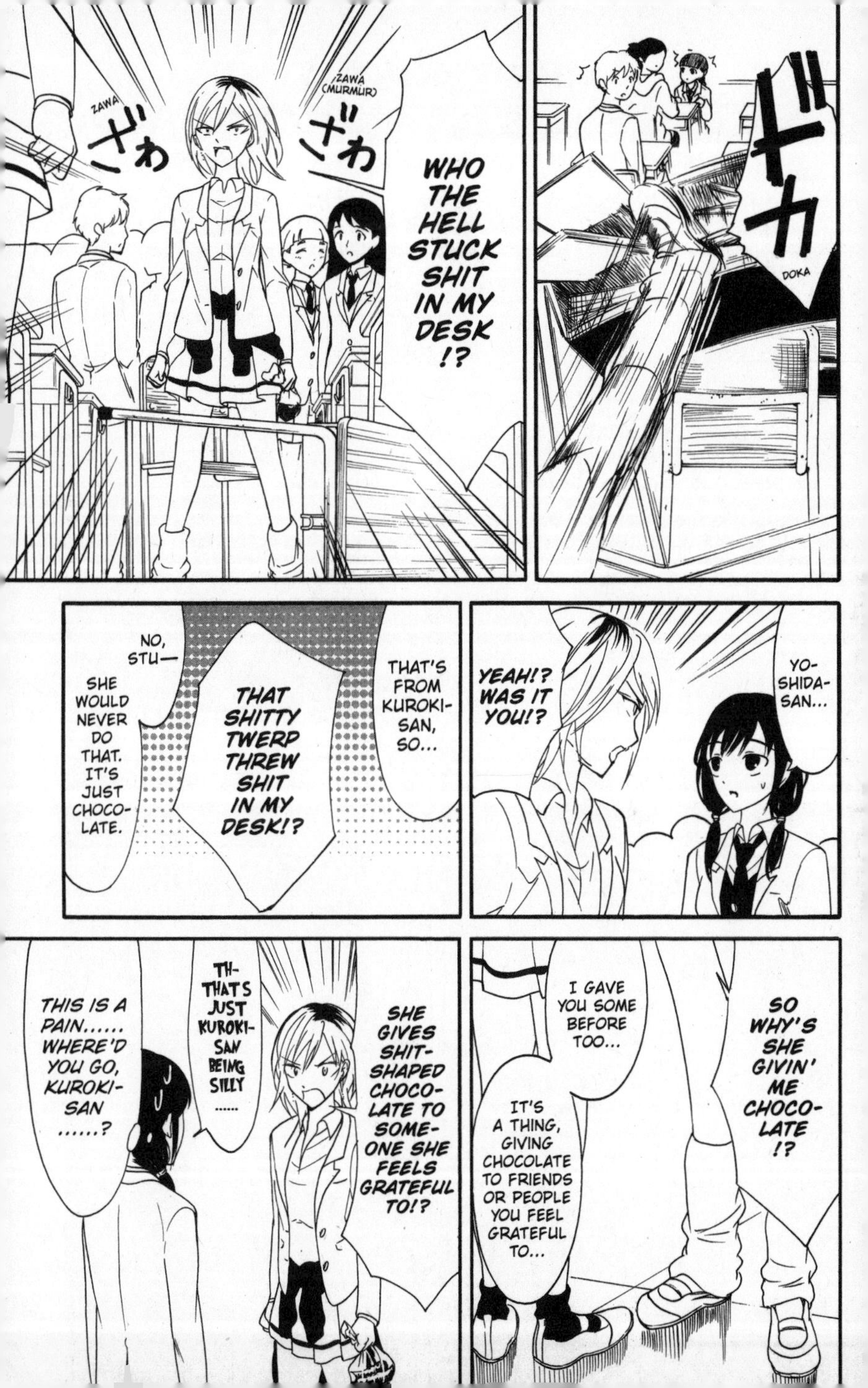

ドカ
DOKA
ZAWA (MURMUR)
ざわ
ZAWA
ざわ
WHO THE HELL STUCK SHIT IN MY DESK!?
YO-SHIDA-SAN...
YEAH!? WAS IT YOU!?
THAT'S FROM KUROKI-SAN, SO...
THAT SHITTY TWERP THREW SHIT IN MY DESK!?
NO, STU—
SHE WOULD NEVER DO THAT. IT'S JUST CHOCO-LATE.
SO WHY'S SHE GIVIN' ME CHOCO-LATE!?
I GAVE YOU SOME BEFORE TOO...
IT'S A THING, GIVING CHOCOLATE TO FRIENDS OR PEOPLE YOU FEEL GRATEFUL TO...
SHE GIVES SHIT-SHAPED CHOCO-LATE TO SOME-ONE SHE FEELS GRATEFUL TO!?
TH-THAT'S JUST KUROKI-SAN BEING SILLY......
THIS IS A PAIN...... WHERE'D YOU GO, KUROKI-SAN ......?

STEALTH CHOCOLATE ②

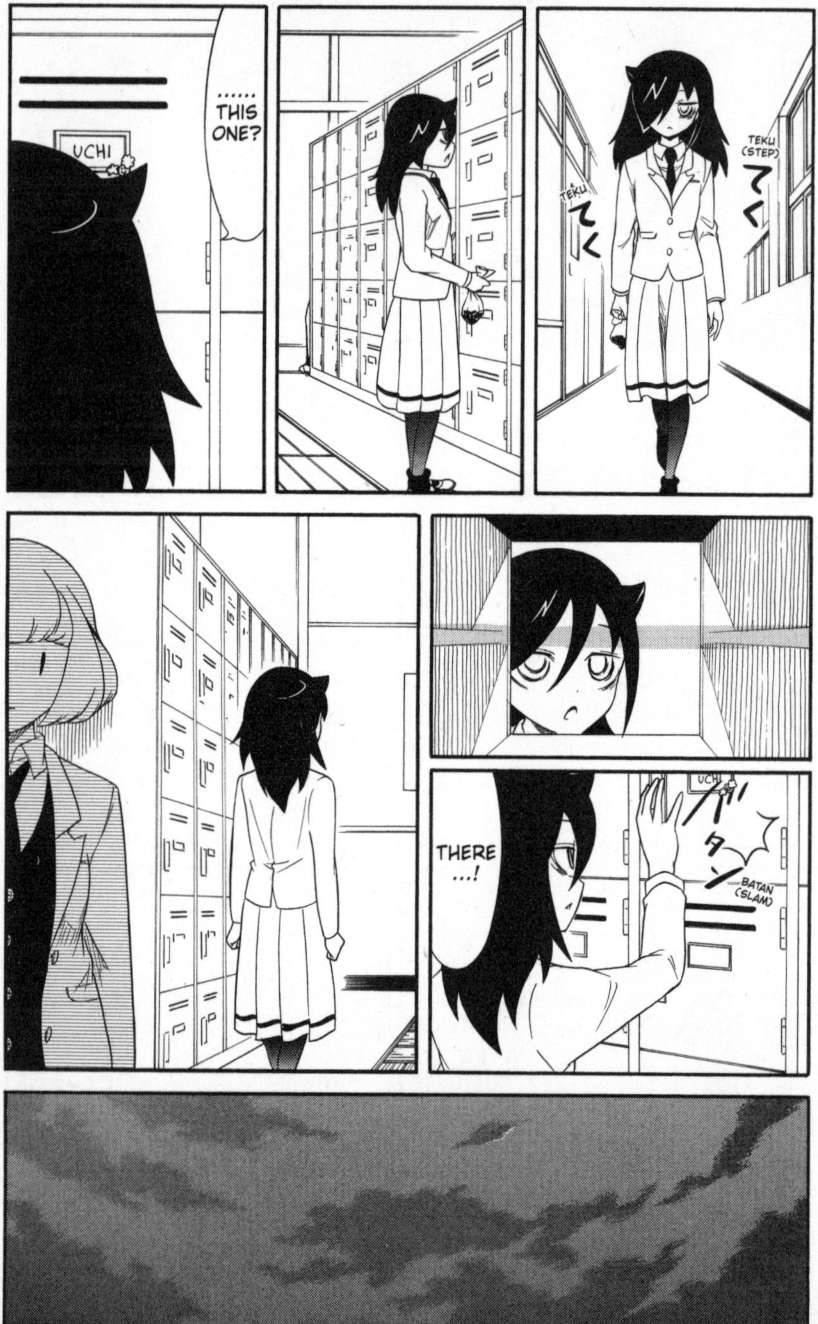
TEKU (STEP)
てく
TEKU
てく
UCHI
......THIS ONE?
UCHI
バタン
BATAN (SLAM)
THERE ...!

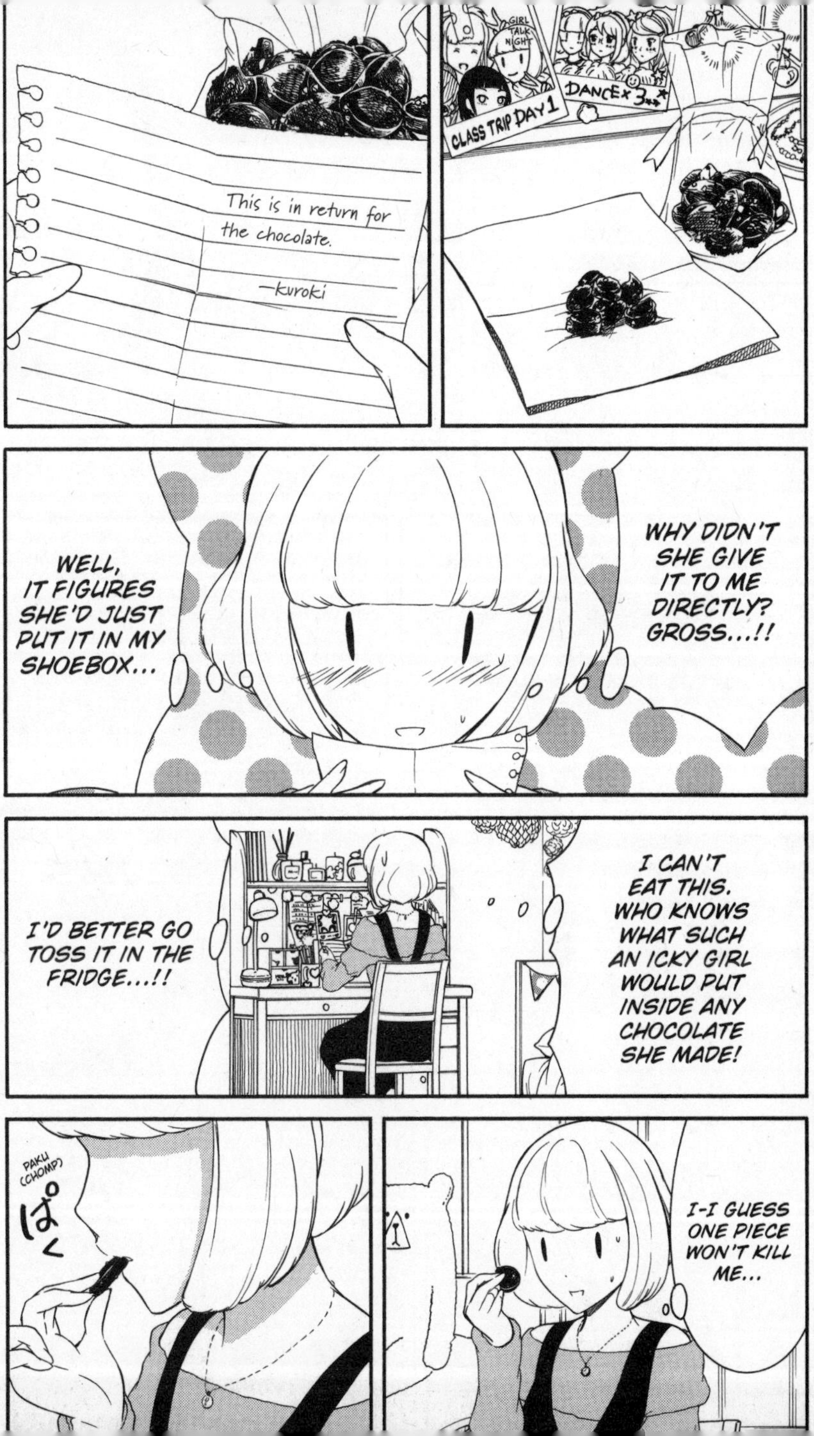
GIRL TALK NIGHT
DANCEx3
CLASS TRIP DAY 1
This is in return for the chocolate.
—kuroki
WHY DIDN'T SHE GIVE IT TO ME DIRECTLY? GROSS...!!
WELL, IT FIGURES SHE'D JUST PUT IT IN MY SHOEBOX...
I CAN'T EAT THIS. WHO KNOWS WHAT SUCH AN ICKY GIRL WOULD PUT INSIDE ANY CHOCOLATE SHE MADE!
I'D BETTER GO TOSS IT IN THE FRIDGE...!!
I-I GUESS ONE PIECE WON'T KILL ME...
PAKU (CHOMP)
ぱく

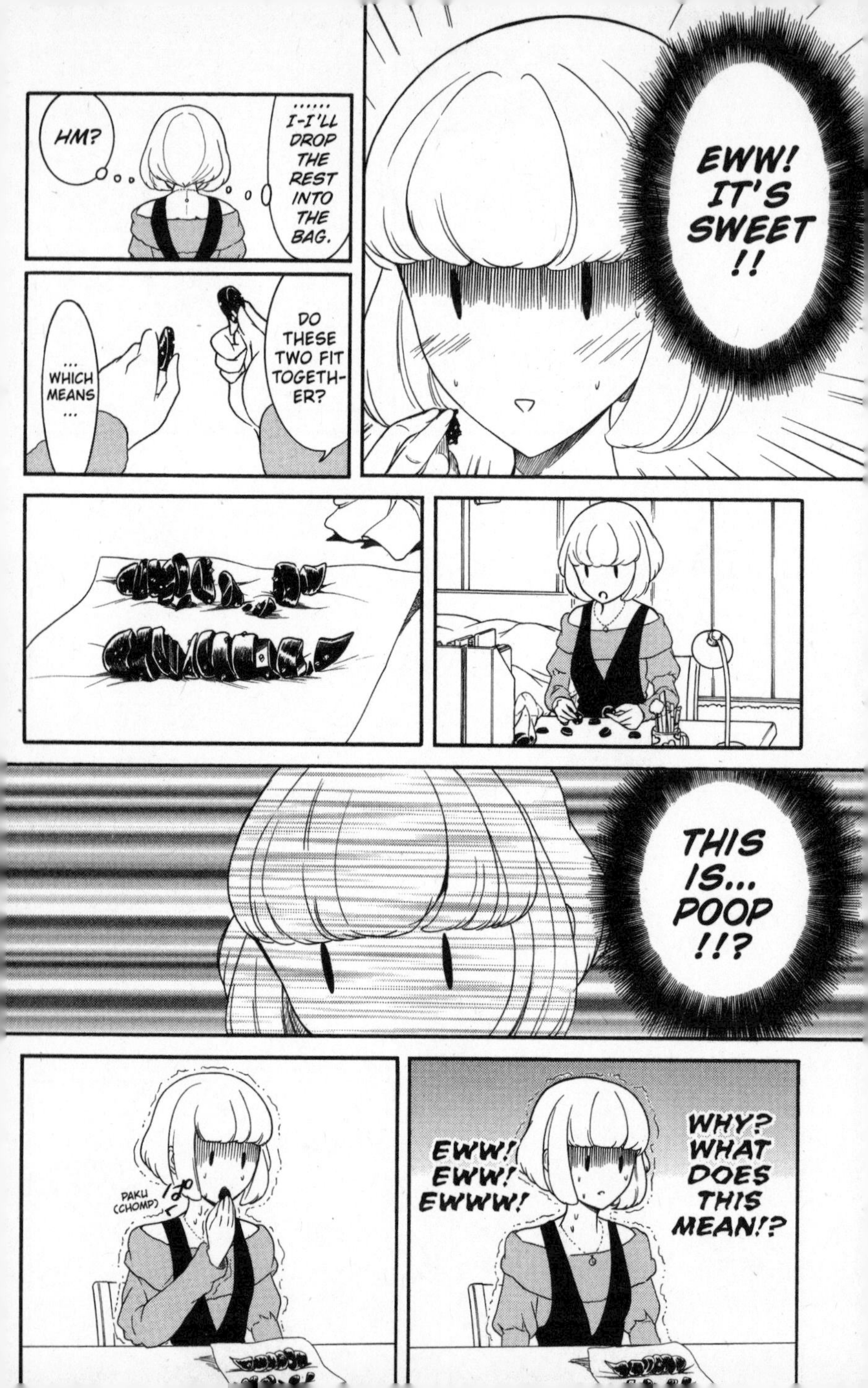
EWW! IT'S SWEET!!
...... I-I'LL DROP THE REST INTO THE BAG.
HM?
DO THESE TWO FIT TOGETH-ER?
... WHICH MEANS ...
THIS IS... POOP!!?
WHY? WHAT DOES THIS MEAN!?
EWW! EWW! EWWW!
PAKU (CHOMP)

No Matter How I Look at It, It's You Guys' Fault I'm Not Popular!

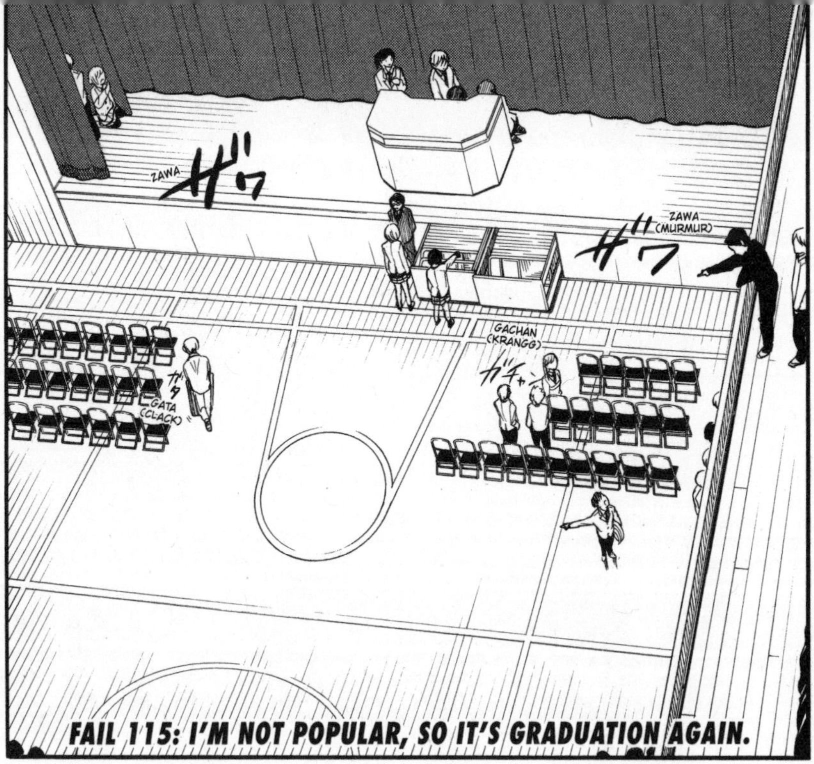
ZAWA (MURMUR)
ザワ
ZAWA
ザワ
GACHAN (KRANGG)
ガチャン
GATA (CLACK)
ガタ
FAIL 115: I'M NOT POPULAR, SO IT'S GRADUATION AGAIN.

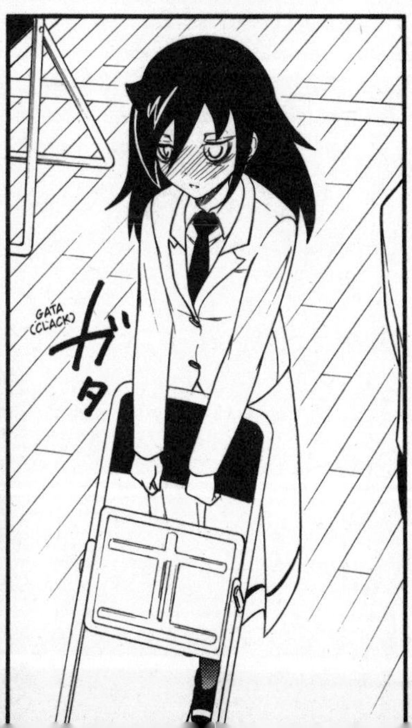
GATA (CLACK)
ガタ

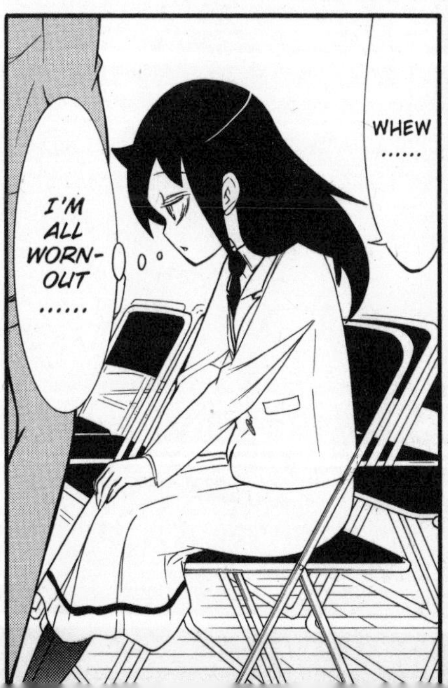
WHEW ......
I'M ALL WORN-OUT ......

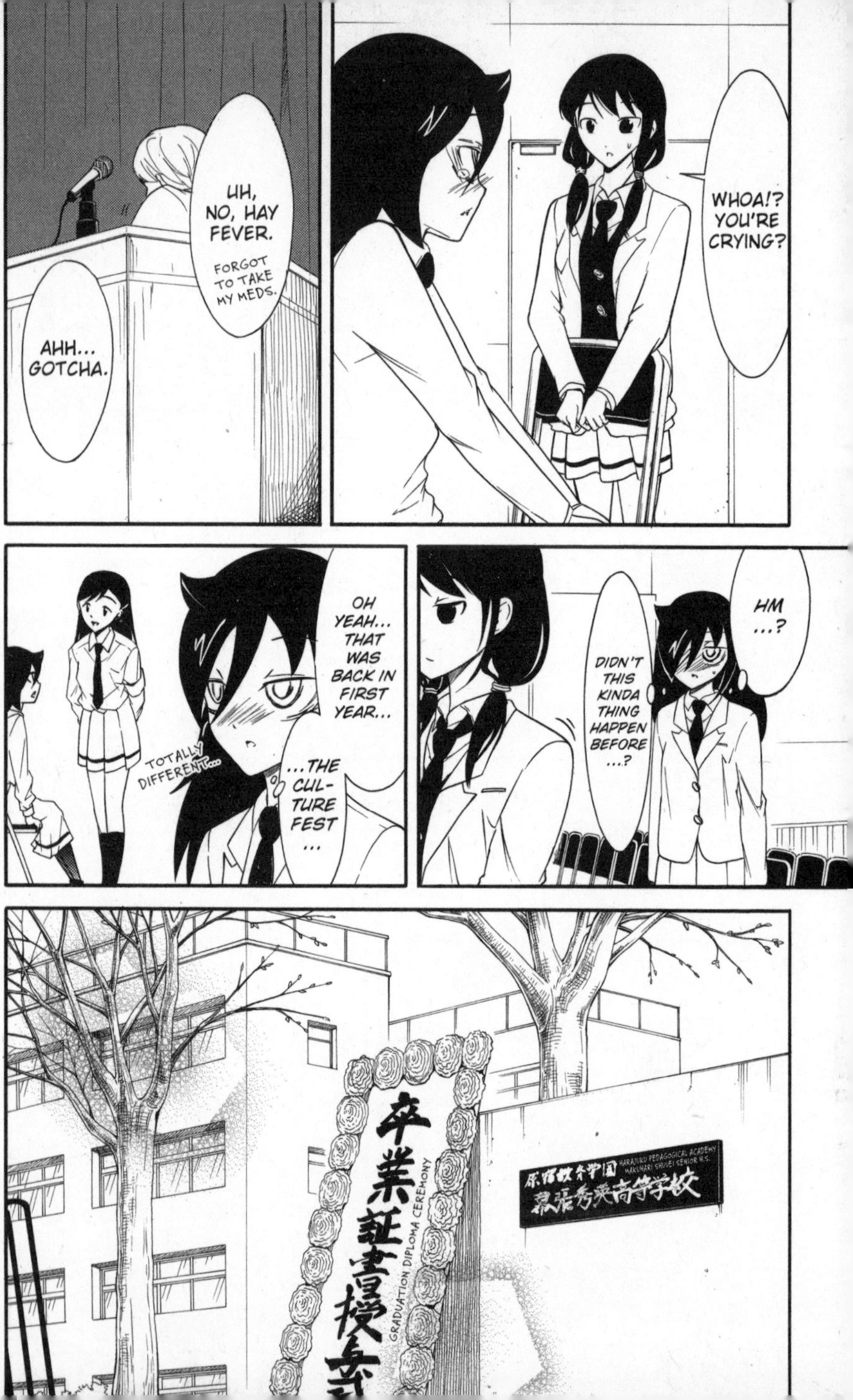
WHOA!? YOU'RE CRYING?
UH, NO, HAY FEVER.
FORGOT TO TAKE MY MEDS.
AHH... GOTCHA.
HM ...?
DIDN'T THIS KINDA THING HAPPEN BEFORE ...?
OH YEAH... THAT WAS BACK IN FIRST YEAR...
...THE CUL-TURE FEST ...
TOTALLY DIFFERENT...
卒業証書授与式
GRADUATION DIPLOMA CEREMONY
原宿教育学園 幕張秀英高等学校
HARAJUKU PEDAGOGICAL ACADEMY MAKUHARI SHUEI SENIOR H.S.

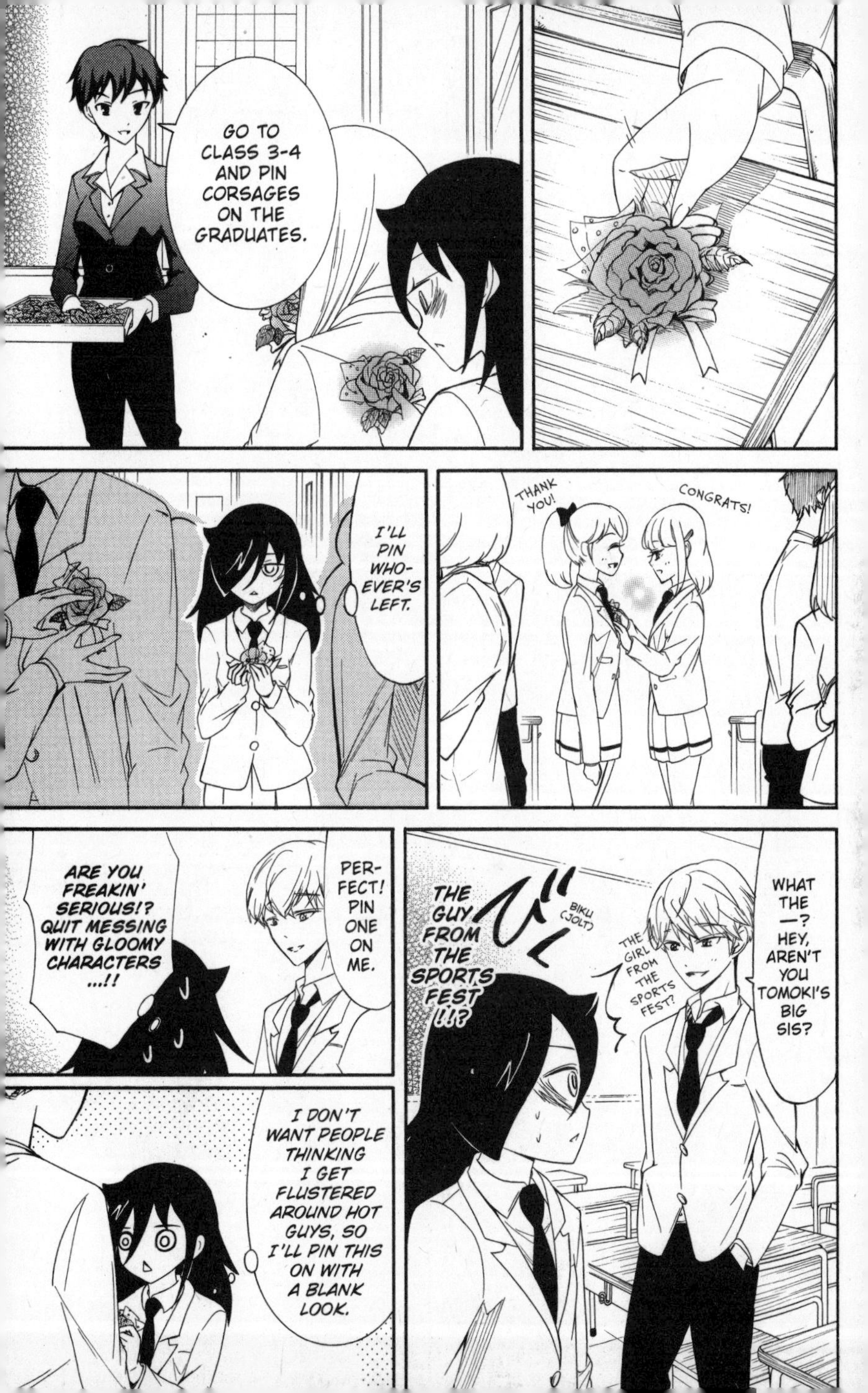
GO TO CLASS 3-4 AND PIN CORSAGES ON THE GRADUATES.
CONGRATS!
THANK YOU!
I'LL PIN WHO-EVER'S LEFT.
WHAT THE —? HEY, AREN'T YOU TOMOKI'S BIG SIS?
THE GIRL FROM THE SPORTS FEST?
BIKU (JOLT)
THE GUY FROM THE SPORTS FEST!!?
PER-FECT! PIN ONE ON ME.
ARE YOU FREAKIN' SERIOUS!? QUIT MESSING WITH GLOOMY CHARACTERS ...!!
I DON'T WANT PEOPLE THINKING I GET FLUSTERED AROUND HOT GUYS, SO I'LL PIN THIS ON WITH A BLANK LOOK.

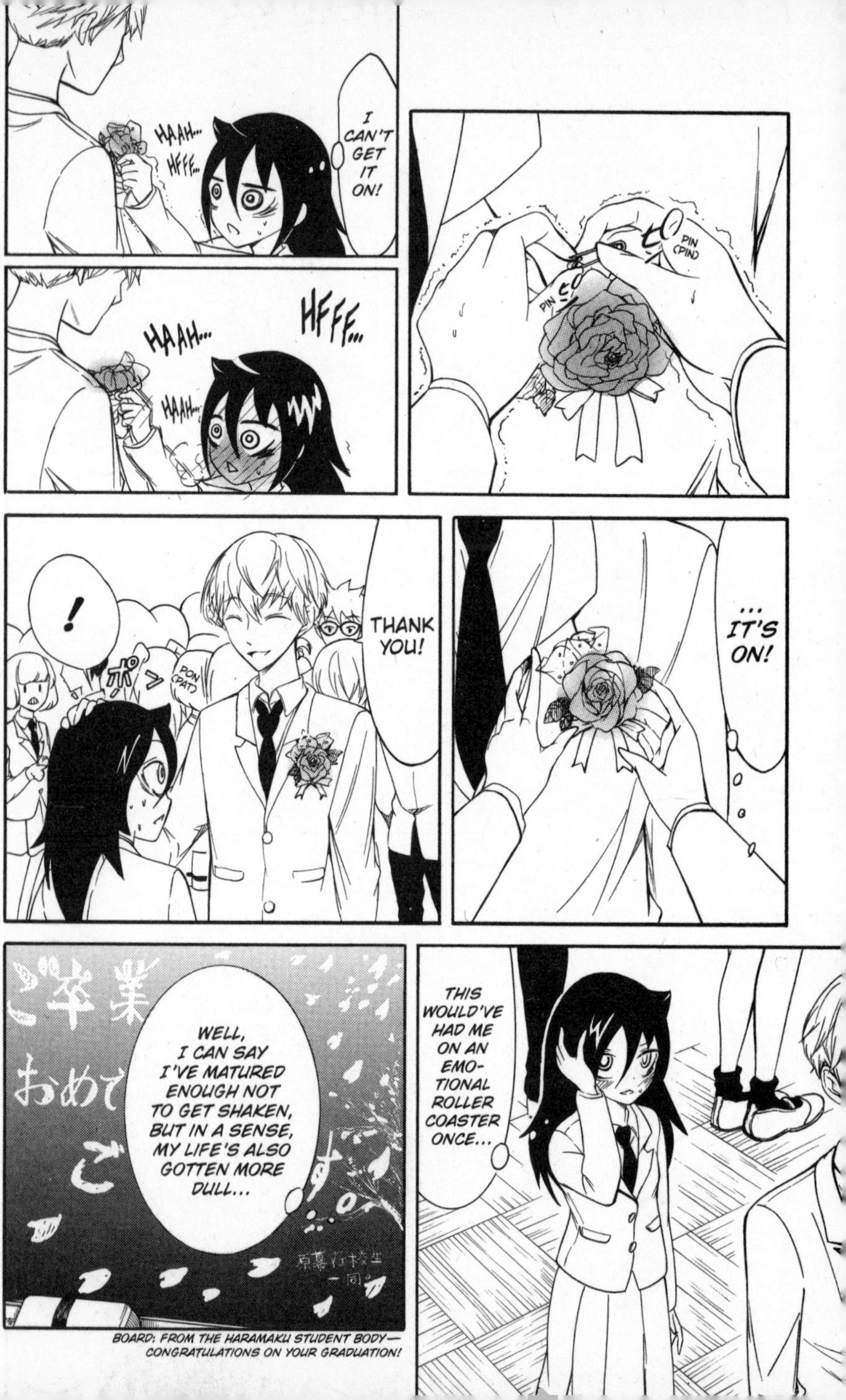
I CAN'T GET IT ON!
HAAH... HFFF...
HAAH... HFFF... HAAH...
PIN (PIN)
PIN
...IT'S ON!
THANK YOU!
!
PON (PAT)
THIS WOULD'VE HAD ME ON AN EMOTIONAL ROLLER COASTER ONCE...
WELL, I CAN SAY I'VE MATURED ENOUGH NOT TO GET SHAKEN, BUT IN A SENSE, MY LIFE'S ALSO GOTTEN MORE DULL...
BOARD: FROM THE HARAMAKU STUDENT BODY— CONGRATULATIONS ON YOUR GRADUATION!

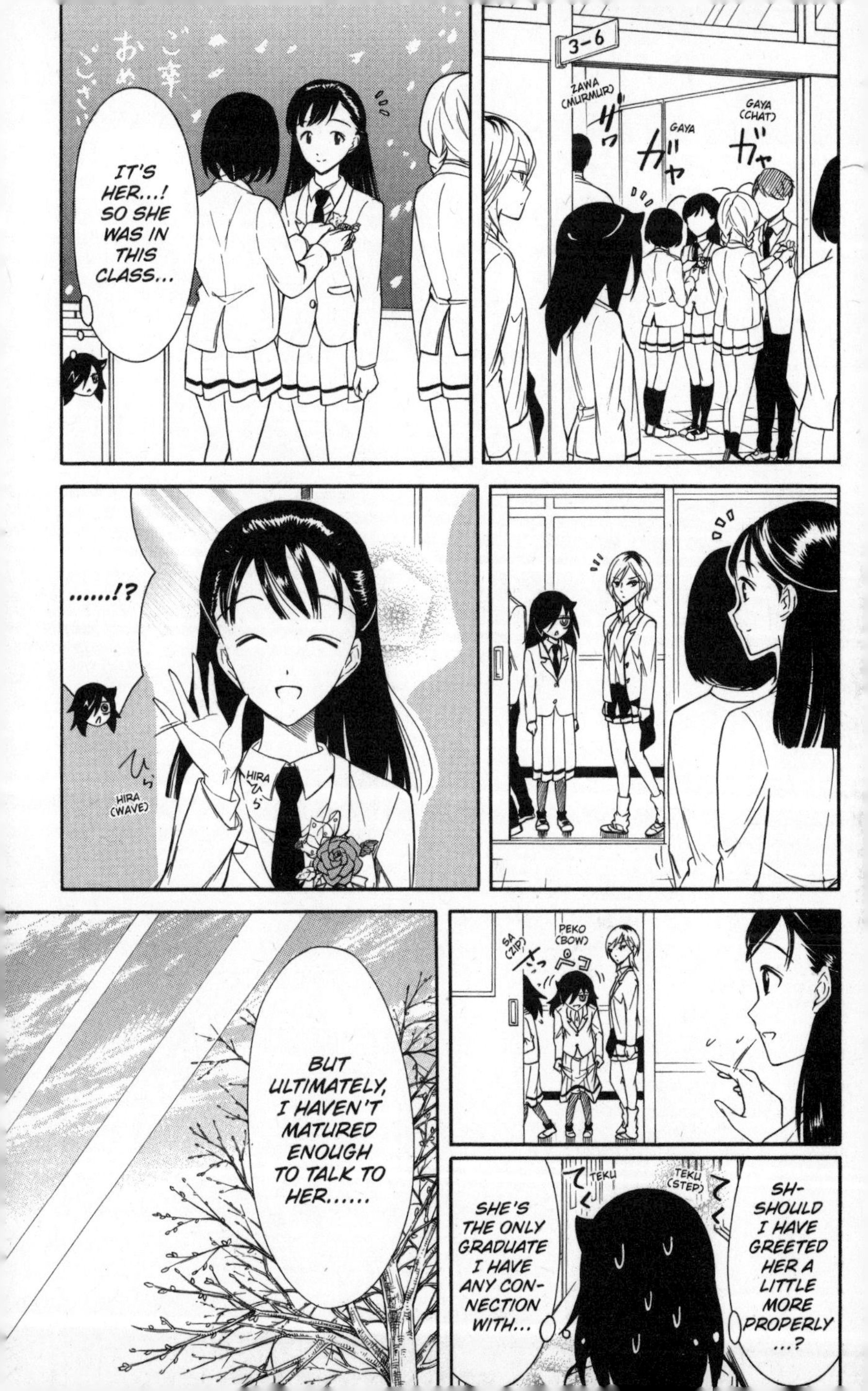
3-6
ZAWA (MURMUR)
GAYA
GAYA (CHAT)
IT'S HER...! SO SHE WAS IN THIS CLASS...
......!?
HIRA (WAVE)
HIRA
SA (ZIP)
PEKO (BOW)
SH-SHOULD I HAVE GREETED HER A LITTLE MORE PROPERLY...?
TEKU (STEP)
TEKU
SHE'S THE ONLY GRADUATE I HAVE ANY CON-NECTION WITH...
BUT ULTIMATELY, I HAVEN'T MATURED ENOUGH TO TALK TO HER......

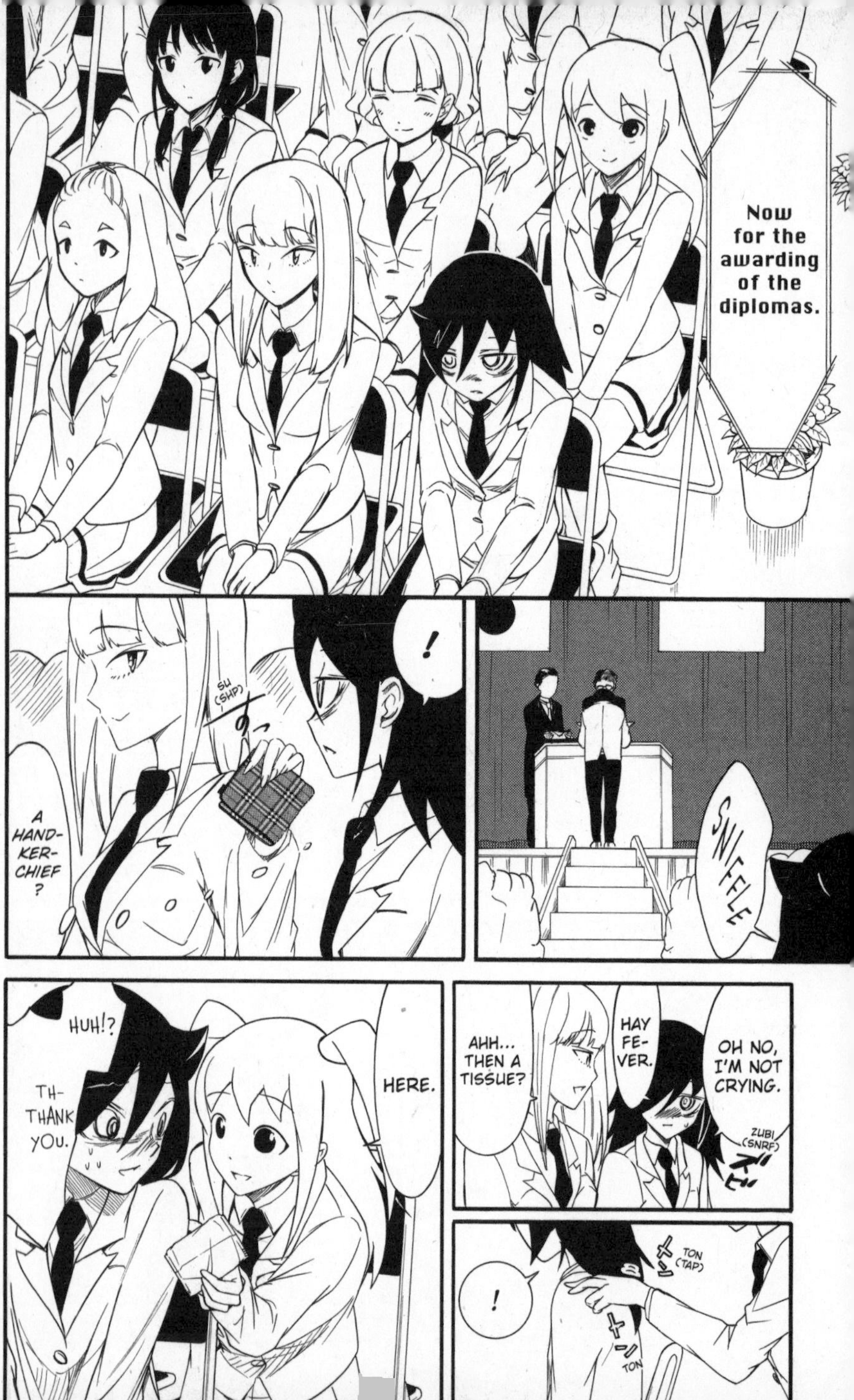
Now for the awarding of the diplomas.
SNIFFLE
!
SU (SHP)
A HANDKERCHIEF?
OH NO, I'M NOT CRYING.
HAY FEVER.
ZUBI (SNRF)
AHH... THEN A TISSUE?
TON (TAP)
!
TON
HERE.
HUH!?
TH-THANK YOU.

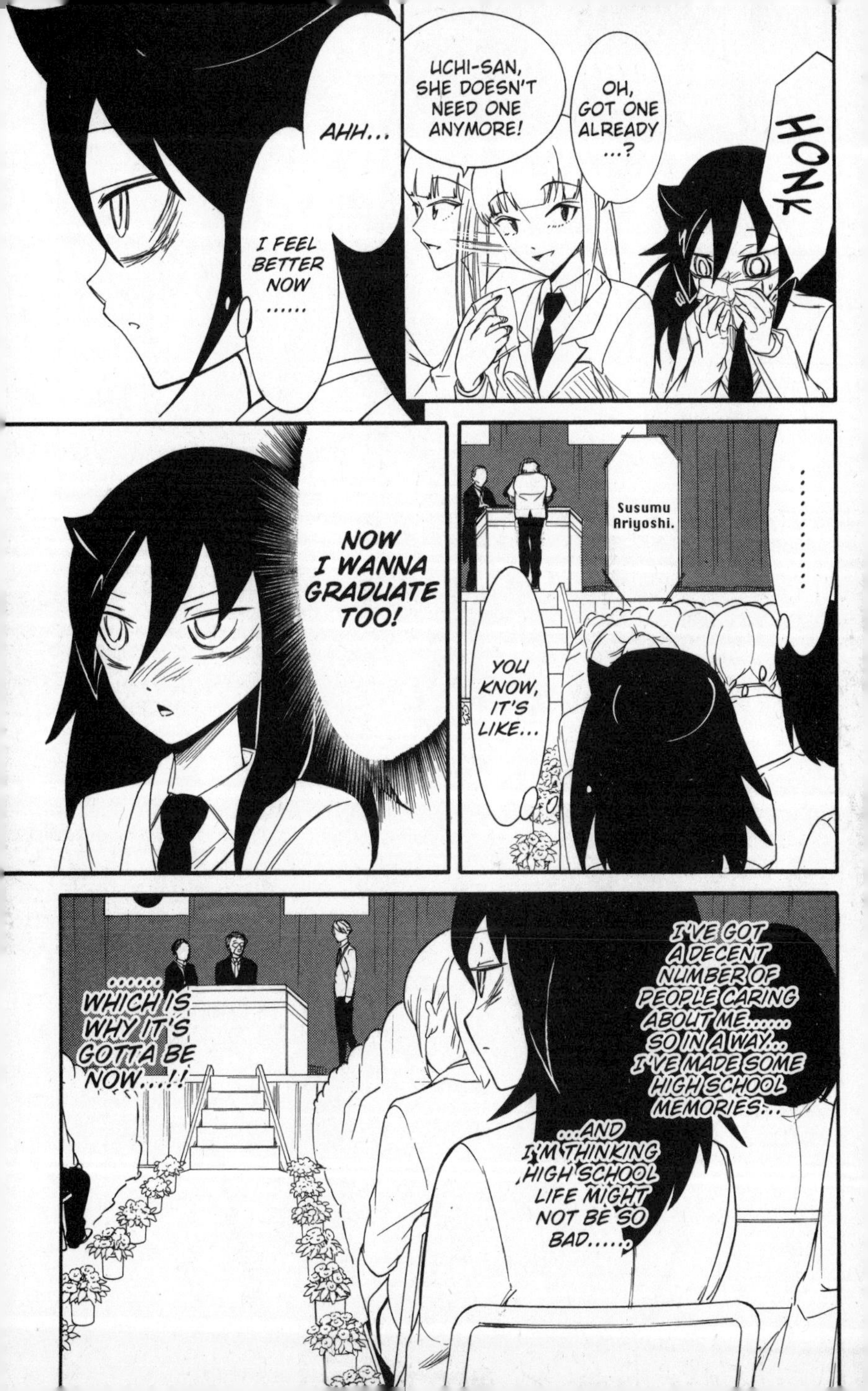
HONK
OH, GOT ONE ALREADY ...?
UCHI-SAN, SHE DOESN'T NEED ONE ANYMORE!
AHH...
I FEEL BETTER NOW ......
......
Susumu Ariyoshi.
YOU KNOW, IT'S LIKE...
NOW I WANNA GRADUATE TOO!
I'VE GOT A DECENT NUMBER OF PEOPLE CARING ABOUT ME...... SO IN A WAY... I'VE MADE SOME HIGH SCHOOL MEMORIES...
...AND I'M THINKING HIGH SCHOOL LIFE MIGHT NOT BE SO BAD.....
...... WHICH IS WHY IT'S GOTTA BE NOW...!!

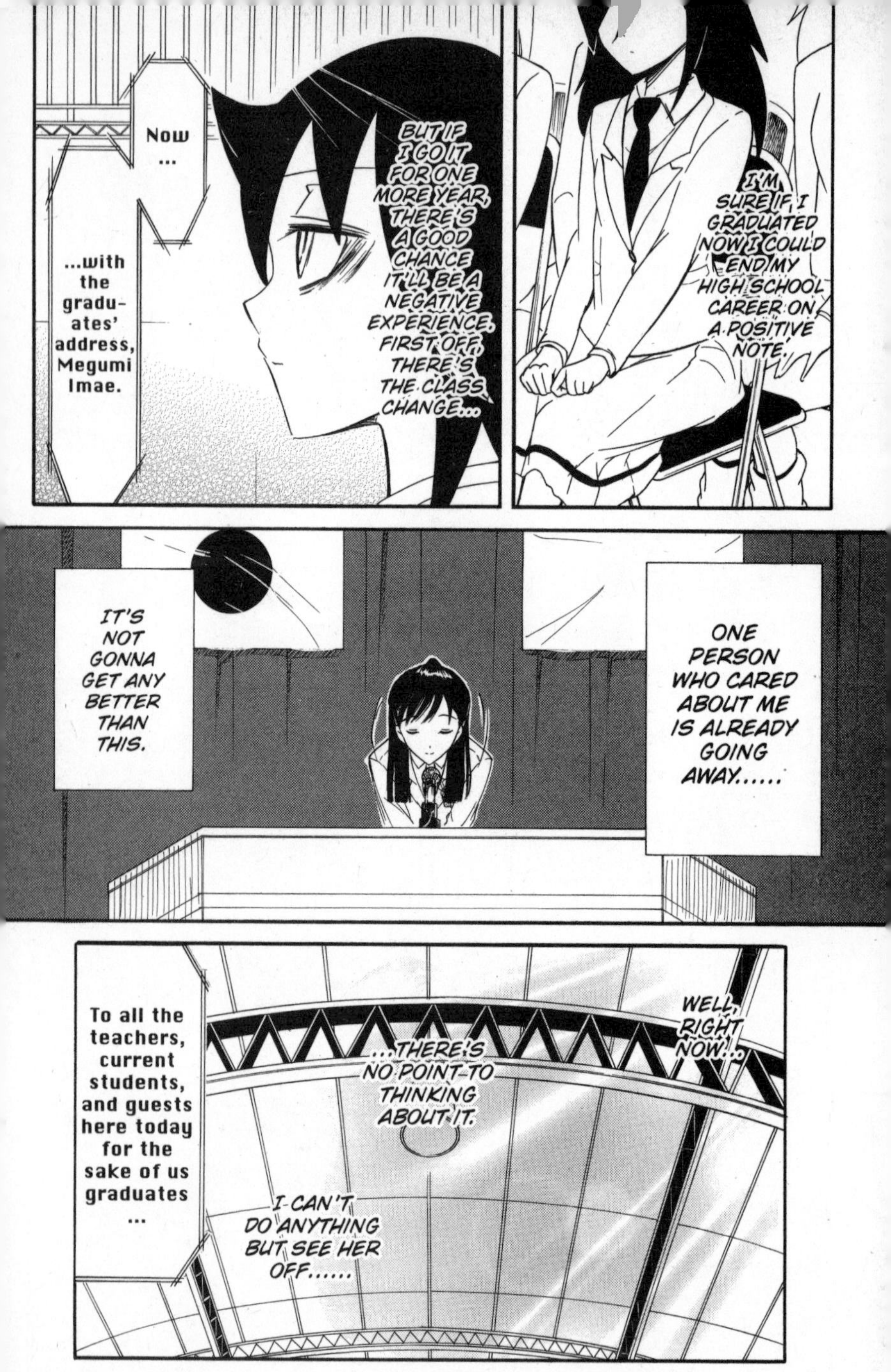
I'M SURE IF I GRADUATED NOW I COULD END MY HIGH SCHOOL CAREER ON A POSITIVE NOTE.
BUT IF I GO IT FOR ONE MORE YEAR, THERE'S A GOOD CHANCE IT'LL BE A NEGATIVE EXPERIENCE. FIRST OFF, THERE'S THE CLASS CHANGE...
Now ...
...with the gradu-ates' address, Megumi Imae.
ONE PERSON WHO CARED ABOUT ME IS ALREADY GOING AWAY......
IT'S NOT GONNA GET ANY BETTER THAN THIS.
WELL, RIGHT NOW...
...THERE'S NO POINT TO THINKING ABOUT IT.
I CAN'T DO ANYTHING BUT SEE HER OFF......
To all the teachers, current students, and guests here today for the sake of us graduates ...

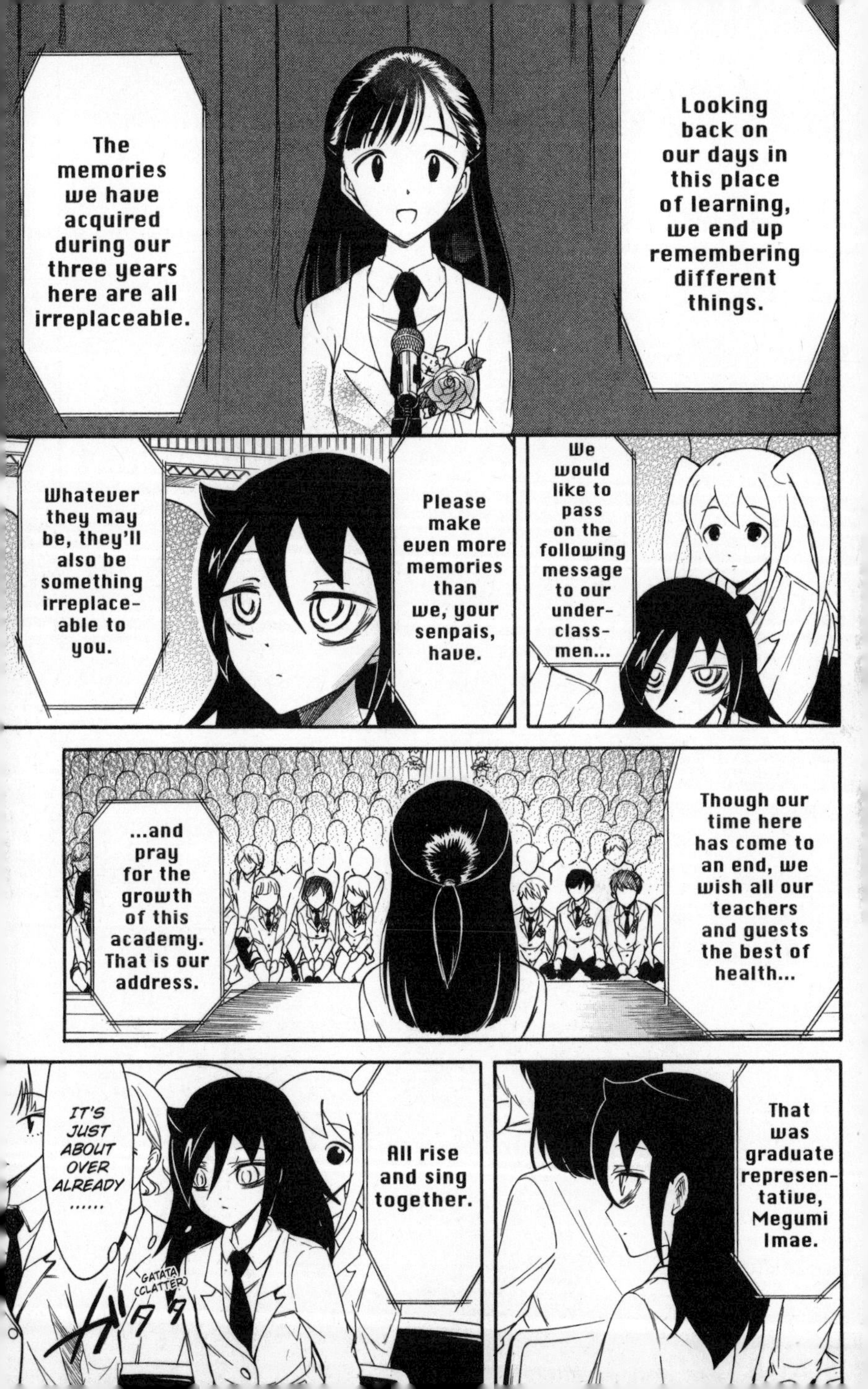
Looking back on our days in this place of learning, we end up remembering different things.
The memories we have acquired during our three years here are all irreplaceable.
We would like to pass on the following message to our under-class-men...
Please make even more memories than we, your senpais, have.
Whatever they may be, they'll also be something irreplace-able to you.
Though our time here has come to an end, we wish all our teachers and guests the best of health...
...and pray for the growth of this academy. That is our address.
That was graduate represen-tative, Megumi Imae.
All rise and sing together.
IT'S JUST ABOUT OVER ALREADY ......
GATATA (CLATTER)

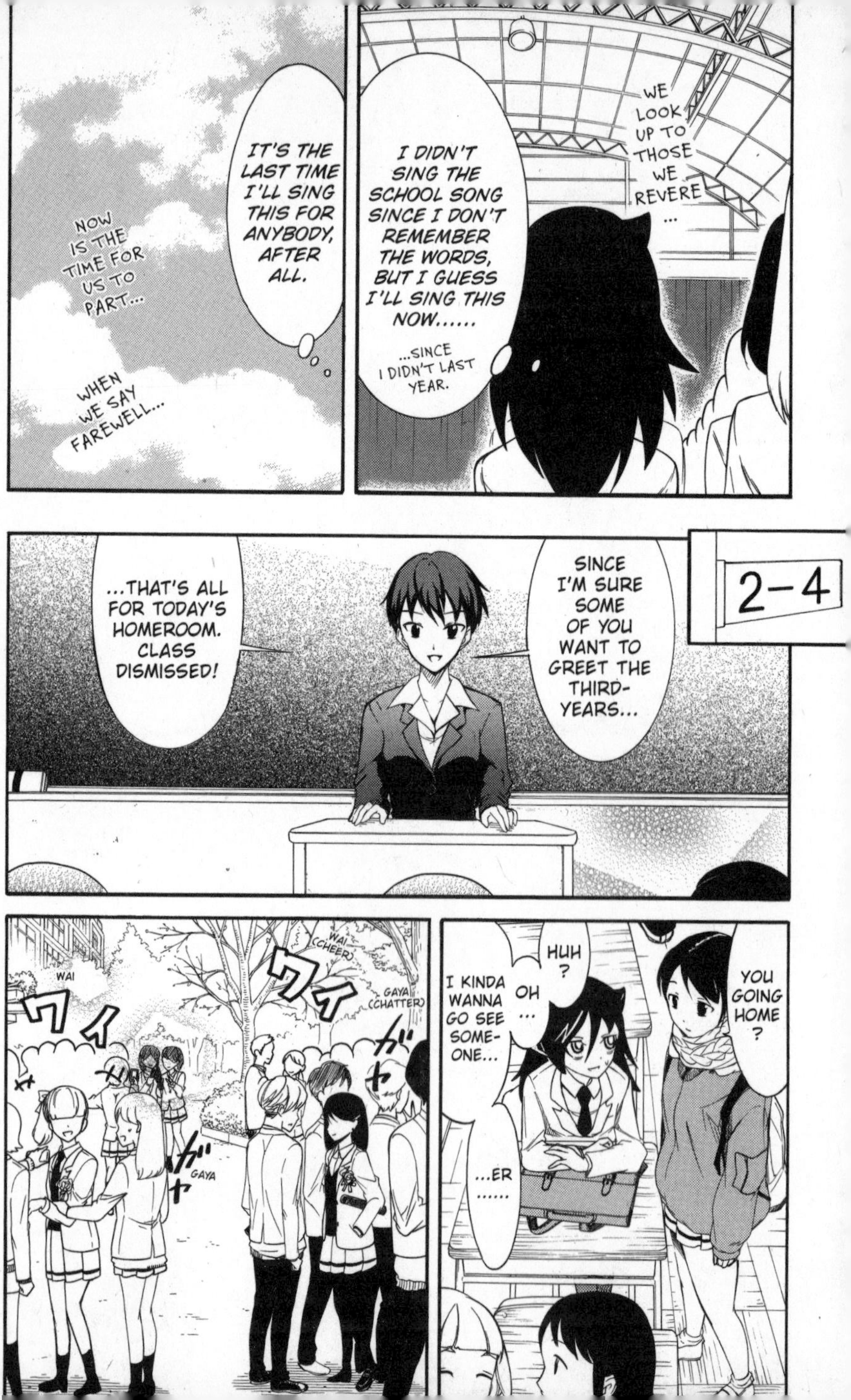
WE LOOK UP TO THOSE WE REVERE ...
I DIDN'T SING THE SCHOOL SONG SINCE I DON'T REMEMBER THE WORDS, BUT I GUESS I'LL SING THIS NOW......
...SINCE I DIDN'T LAST YEAR.
IT'S THE LAST TIME I'LL SING THIS FOR ANYBODY, AFTER ALL.
NOW IS THE TIME FOR US TO PART...
WHEN WE SAY FAREWELL...
2-4
SINCE I'M SURE SOME OF YOU WANT TO GREET THE THIRD-YEARS...
...THAT'S ALL FOR TODAY'S HOMEROOM. CLASS DISMISSED!
YOU GOING HOME?
HUH?
OH...
I KINDA WANNA GO SEE SOMEONE...
...ER......
ワイ
WAI (CHEER)
ガヤ
GAYA (CHATTER)
ワイ
WAI
ガヤ
GAYA

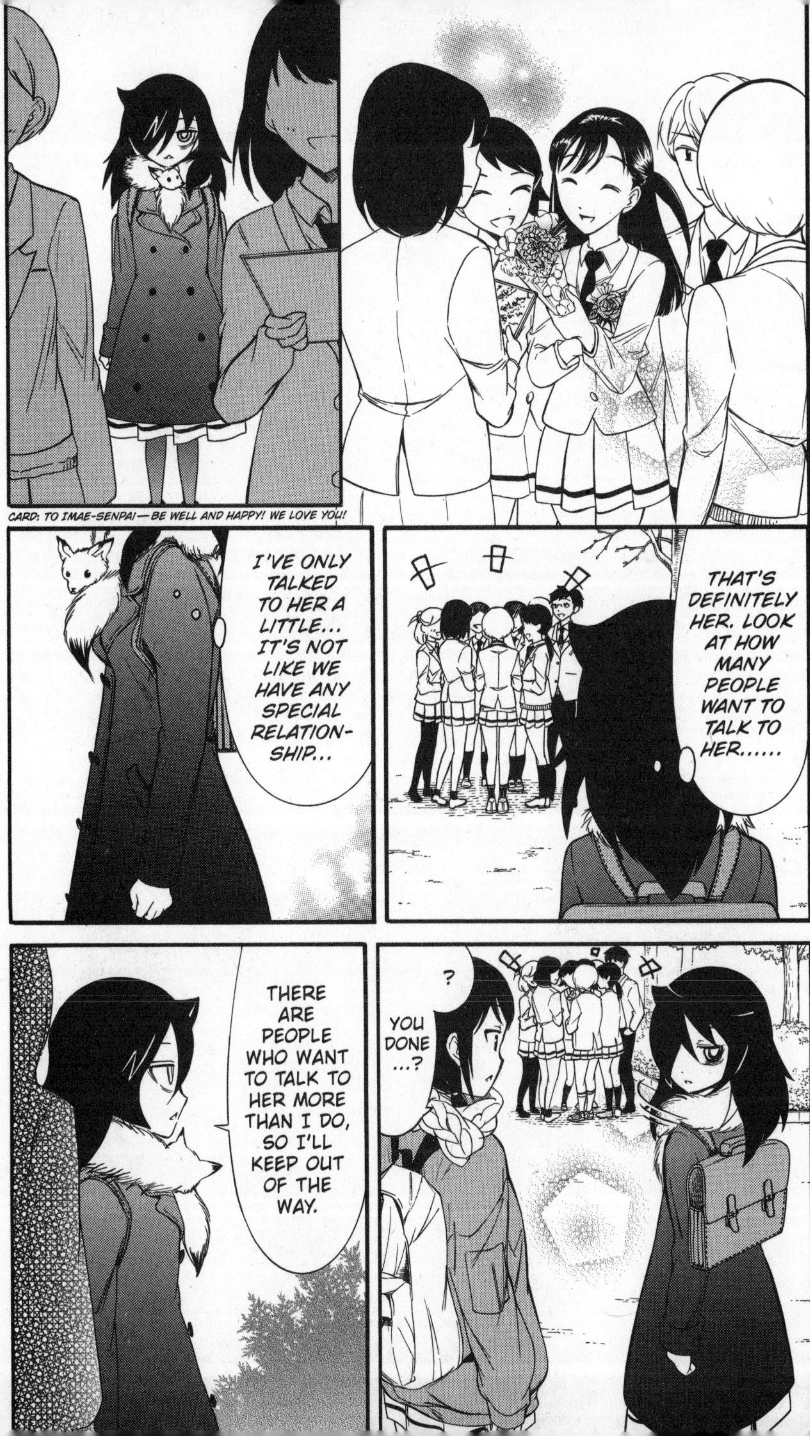
CARD: TO IMAE-SENPAI—BE WELL AND HAPPY! WE LOVE YOU!
THAT'S DEFINITELY HER. LOOK AT HOW MANY PEOPLE WANT TO TALK TO HER......
I'VE ONLY TALKED TO HER A LITTLE... IT'S NOT LIKE WE HAVE ANY SPECIAL RELATION-SHIP...
?
YOU DONE ...?
THERE ARE PEOPLE WHO WANT TO TALK TO HER MORE THAN I DO, SO I'LL KEEP OUT OF THE WAY.

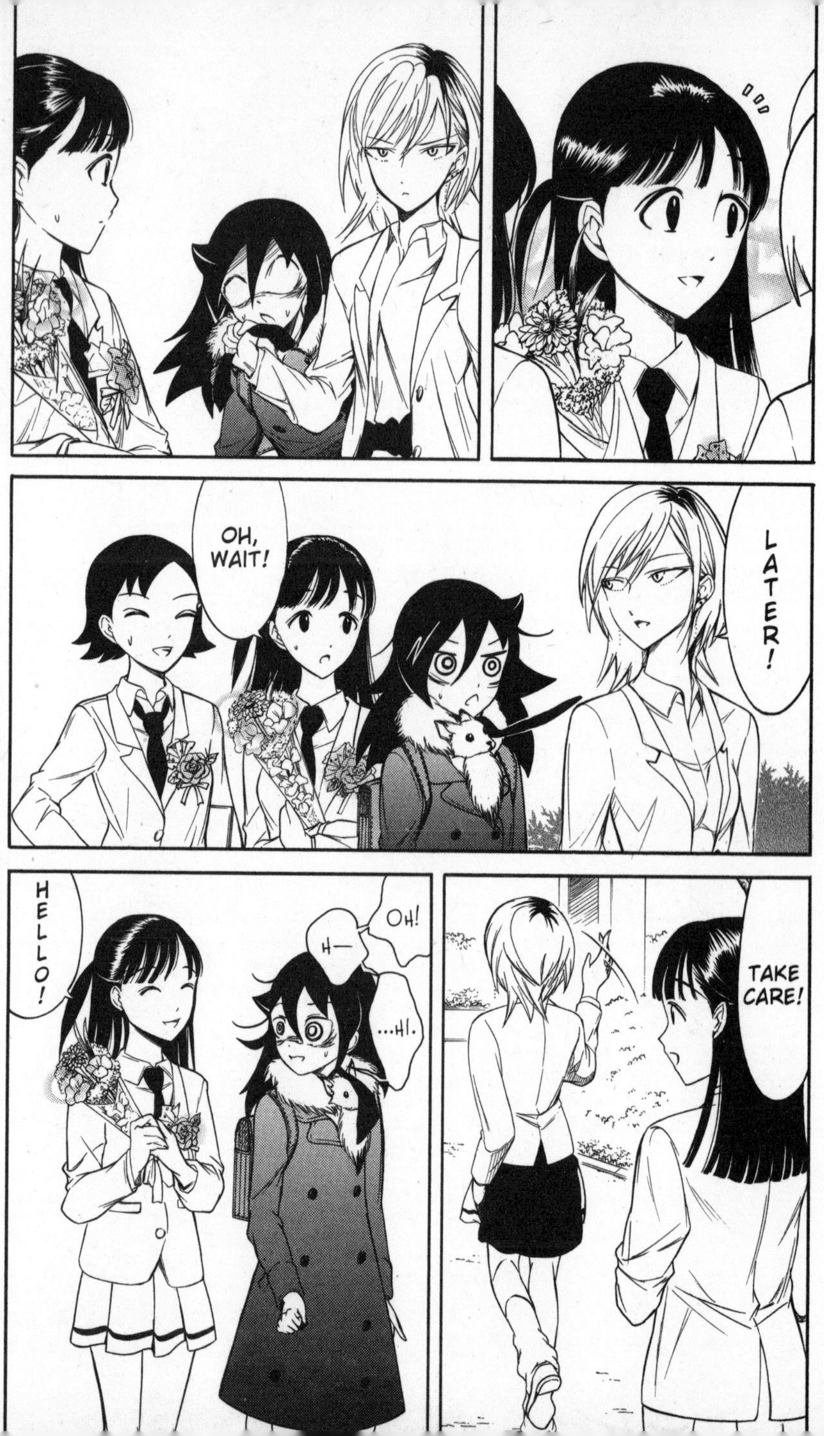
LATER!
OH, WAIT!
TAKE CARE!
OH!
H—
HELLO!
...HI.

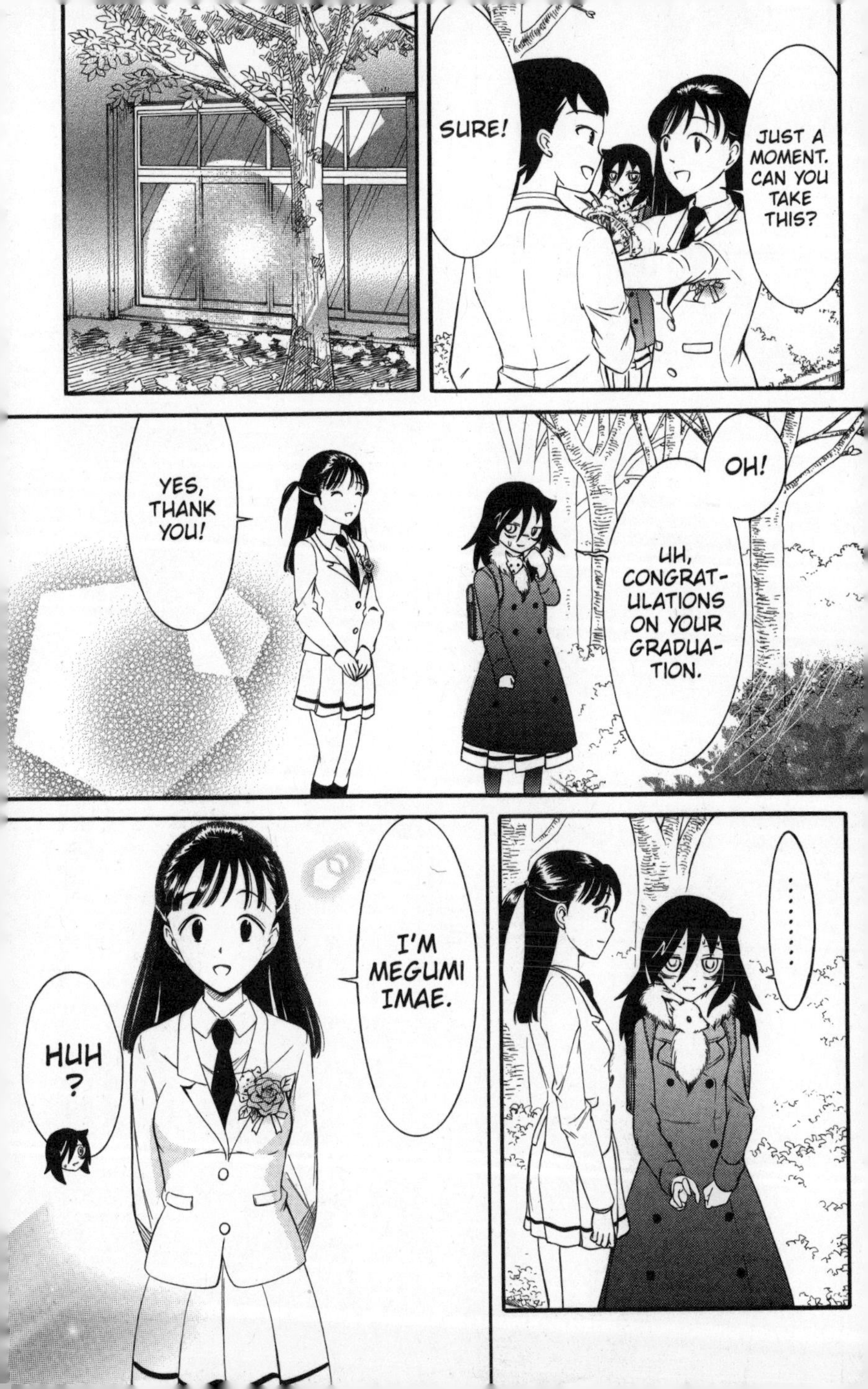
JUST A MOMENT. CAN YOU TAKE THIS?
SURE!
OH!
UH, CONGRATULATIONS ON YOUR GRADUATION.
YES, THANK YOU!
......
I'M MEGUMI IMAE.
HUH?

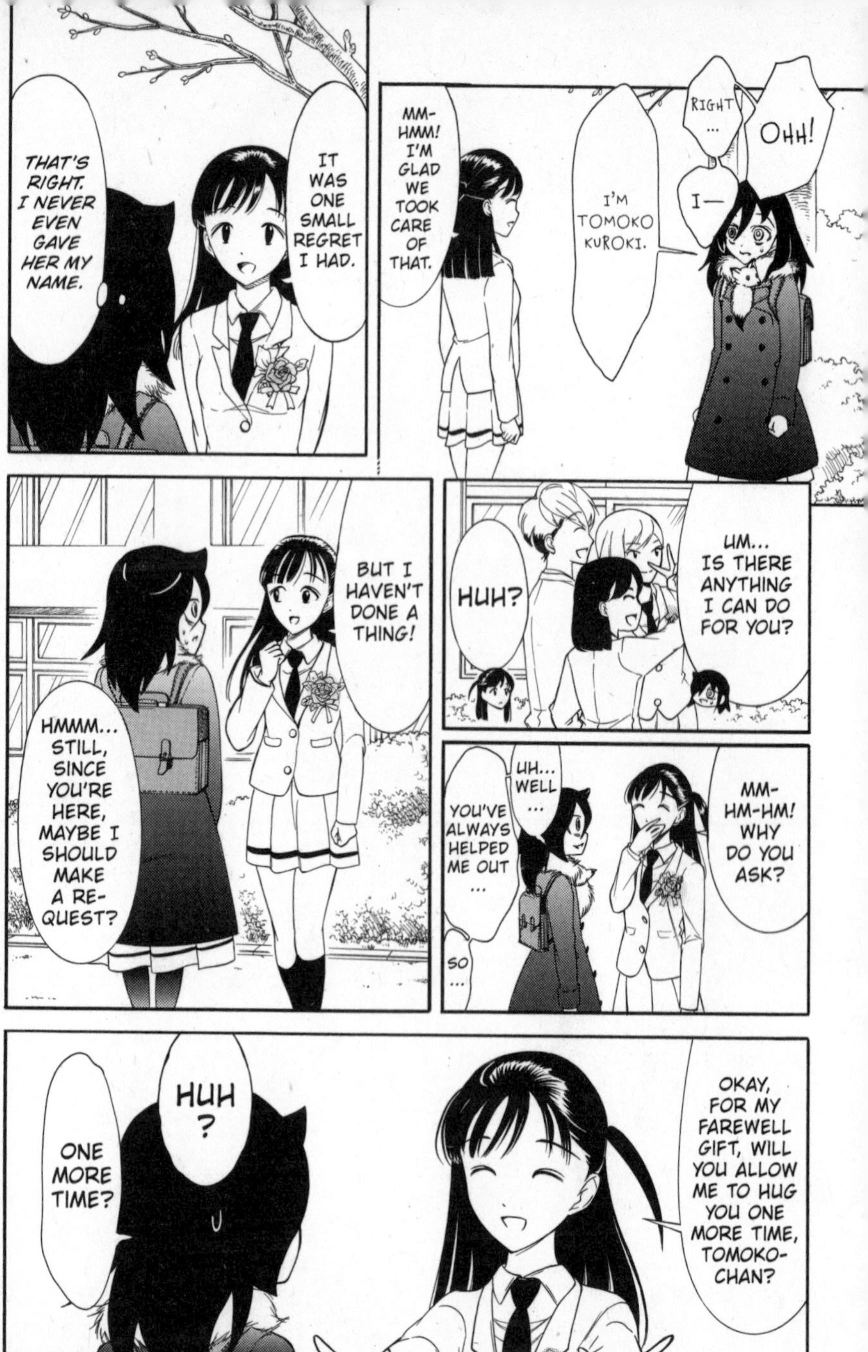
OHH!
RIGHT ...
I—
I'M TOMOKO KUROKI.
MM-HMM! I'M GLAD WE TOOK CARE OF THAT.
IT WAS ONE SMALL REGRET I HAD.
THAT'S RIGHT. I NEVER EVEN GAVE HER MY NAME.
UM... IS THERE ANYTHING I CAN DO FOR YOU?
HUH?
MM-HM-HM! WHY DO YOU ASK?
UH... WELL ...
YOU'VE ALWAYS HELPED ME OUT ...
SO ...
BUT I HAVEN'T DONE A THING!
HMMM... STILL, SINCE YOU'RE HERE, MAYBE I SHOULD MAKE A RE-QUEST?
OKAY, FOR MY FAREWELL GIFT, WILL YOU ALLOW ME TO HUG YOU ONE MORE TIME, TOMOKO-CHAN?
HUH?
ONE MORE TIME?

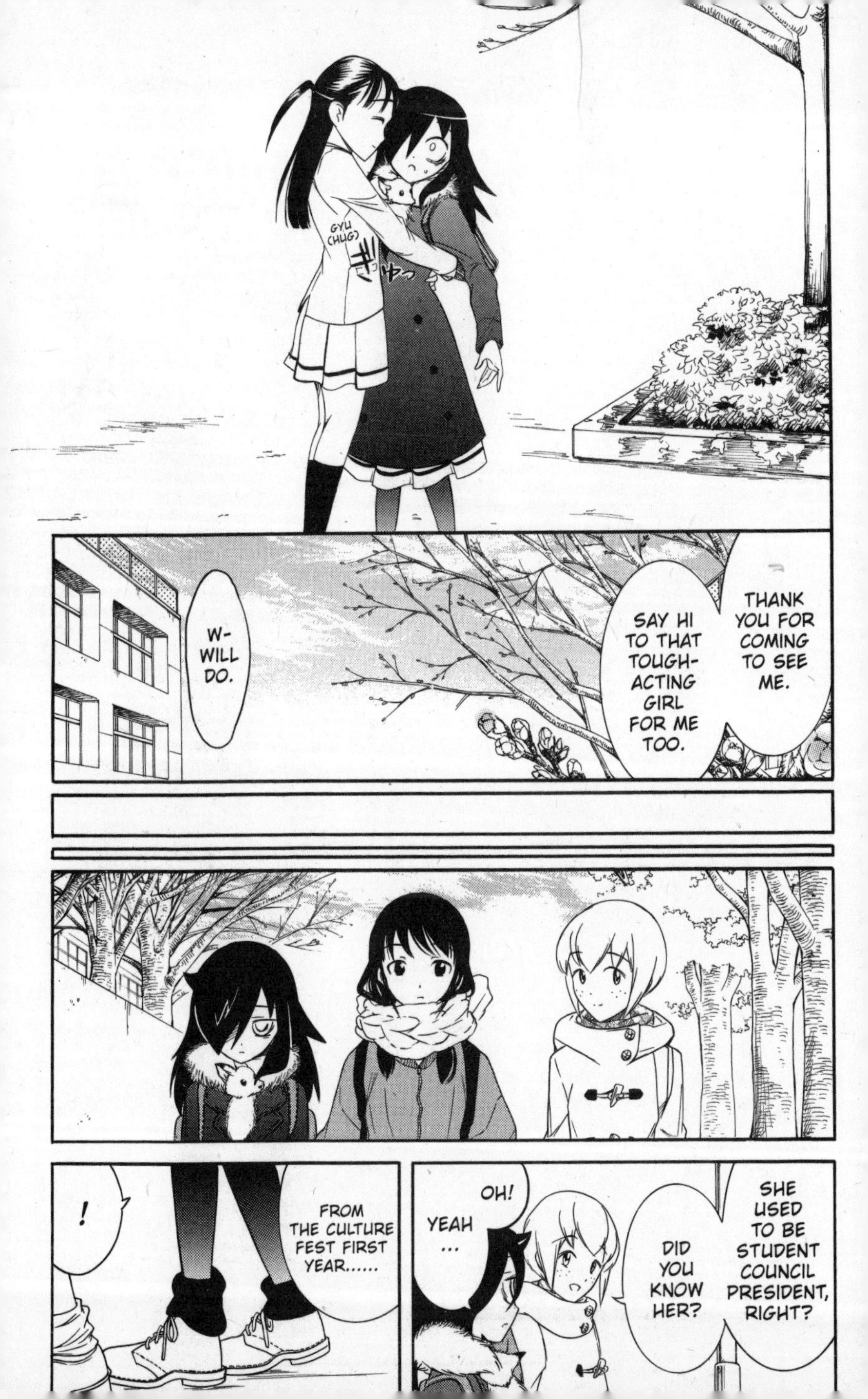
GYU (HUG)
THANK YOU FOR COMING TO SEE ME.
SAY HI TO THAT TOUGH-ACTING GIRL FOR ME TOO.
W-WILL DO.
SHE USED TO BE STUDENT COUNCIL PRESIDENT, RIGHT?
DID YOU KNOW HER?
OH!
YEAH ...
FROM THE CULTURE FEST FIRST YEAR......
!

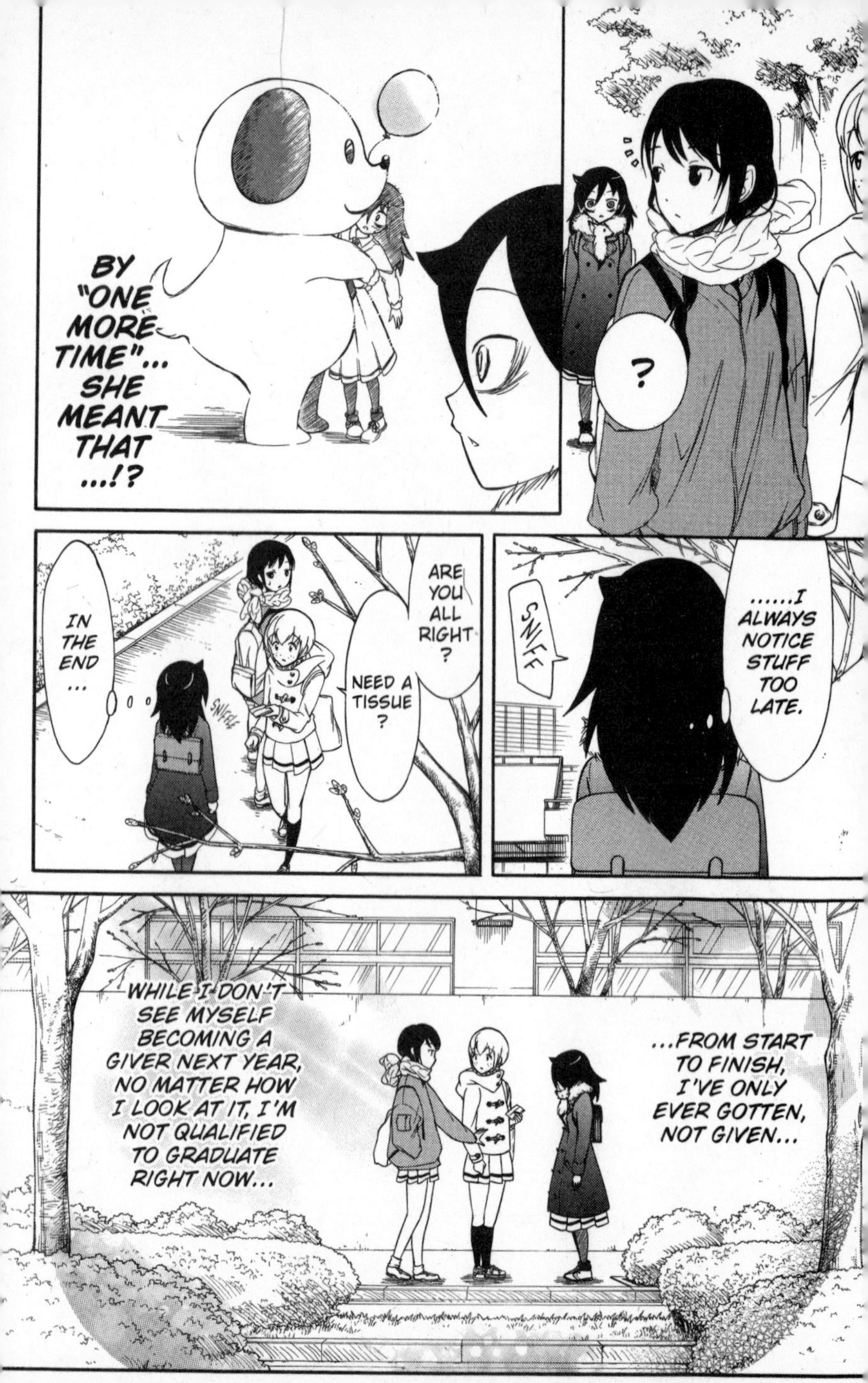
?
BY "ONE MORE TIME"... SHE MEANT THAT ...!?
SNIFF
......I ALWAYS NOTICE STUFF TOO LATE.
ARE YOU ALL RIGHT?
NEED A TISSUE?
IN THE END ...
SNIFFLE
...FROM START TO FINISH, I'VE ONLY EVER GOTTEN, NOT GIVEN...
WHILE I DON'T SEE MYSELF BECOMING A GIVER NEXT YEAR, NO MATTER HOW I LOOK AT IT, I'M NOT QUALIFIED TO GRADUATE RIGHT NOW...

No Matter How I Look at It, It's You Guys' Fault I'm Not Popular!

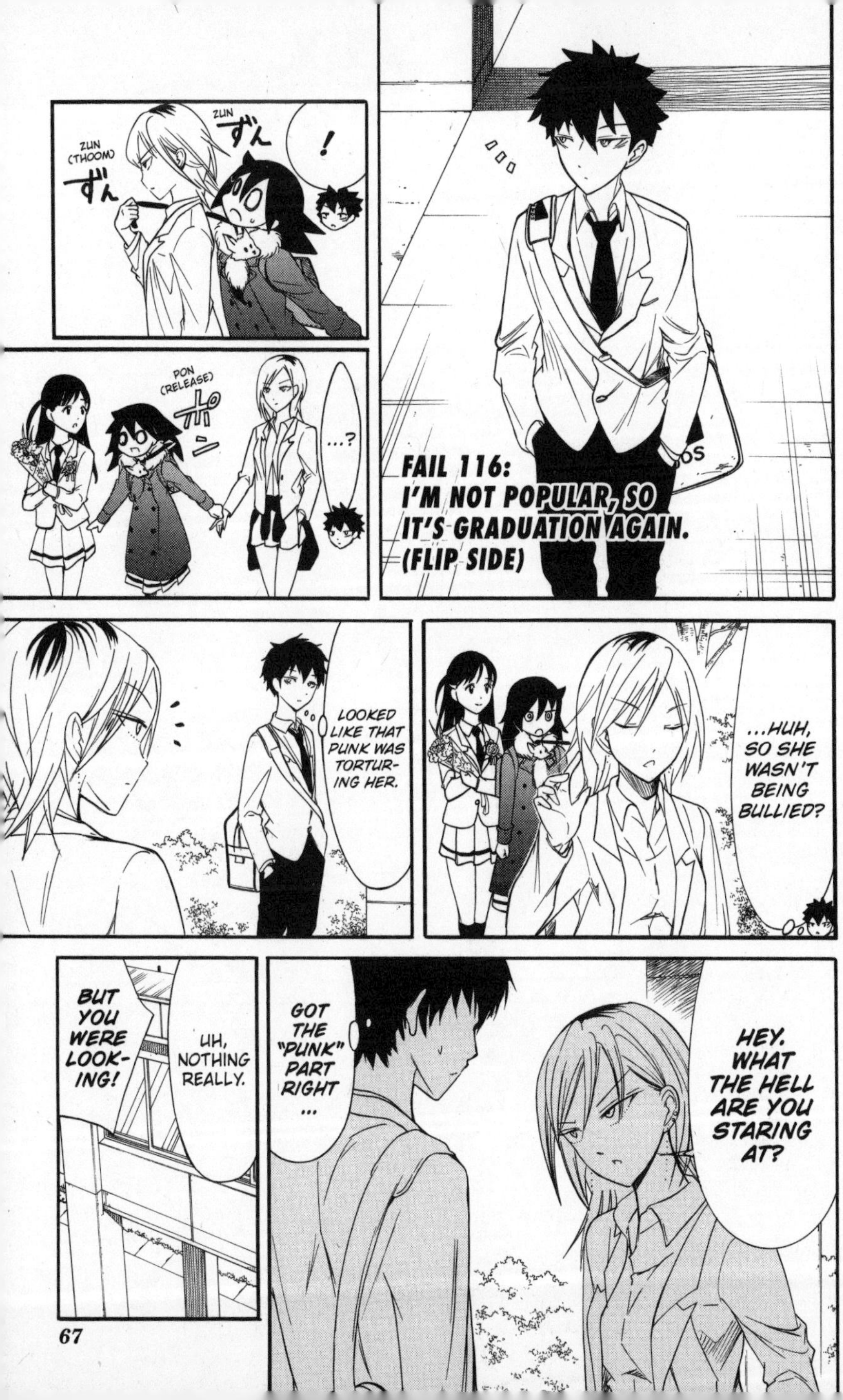
FAIL 116:
I'M NOT POPULAR, SO IT'S GRADUATION AGAIN.
(FLIP SIDE)
!
ZUN
ずん
ZUN (THOOM)
ずん
...?
PON (RELEASE)
ポン
...HUH, SO SHE WASN'T BEING BULLIED?
LOOKED LIKE THAT PUNK WAS TORTURING HER.
HEY. WHAT THE HELL ARE YOU STARING AT?
GOT THE "PUNK" PART RIGHT ...
UH, NOTHING REALLY.
BUT YOU WERE LOOKING!

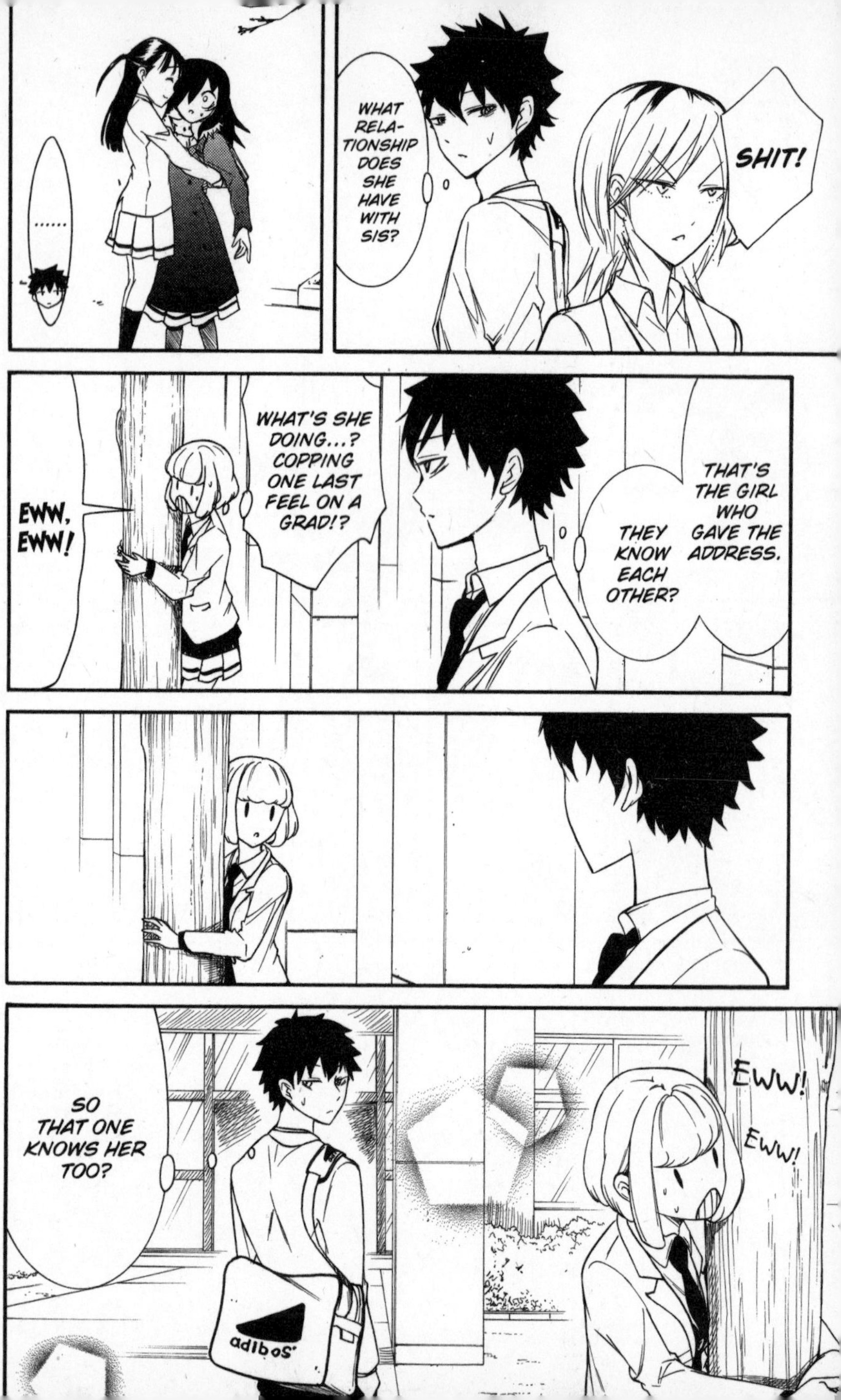
SHIT!
WHAT RELATIONSHIP DOES SHE HAVE WITH SIS?
......
THAT'S THE GIRL WHO GAVE THE ADDRESS.
THEY KNOW EACH OTHER?
WHAT'S SHE DOING...? COPPING ONE LAST FEEL ON A GRAD!?
EWW, EWW!
EWW!
EWW!
SO THAT ONE KNOWS HER TOO?
adiboS

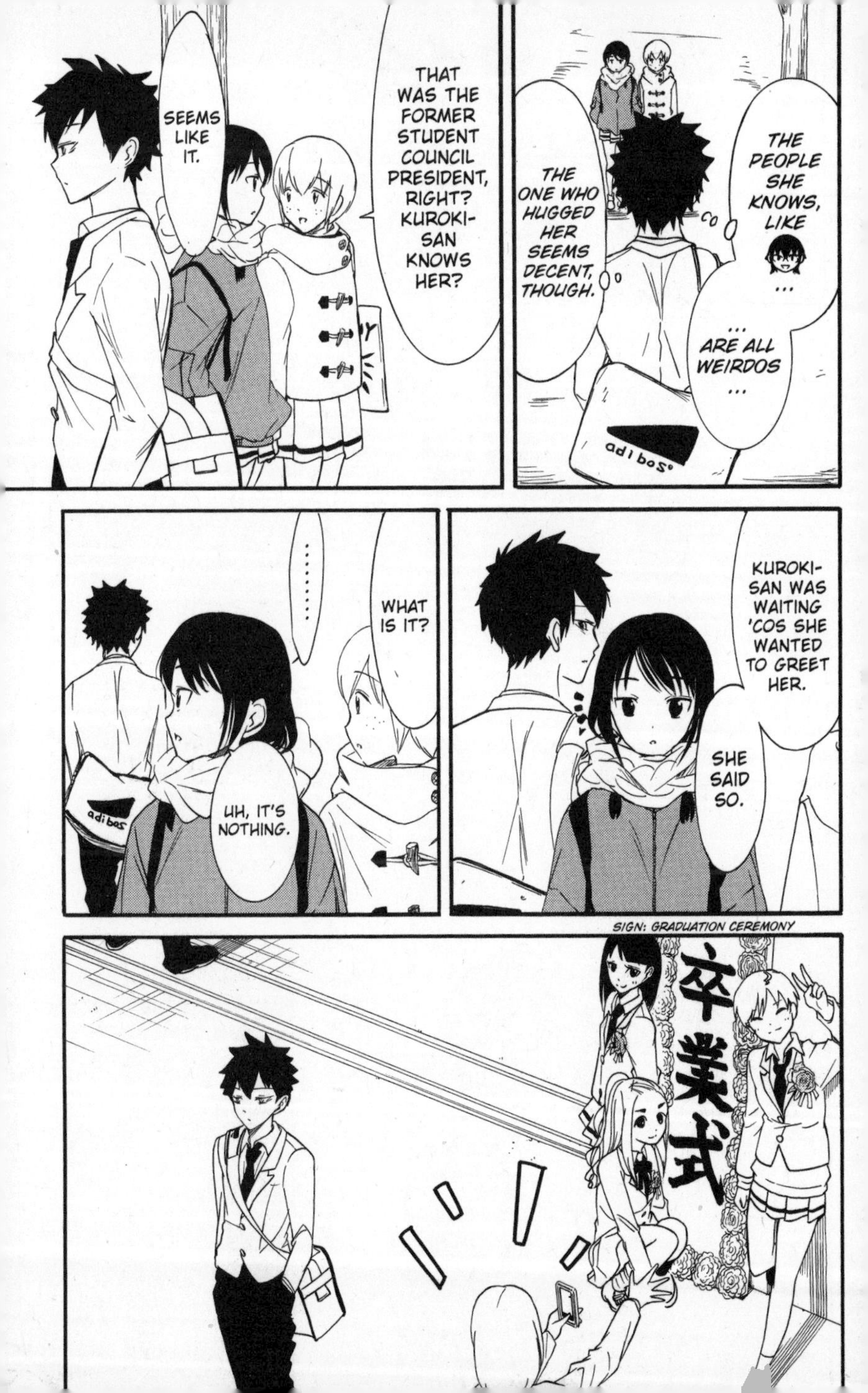
THE PEOPLE SHE KNOWS, LIKE ... ... ARE ALL WEIRDOS ...
THE ONE WHO HUGGED HER SEEMS DECENT, THOUGH.
adibos
THAT WAS THE FORMER STUDENT COUNCIL PRESIDENT, RIGHT? KUROKI-SAN KNOWS HER?
SEEMS LIKE IT.
KUROKI-SAN WAS WAITING 'COS SHE WANTED TO GREET HER.
SHE SAID SO.
WHAT IS IT?
......
UH, IT'S NOTHING.
adibos
SIGN: GRADUATION CEREMONY
卒業式

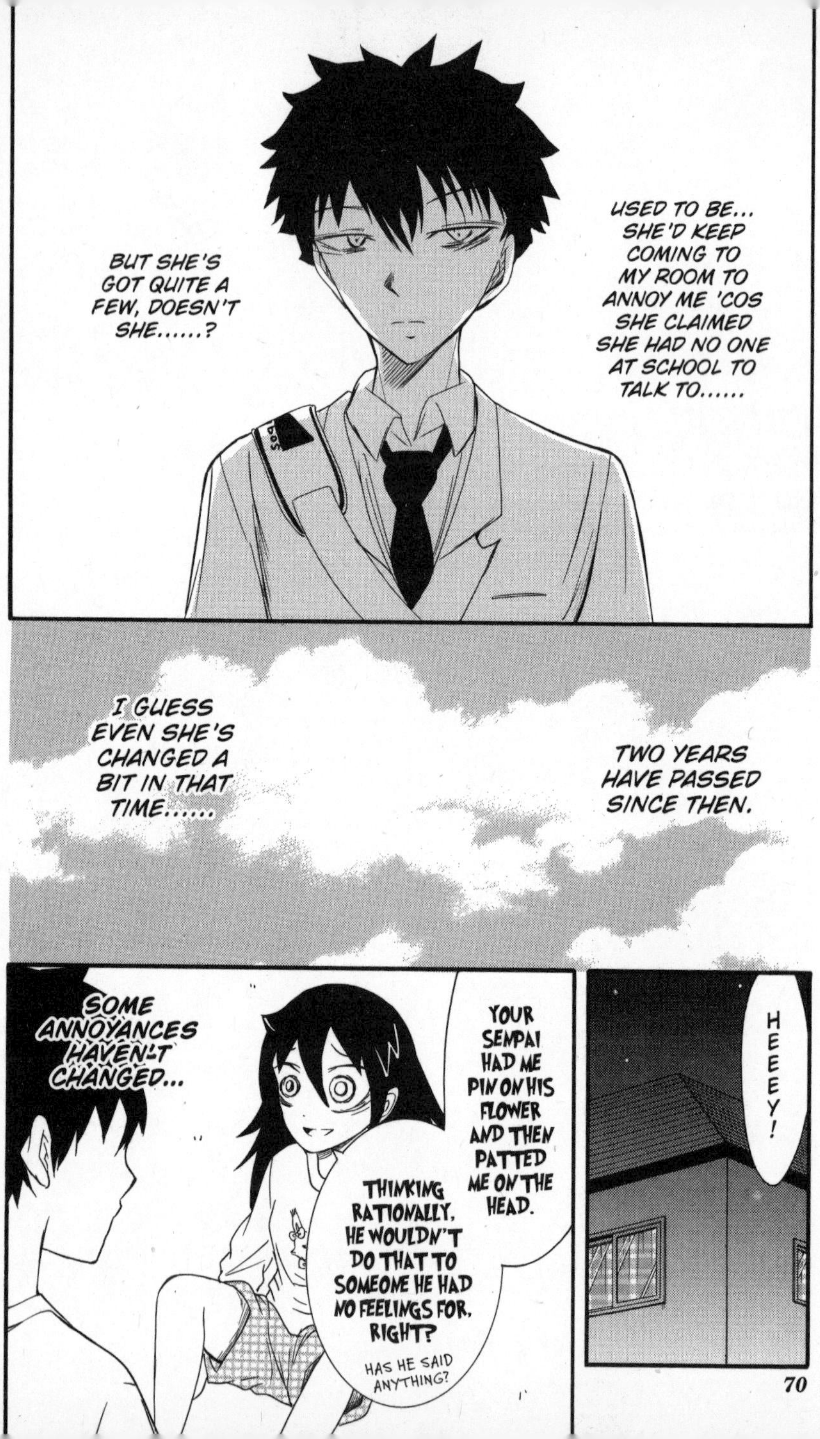
USED TO BE... SHE'D KEEP COMING TO MY ROOM TO ANNOY ME 'COS SHE CLAIMED SHE HAD NO ONE AT SCHOOL TO TALK TO......
BUT SHE'S GOT QUITE A FEW, DOESN'T SHE......?
TWO YEARS HAVE PASSED SINCE THEN.
I GUESS EVEN SHE'S CHANGED A BIT IN THAT TIME......
HEEEY!
YOUR SENPAI HAD ME PIN ON HIS FLOWER AND THEN PATTED ME ON THE HEAD.
THINKING RATIONALLY, HE WOULDN'T DO THAT TO SOMEONE HE HAD NO FEELINGS FOR, RIGHT?
HAS HE SAID ANYTHING?
SOME ANNOYANCES HAVEN'T CHANGED...

No Matter How I Look at It, It's You Guys' Fault I'm Not Popular!

FAIL 117: I'M NOT POPULAR, SO IT'S THE END OF SECOND YEAR.

CLOSE CONTACT

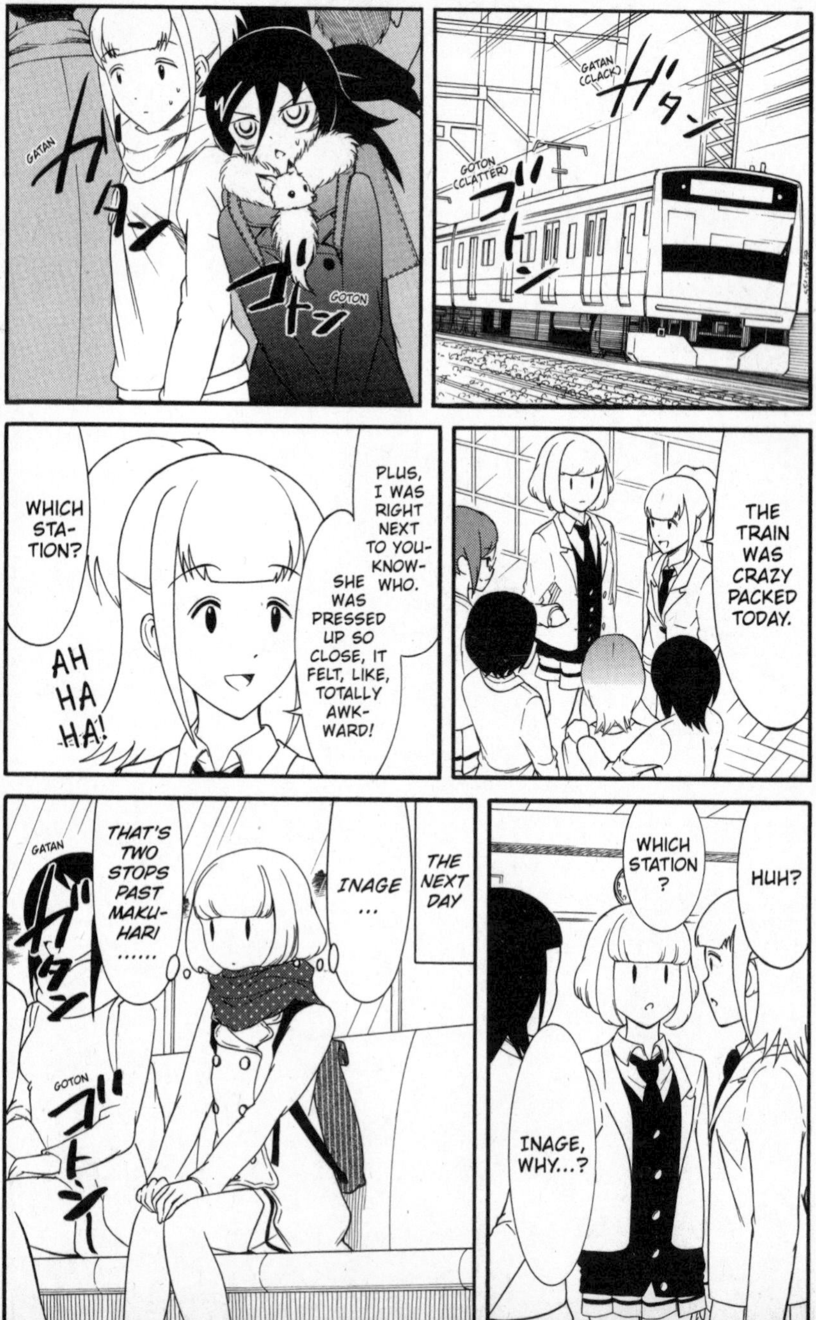
GATAN (CLACK)
ガタン
GOTON (CLATTER)
ゴトン
GATAN
ガタン
GOTON
ゴトン
THE TRAIN WAS CRAZY PACKED TODAY.
PLUS, I WAS RIGHT NEXT TO YOU-KNOW-WHO.
SHE WAS PRESSED UP SO CLOSE, IT FELT, LIKE, TOTALLY AWK-WARD!
WHICH STA-TION?
AH HA HA!
HUH?
WHICH STATION?
INAGE, WHY...?
THE NEXT DAY
INAGE...
THAT'S TWO STOPS PAST MAKU-HARI.......
GATAN
ガタン
GOTON
ゴトン

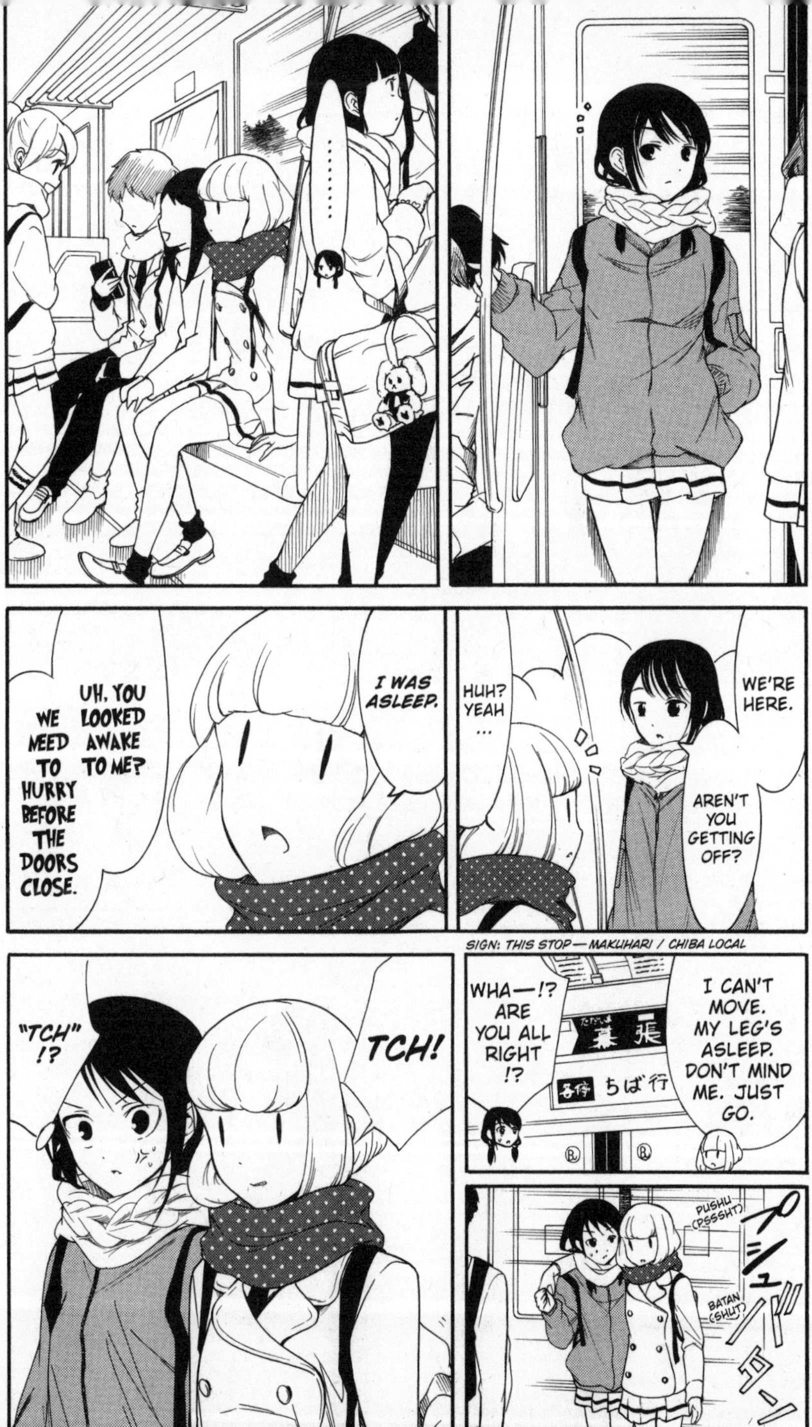
WE'RE HERE.
AREN'T YOU GETTING OFF?
HUH? YEAH ...
I WAS ASLEEP.
UH, YOU LOOKED AWAKE TO ME?
WE NEED TO HURRY BEFORE THE DOORS CLOSE.
SIGN: THIS STOP—MAKUHARI / CHIBA LOCAL
幕張
各停 ちば行
I CAN'T MOVE. MY LEG'S ASLEEP. DON'T MIND ME. JUST GO.
WHA—!? ARE YOU ALL RIGHT!?
PUSHU (PSSSHT)
BATAN (SHUT)
TCH!
"TCH"!?

ANEW......

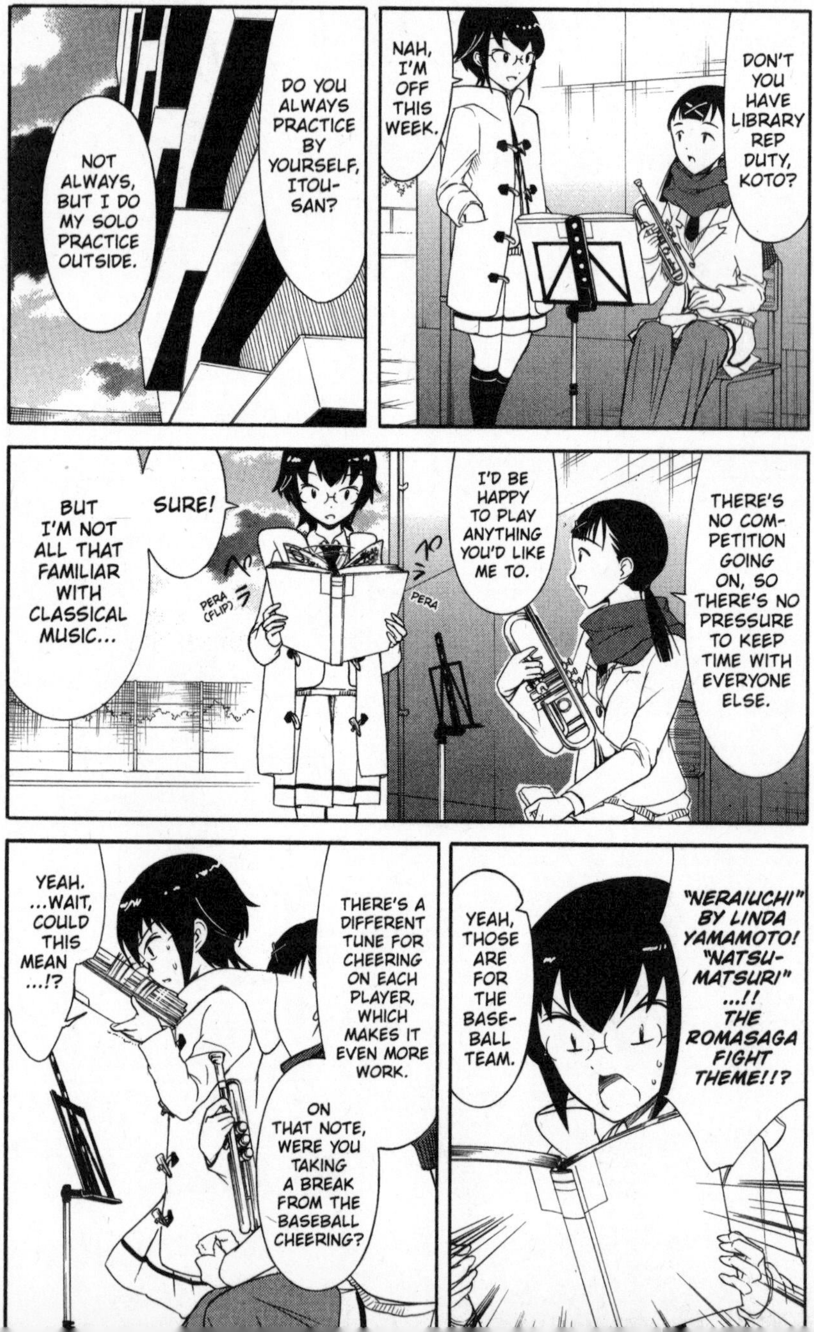

DON'T YOU HAVE LIBRARY REP DUTY, KOTO?
NAH, I'M OFF THIS WEEK.
DO YOU ALWAYS PRACTICE BY YOURSELF, ITOU-SAN?
NOT ALWAYS, BUT I DO MY SOLO PRACTICE OUTSIDE.
THERE'S NO COMPETITION GOING ON, SO THERE'S NO PRESSURE TO KEEP TIME WITH EVERYONE ELSE.
I'D BE HAPPY TO PLAY ANYTHING YOU'D LIKE ME TO.
PERA
PERA (FLIP)
SURE!
BUT I'M NOT ALL THAT FAMILIAR WITH CLASSICAL MUSIC...
"NERAIUCHI" BY LINDA YAMAMOTO! "NATSU-MATSURI" ...!! THE ROMASAGA FIGHT THEME!!?
YEAH, THOSE ARE FOR THE BASE-BALL TEAM.
THERE'S A DIFFERENT TUNE FOR CHEERING ON EACH PLAYER, WHICH MAKES IT EVEN MORE WORK.
ON THAT NOTE, WERE YOU TAKING A BREAK FROM THE BASEBALL CHEERING?
YEAH. ...WAIT, COULD THIS MEAN ...!?

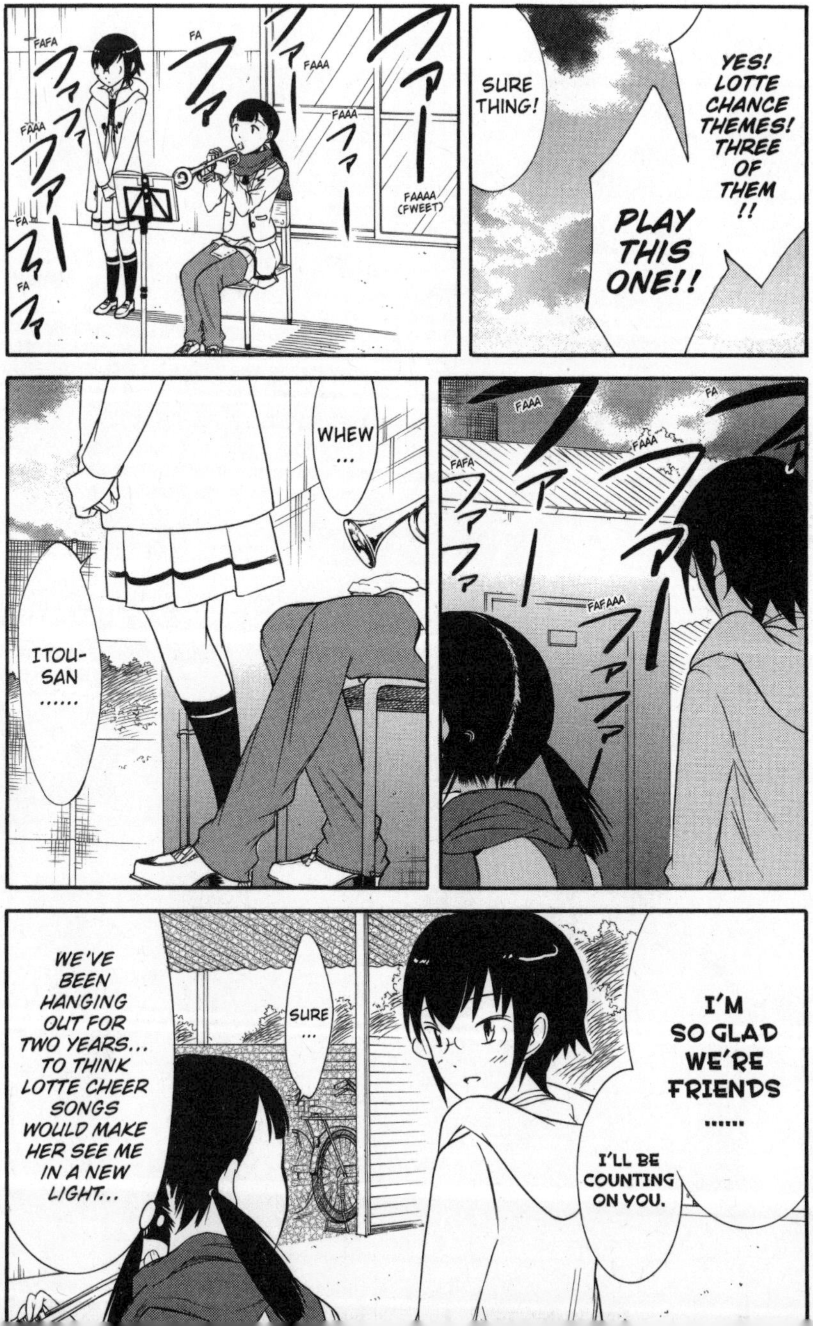
YES! LOTTE CHANCE THEMES! THREE OF THEM!!
PLAY THIS ONE!!
SURE THING!
FAAAA (FWEET)
FAAA
FAAA
FA
FAFA
FAAA
FA
FA
FA
FAAA
FAAA
FAFA
FAFAAA
WHEW ...
ITOU-SAN ......
I'M SO GLAD WE'RE FRIENDS ......
I'LL BE COUNTING ON YOU.
SURE ...
WE'VE BEEN HANGING OUT FOR TWO YEARS... TO THINK LOTTE CHEER SONGS WOULD MAKE HER SEE ME IN A NEW LIGHT...

AN UNKNOWN FACE

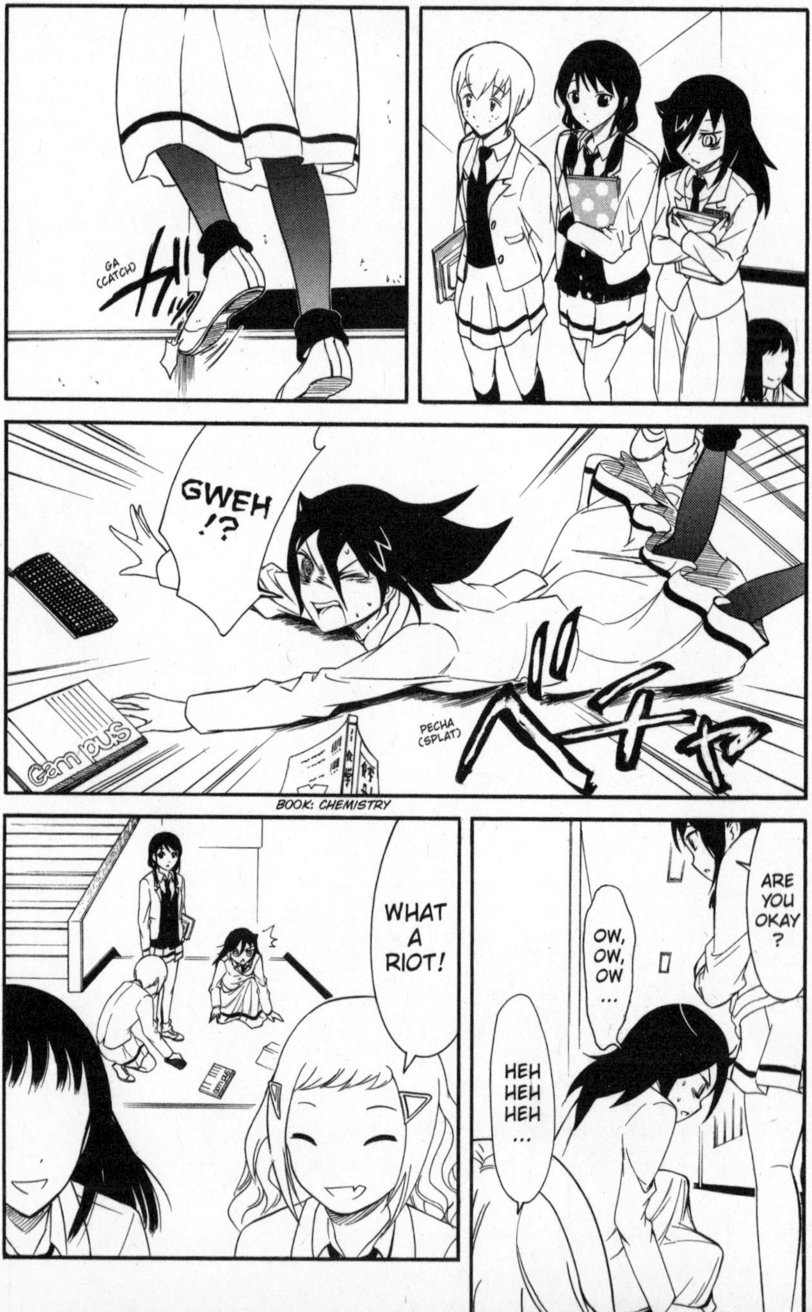

GA (CATCH)
GWEH !?
PECHA (SPLAT)
BOOK: CHEMISTRY
ARE YOU OKAY?
OW, OW, OW...
HEH HEH HEH...
WHAT A RIOT!

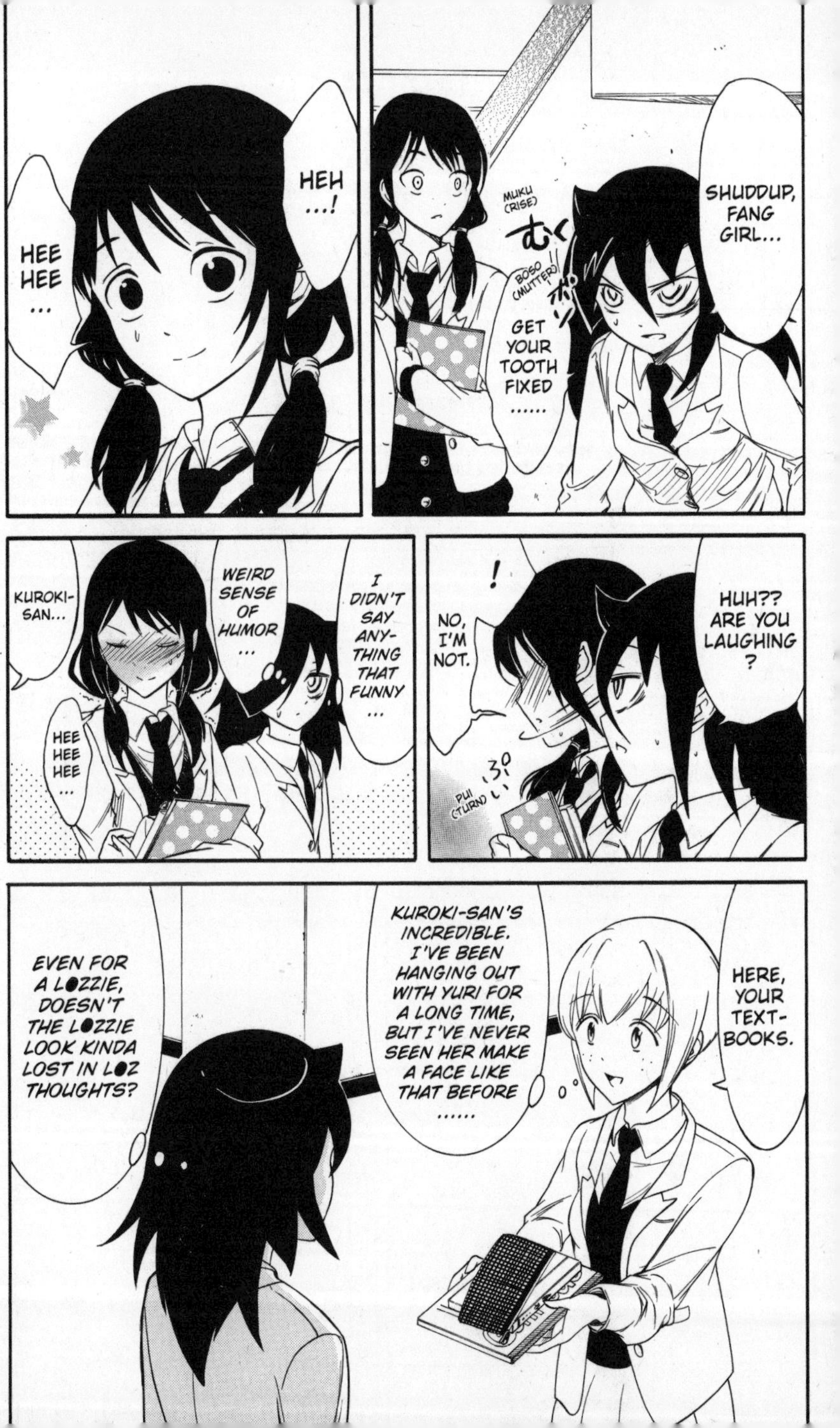
SHUDDUP, FANG GIRL...
MUKU (RISE)
BOSO (MUTTER)
GET YOUR TOOTH FIXED ......
HEH ...!
HEE HEE ...
HUH?? ARE YOU LAUGHING ?
!
NO, I'M NOT.
PUI (TURN)
I DIDN'T SAY ANYTHING THAT FUNNY ...
WEIRD SENSE OF HUMOR ...
KUROKI-SAN...
HEE HEE HEE ...
HERE, YOUR TEXT-BOOKS.
KUROKI-SAN'S INCREDIBLE. I'VE BEEN HANGING OUT WITH YURI FOR A LONG TIME, BUT I'VE NEVER SEEN HER MAKE A FACE LIKE THAT BEFORE ......
EVEN FOR A LOZZIE, DOESN'T THE LOZZIE LOOK KINDA LOST IN LOZ THOUGHTS?

TOGETHER

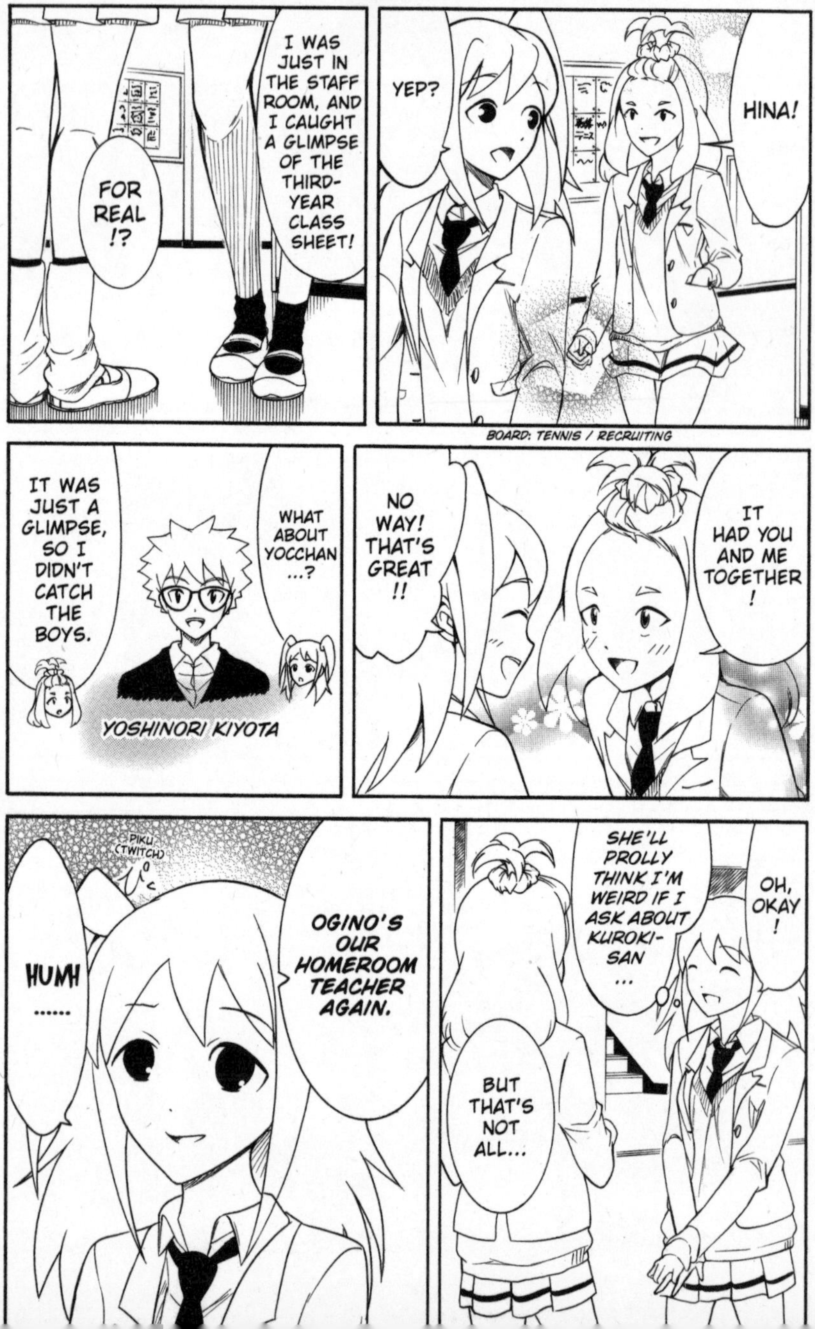
HINA!
YEP?
I WAS JUST IN THE STAFF ROOM, AND I CAUGHT A GLIMPSE OF THE THIRD-YEAR CLASS SHEET!
FOR REAL!?
BOARD: TENNIS / RECRUITING
IT HAD YOU AND ME TOGETHER!
NO WAY! THAT'S GREAT!!
WHAT ABOUT YOCCHAN...?
IT WAS JUST A GLIMPSE, SO I DIDN'T CATCH THE BOYS.
YOSHINORI KIYOTA
OH, OKAY!
SHE'LL PROLLY THINK I'M WEIRD IF I ASK ABOUT KUROKI-SAN...
BUT THAT'S NOT ALL...
OGINO'S OUR HOMEROOM TEACHER AGAIN.
PIKU (TWITCH)
HUMH ......

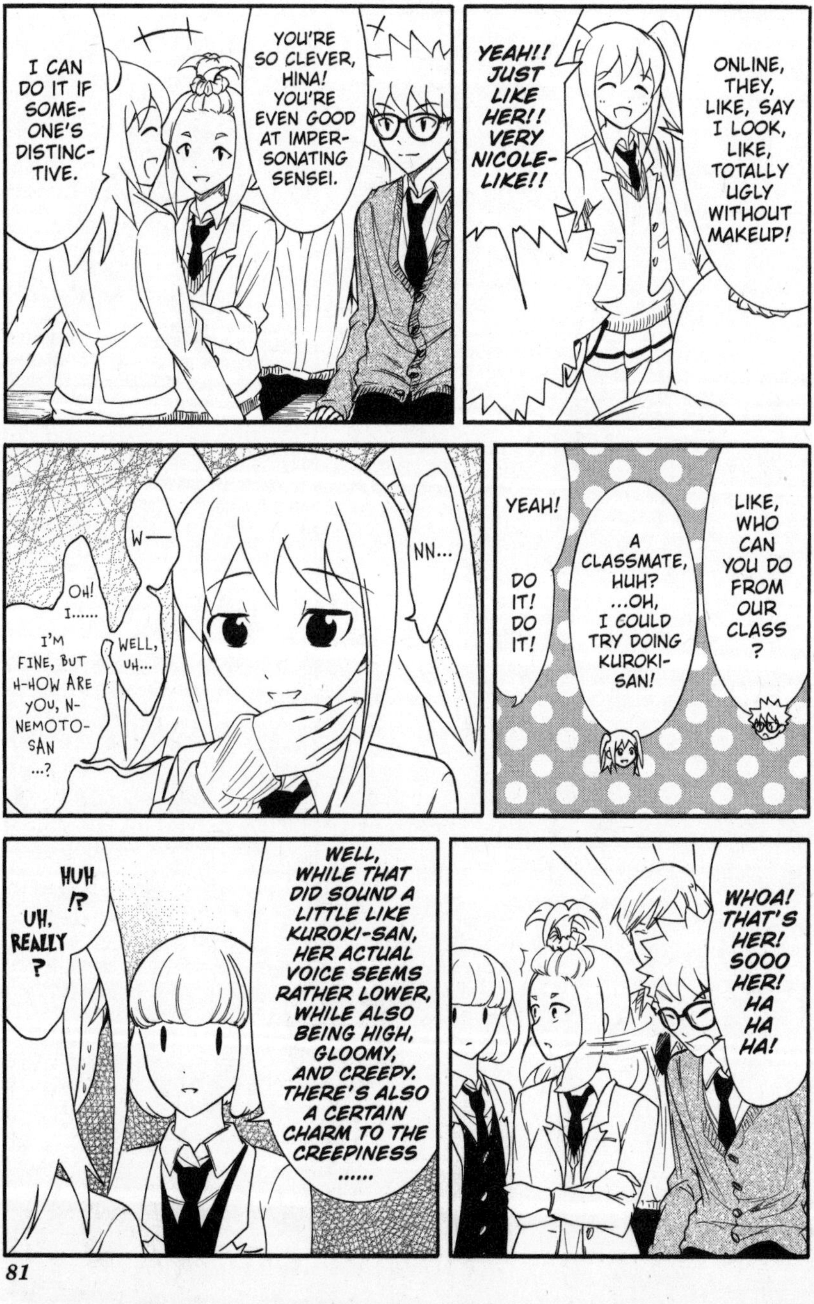
ONLINE, THEY, LIKE, SAY I LOOK, LIKE, TOTALLY UGLY WITHOUT MAKEUP!
YEAH!! JUST LIKE HER!! VERY NICOLE-LIKE!!
YOU'RE SO CLEVER, HINA! YOU'RE EVEN GOOD AT IMPERSONATING SENSEI.
I CAN DO IT IF SOMEONE'S DISTINCTIVE.
LIKE, WHO CAN YOU DO FROM OUR CLASS?
A CLASSMATE, HUH? ...OH, I COULD TRY DOING KUROKI-SAN!
YEAH!
DO IT! DO IT!
NN...
W—
WELL, UH...
OH! I......
I'M FINE, BUT H-HOW ARE YOU, N-NEMOTO-SAN...?
WHOA! THAT'S HER! SOOO HER! HA HA HA!
WELL, WHILE THAT DID SOUND A LITTLE LIKE KUROKI-SAN, HER ACTUAL VOICE SEEMS RATHER LOWER, WHILE ALSO BEING HIGH, GLOOMY, AND CREEPY. THERE'S ALSO A CERTAIN CHARM TO THE CREEPINESS ......
HUH!?
UH, REALLY?

I REMEMBER

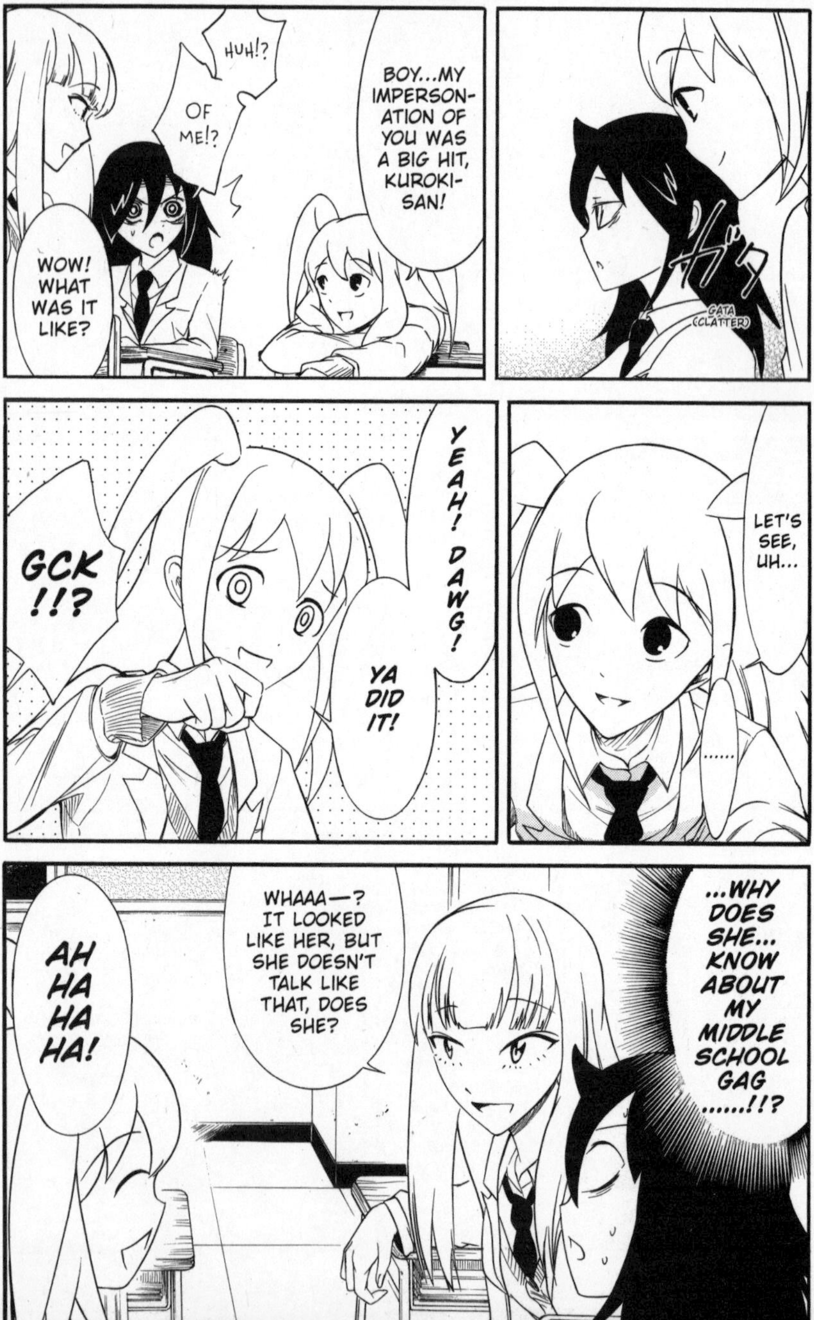
GATA (CLATTER)
BOY...MY IMPERSONATION OF YOU WAS A BIG HIT, KUROKI-SAN!
HUH!?
OF ME!?
WOW! WHAT WAS IT LIKE?
LET'S SEE, UH...
......
YEAH! DAWG!
YA DID IT!
GCK!!?
...WHY DOES SHE... KNOW ABOUT MY MIDDLE SCHOOL GAG ......!!?
WHAAA—? IT LOOKED LIKE HER, BUT SHE DOESN'T TALK LIKE THAT, DOES SHE?
AH HA HA HA HA!

No Matter How I Look at It, It's You Guys' Fault I'm Not Popular!

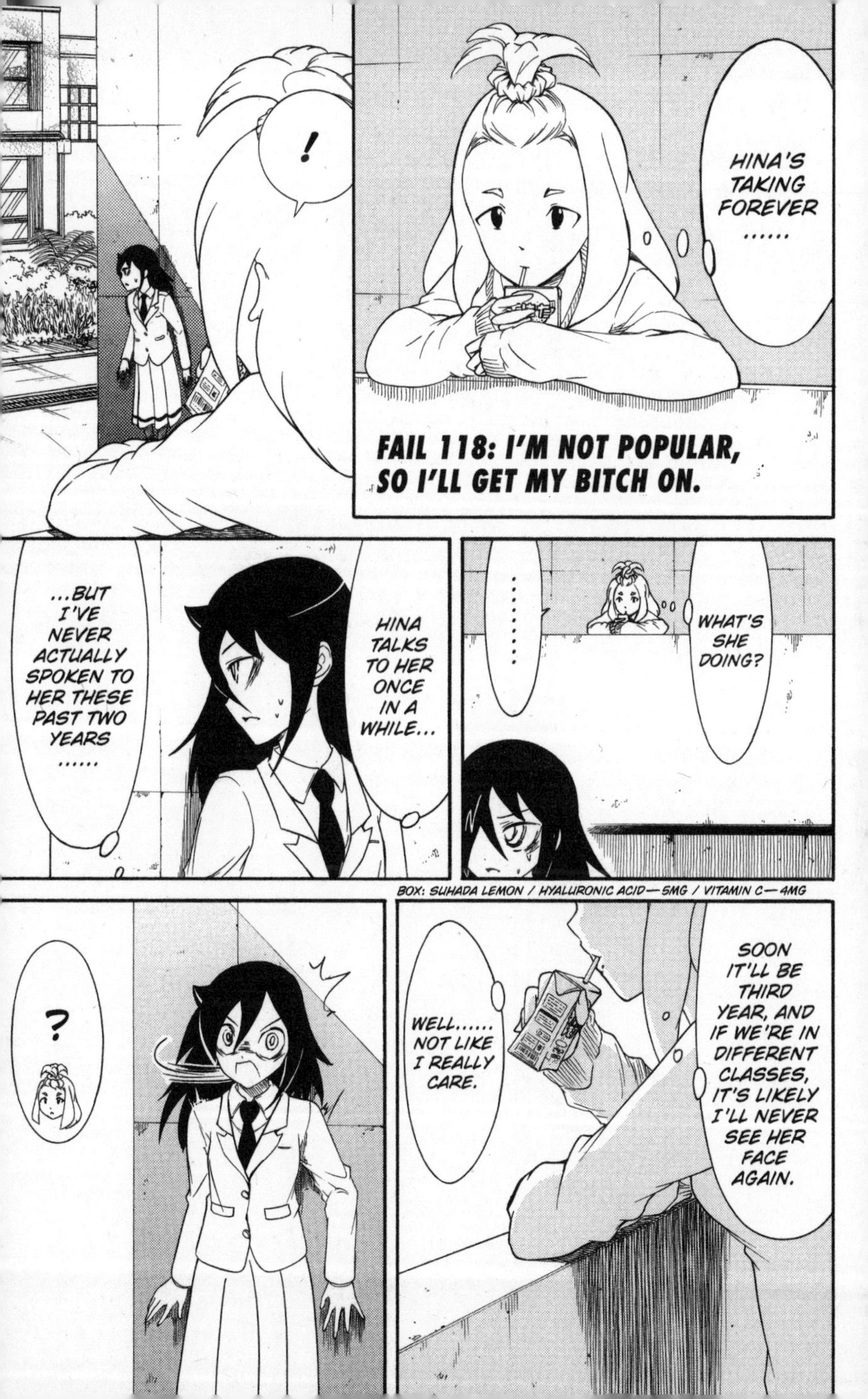
HINA'S TAKING FOREVER ......
FAIL 118: I'M NOT POPULAR, SO I'LL GET MY BITCH ON.
!
WHAT'S SHE DOING?
......
HINA TALKS TO HER ONCE IN A WHILE...
...BUT I'VE NEVER ACTUALLY SPOKEN TO HER THESE PAST TWO YEARS ......
BOX: SUHADA LEMON / HYALURONIC ACID—5MG / VITAMIN C—4MG
SOON IT'LL BE THIRD YEAR, AND IF WE'RE IN DIFFERENT CLASSES, IT'S LIKELY I'LL NEVER SEE HER FACE AGAIN.
WELL...... NOT LIKE I REALLY CARE.
?

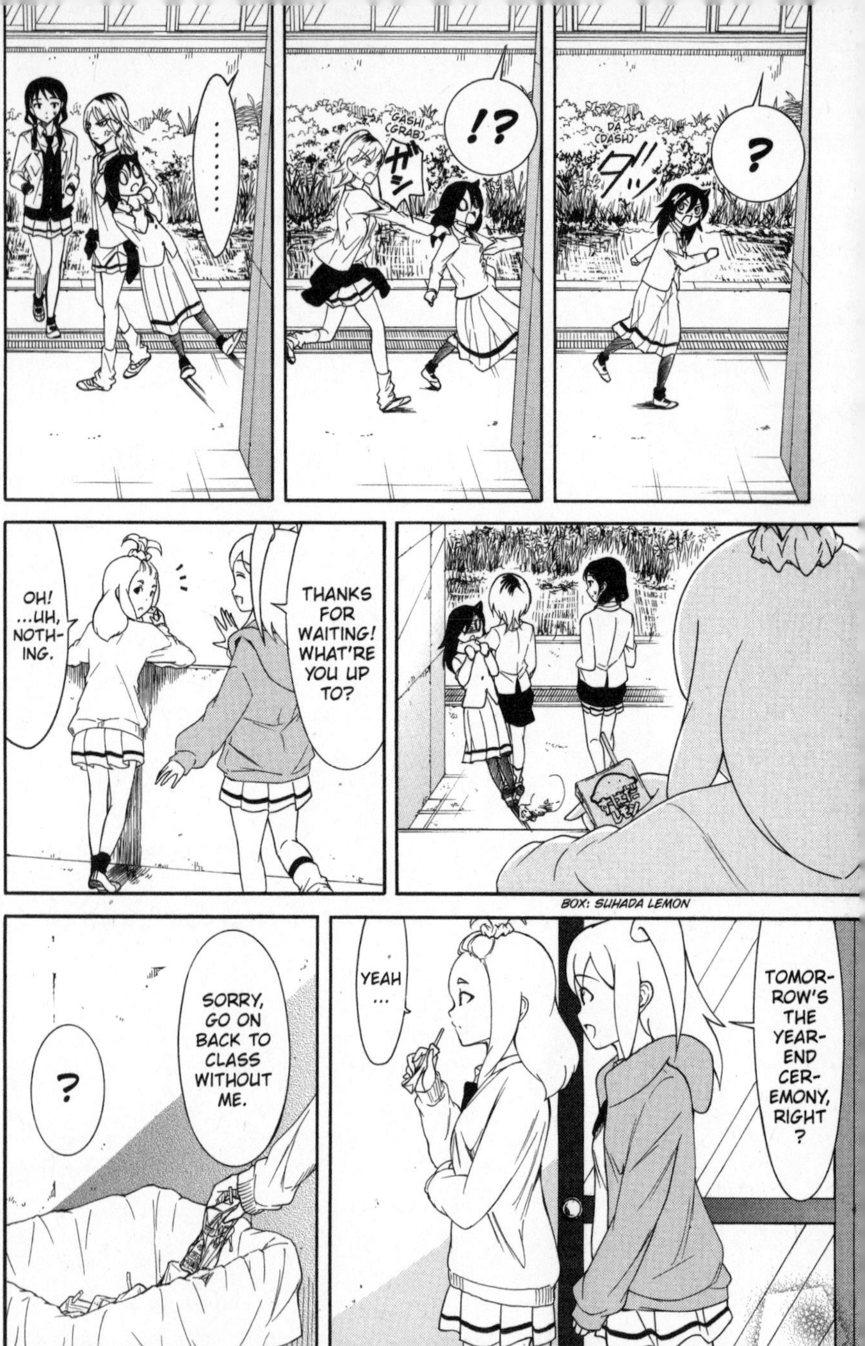
DA (DASH)
ダッ
?
GASHI (GRAB)
ガシ
!?
......
BOX: SUHADA LEMON
THANKS FOR WAITING! WHAT'RE YOU UP TO?
OH! ...UH, NOTHING.
TOMORROW'S THE YEAR-END CEREMONY, RIGHT?
YEAH ...
SORRY, GO ON BACK TO CLASS WITHOUT ME.
?

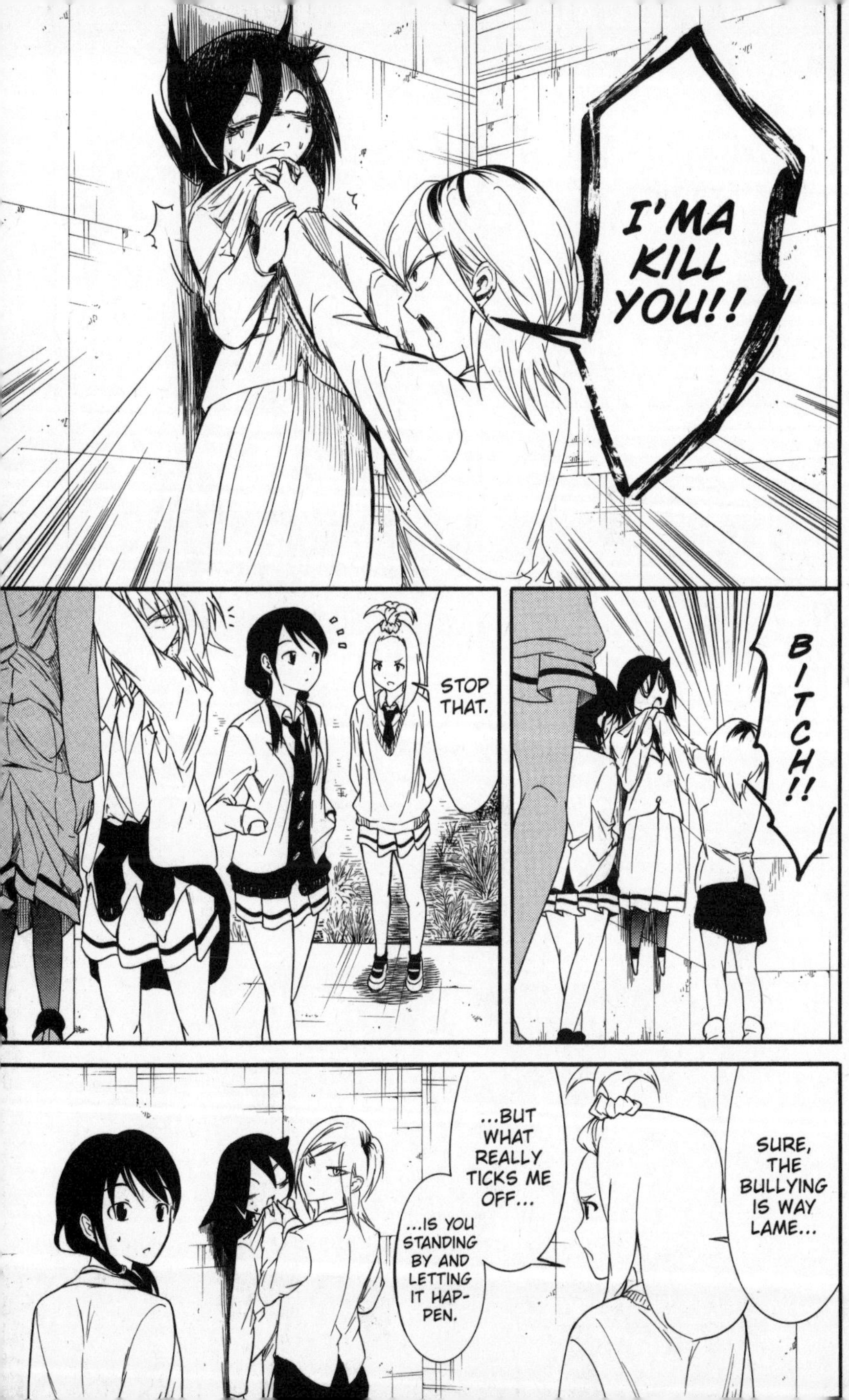
I'MA KILL YOU!!
BITCH!!
STOP THAT.
SURE, THE BULLYING IS WAY LAME...
...BUT WHAT REALLY TICKS ME OFF...
...IS YOU STANDING BY AND LETTING IT HAP-PEN.

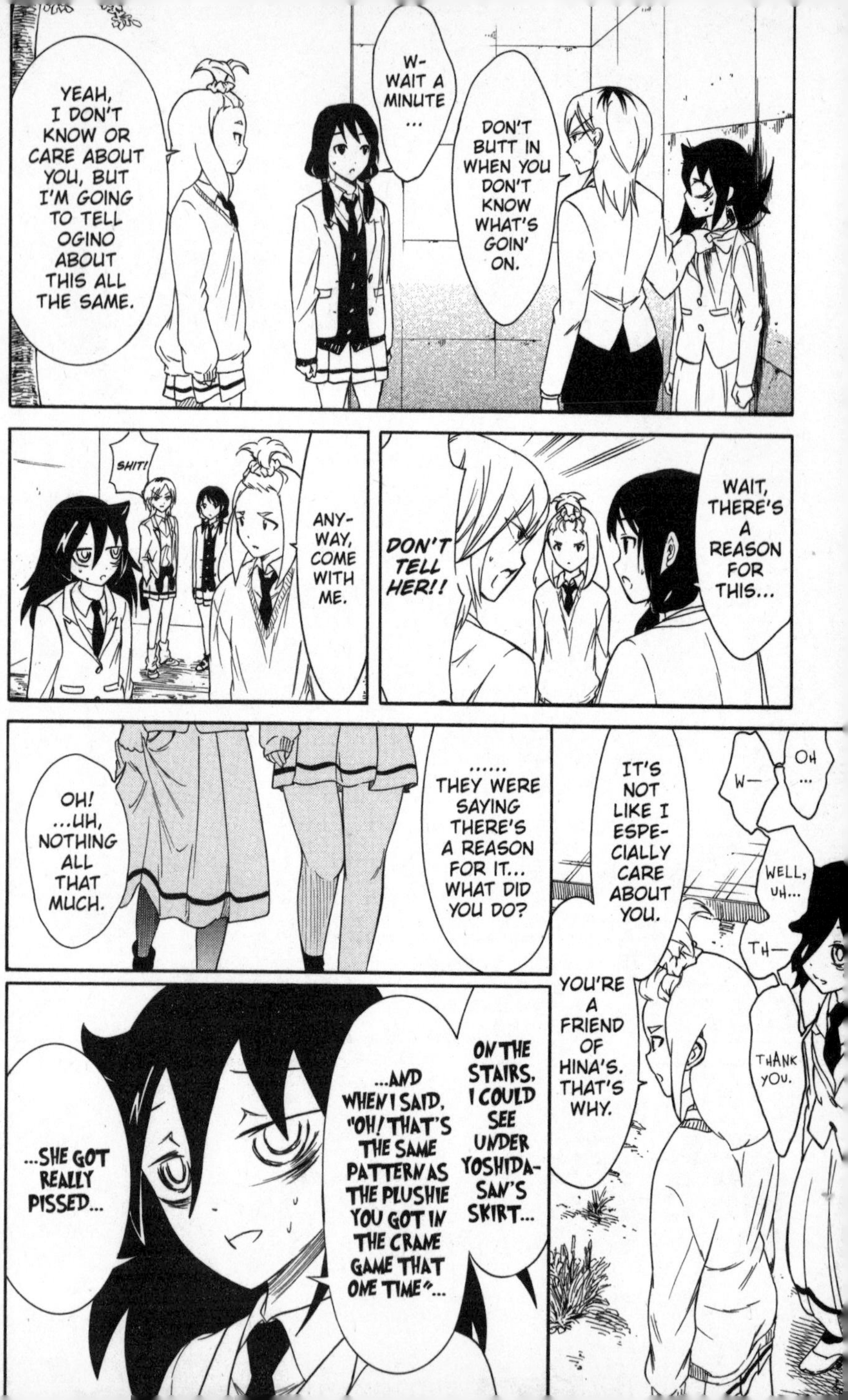
DON'T BUTT IN WHEN YOU DON'T KNOW WHAT'S GOIN' ON.
W- WAIT A MINUTE ...
YEAH, I DON'T KNOW OR CARE ABOUT YOU, BUT I'M GOING TO TELL OGINO ABOUT THIS ALL THE SAME.
WAIT, THERE'S A REASON FOR THIS...
DON'T TELL HER!!
ANY-WAY, COME WITH ME.
SHIT!
IT'S NOT LIKE I ESPE-CIALLY CARE ABOUT YOU.
YOU'RE A FRIEND OF HINA'S. THAT'S WHY.
W—
OH ...
WELL, UH...
TH—
THANK YOU.
...... THEY WERE SAYING THERE'S A REASON FOR IT... WHAT DID YOU DO?
OH! ...UH, NOTHING ALL THAT MUCH.
ON THE STAIRS, I COULD SEE UNDER YOSHIDA-SAN'S SKIRT...
...AND WHEN I SAID, "OH! THAT'S THE SAME PATTERN AS THE PLUSHIE YOU GOT IN THE CRANE GAME THAT ONE TIME"...
...SHE GOT REALLY PISSED...

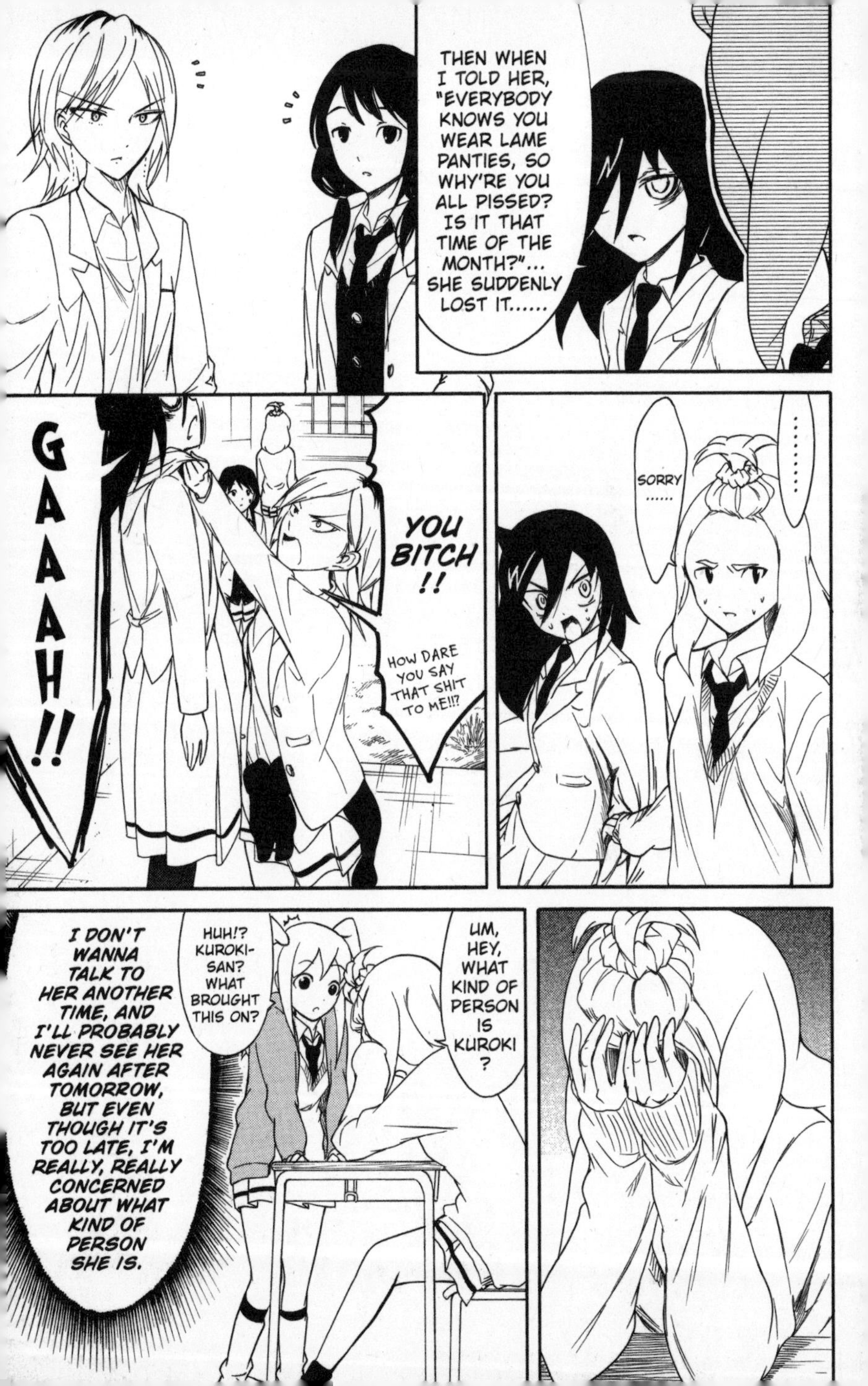
THEN WHEN I TOLD HER, "EVERYBODY KNOWS YOU WEAR LAME PANTIES, SO WHY'RE YOU ALL PISSED? IS IT THAT TIME OF THE MONTH?"... SHE SUDDENLY LOST IT......
......
SORRY ......
YOU BITCH!!
HOW DARE YOU SAY THAT SHIT TO ME!!?
GAAAH!!
UM, HEY, WHAT KIND OF PERSON IS KUROKI?
HUH!? KUROKI-SAN? WHAT BROUGHT THIS ON?
I DON'T WANNA TALK TO HER ANOTHER TIME, AND I'LL PROBABLY NEVER SEE HER AGAIN AFTER TOMORROW, BUT EVEN THOUGH IT'S TOO LATE, I'M REALLY, REALLY CONCERNED ABOUT WHAT KIND OF PERSON SHE IS.

No Matter How I Look at It, It's You Guys' Fault I'm Not Popular!

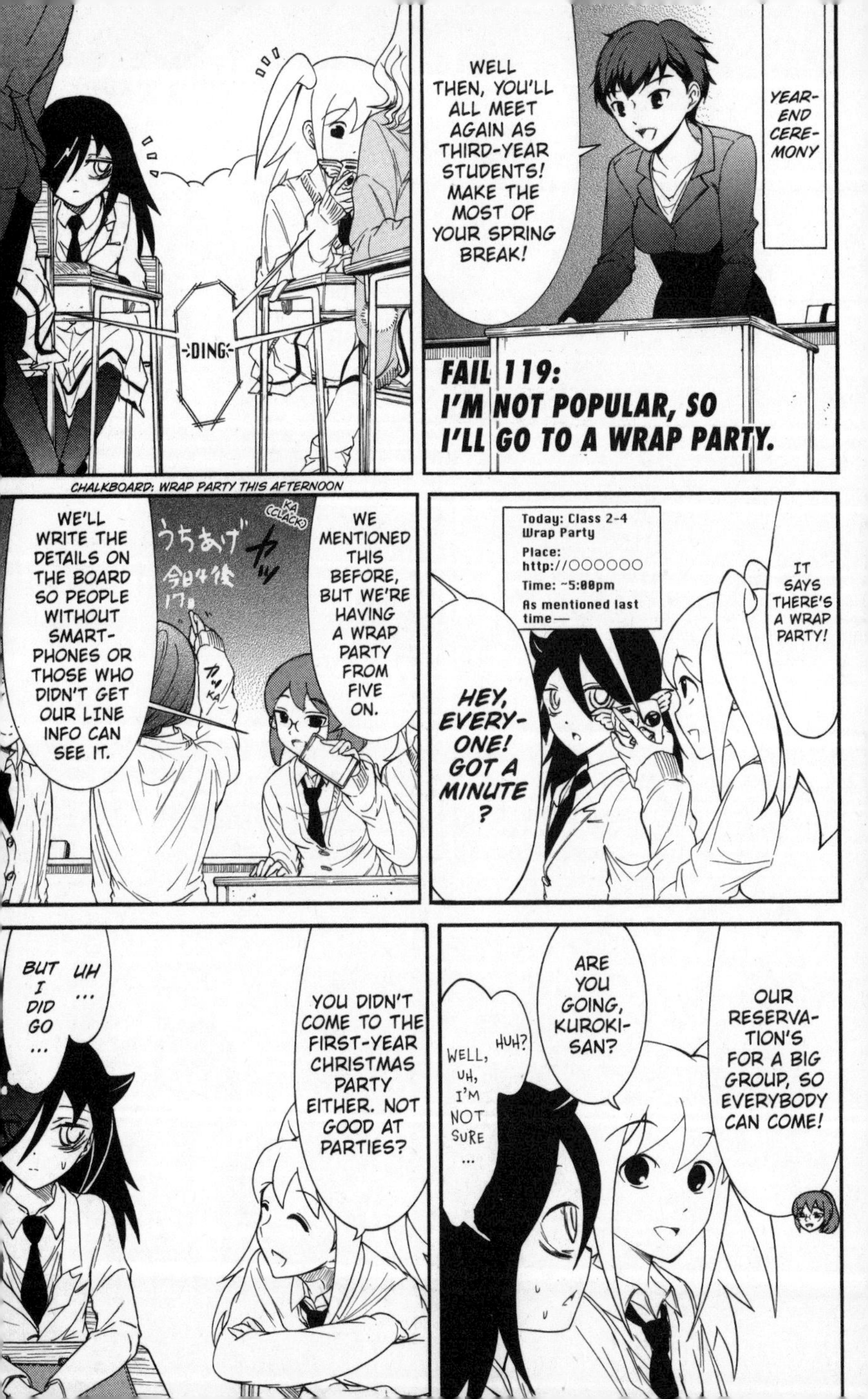
YEAR-END CEREMONY
WELL THEN, YOU'LL ALL MEET AGAIN AS THIRD-YEAR STUDENTS! MAKE THE MOST OF YOUR SPRING BREAK!
FAIL 119: I'M NOT POPULAR, SO I'LL GO TO A WRAP PARTY.
DING
CHALKBOARD: WRAP PARTY THIS AFTERNOON
Today: Class 2-4 Wrap Party
Place: http://○○○○○○
Time: ~5:00pm
As mentioned last time—
IT SAYS THERE'S A WRAP PARTY!
HEY, EVERYONE! GOT A MINUTE?
WE MENTIONED THIS BEFORE, BUT WE'RE HAVING A WRAP PARTY FROM FIVE ON.
KA (CLACK)
カッ
うちあげ
WE'LL WRITE THE DETAILS ON THE BOARD SO PEOPLE WITHOUT SMARTPHONES OR THOSE WHO DIDN'T GET OUR LINE INFO CAN SEE IT.
カッ KA
OUR RESERVATION'S FOR A BIG GROUP, SO EVERYBODY CAN COME!
ARE YOU GOING, KUROKI-SAN?
HUH?
WELL, UH, I'M NOT SURE ...
YOU DIDN'T COME TO THE FIRST-YEAR CHRISTMAS PARTY EITHER. NOT GOOD AT PARTIES?
UH ...
BUT I DID GO ...

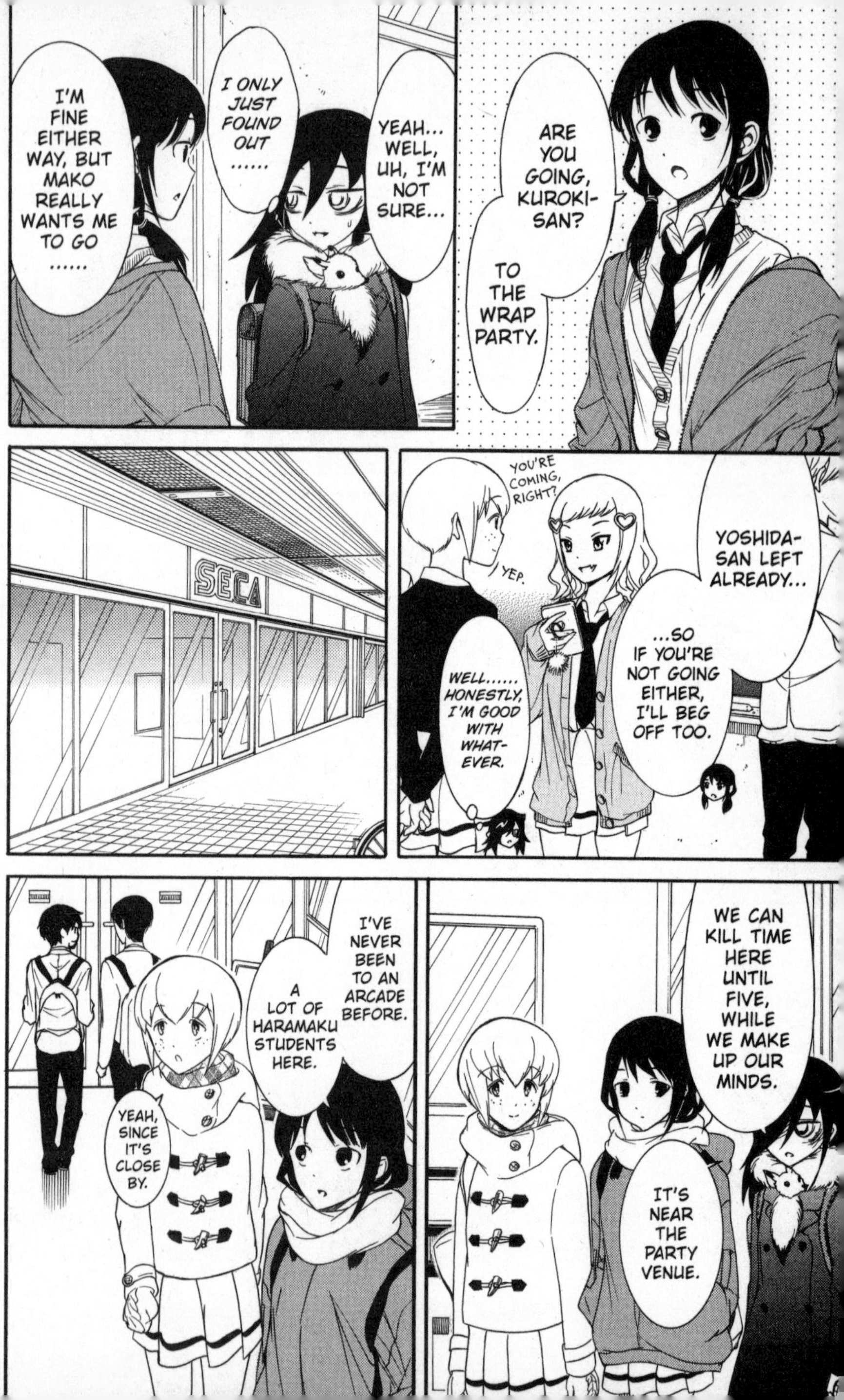
ARE YOU GOING, KUROKI-SAN?
TO THE WRAP PARTY.
YEAH... WELL, UH, I'M NOT SURE...
I ONLY JUST FOUND OUT......
I'M FINE EITHER WAY, BUT MAKO REALLY WANTS ME TO GO......
YOSHIDA-SAN LEFT ALREADY...
...SO IF YOU'RE NOT GOING EITHER, I'LL BEG OFF TOO.
YOU'RE COMING, RIGHT?
YEP.
WELL...... HONESTLY, I'M GOOD WITH WHAT-EVER.
SEGA
WE CAN KILL TIME HERE UNTIL FIVE, WHILE WE MAKE UP OUR MINDS.
IT'S NEAR THE PARTY VENUE.
I'VE NEVER BEEN TO AN ARCADE BEFORE.
A LOT OF HARAMAKU STUDENTS HERE.
YEAH, SINCE IT'S CLOSE BY.

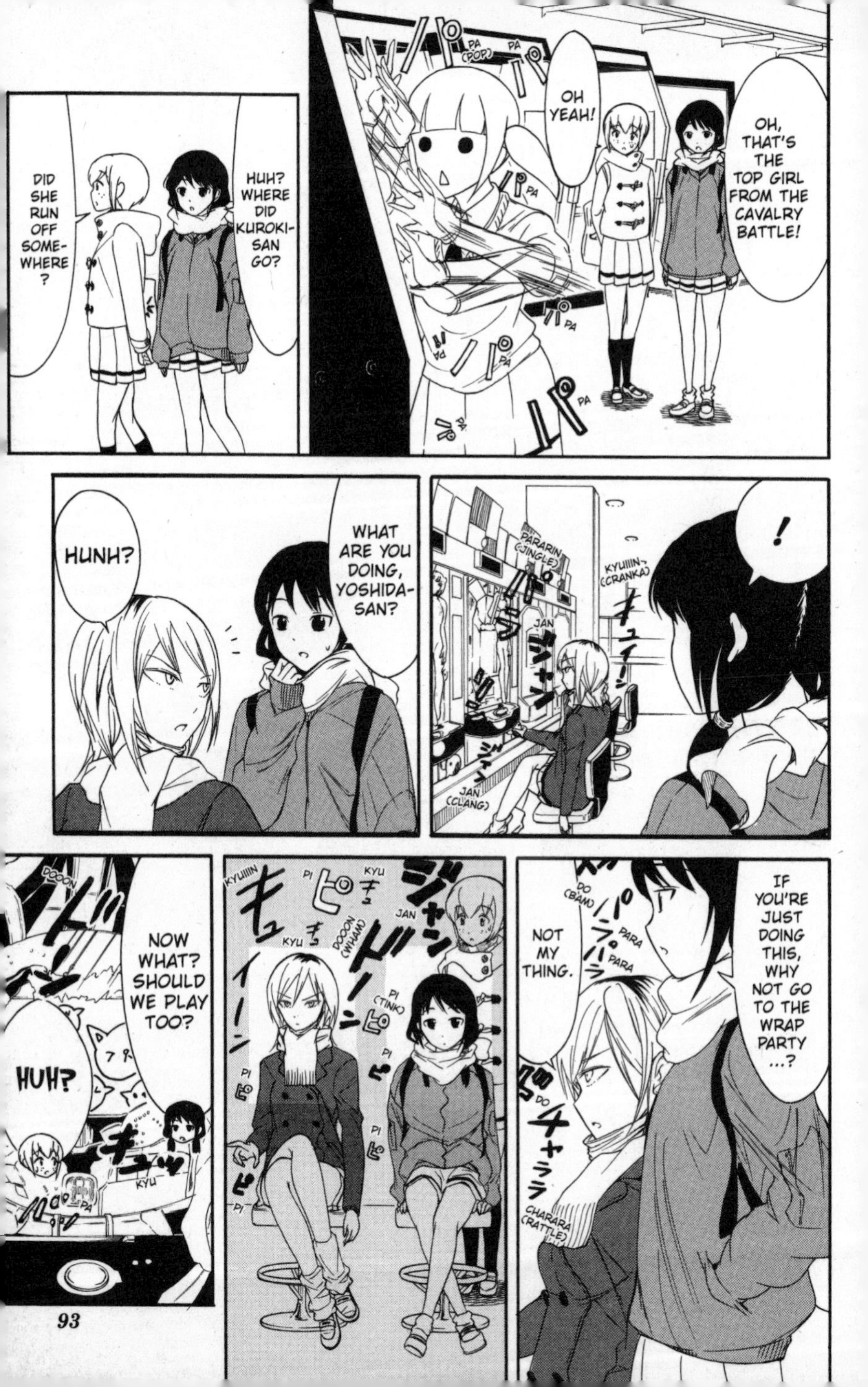

OH, THAT'S THE TOP GIRL FROM THE CAVALRY BATTLE!
OH YEAH!
PA (POP) PA
PA
PA
PA
PA
HUH? WHERE DID KUROKI-SAN GO?
DID SHE RUN OFF SOME-WHERE?
!
KYUIIIN (CRANKA)
PARARIN (JINGLE)
JAN
JAN (CLANG)
WHAT ARE YOU DOING, YOSHIDA-SAN?
HUNH?
IF YOU'RE JUST DOING THIS, WHY NOT GO TO THE WRAP PARTY...?
NOT MY THING.
DO (BAM)
PARA PARA
DO
CHARARA (RATTLE)
KYU
PI
KYUIIIN
JAN
DOOON (WHAM)
KYU
PI (TINK)
PI
PI
PI
PI
NOW WHAT? SHOULD WE PLAY TOO?
HUH?
DOOON
KYU
PA

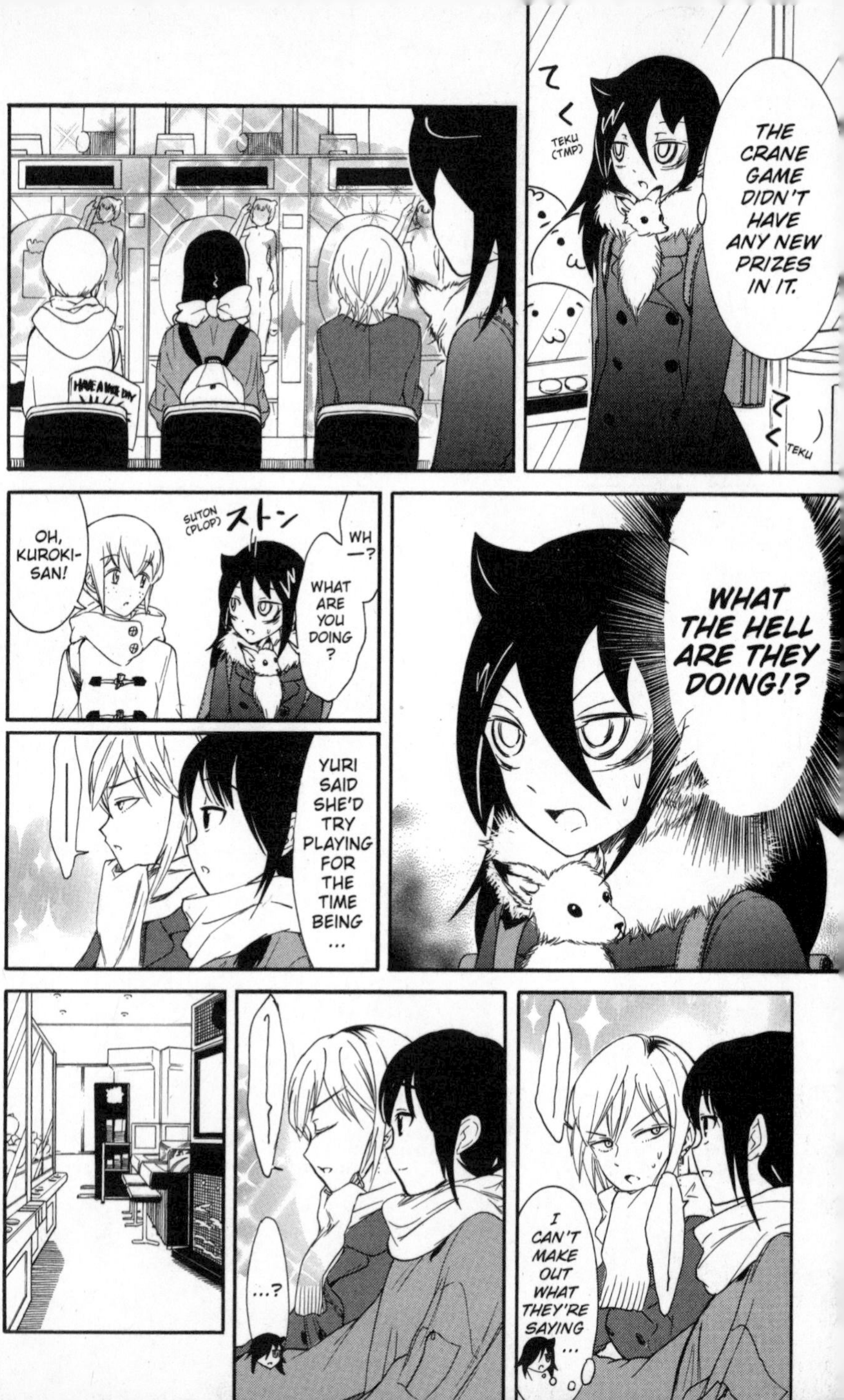
てく
TEKU (TMP)
THE CRANE GAME DIDN'T HAVE ANY NEW PRIZES IN IT.
てく
TEKU
HAVE A NICE DAY
WHAT THE HELL ARE THEY DOING!?
SUTON (PLOP) ストン
WH—?
WHAT ARE YOU DOING?
OH, KUROKI-SAN!
YURI SAID SHE'D TRY PLAYING FOR THE TIME BEING...
!
I CAN'T MAKE OUT WHAT THEY'RE SAYING...
!
...?

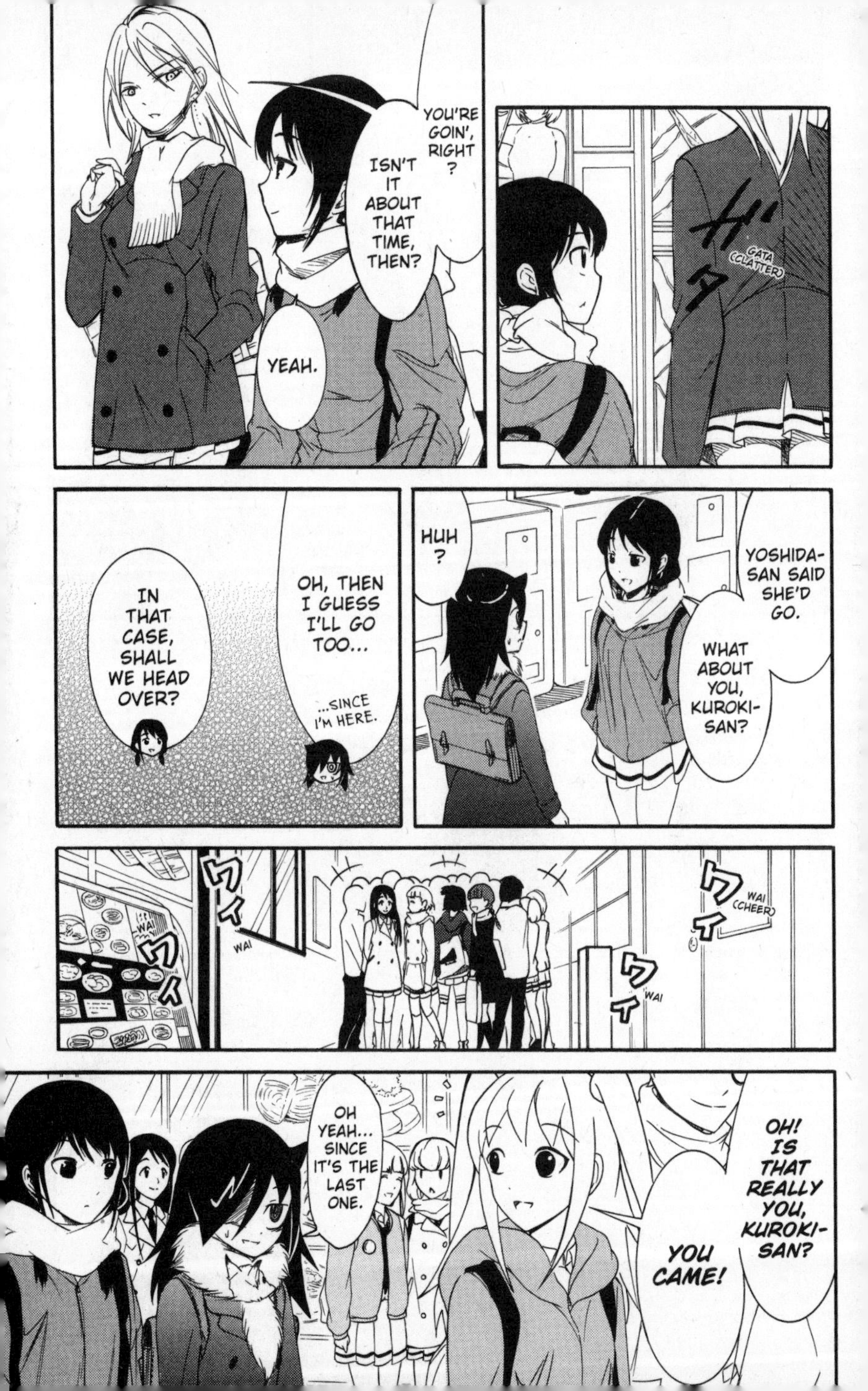
GATA (CLATTER)
YOU'RE GOIN', RIGHT?
ISN'T IT ABOUT THAT TIME, THEN?
YEAH.
YOSHIDA-SAN SAID SHE'D GO.
WHAT ABOUT YOU, KUROKI-SAN?
HUH?
OH, THEN I GUESS I'LL GO TOO...
...SINCE I'M HERE.
IN THAT CASE, SHALL WE HEAD OVER?
WAI (CHEER)
WAI
WAI
WAI
OH! IS THAT REALLY YOU, KUROKI-SAN?
YOU CAME!
OH YEAH... SINCE IT'S THE LAST ONE.

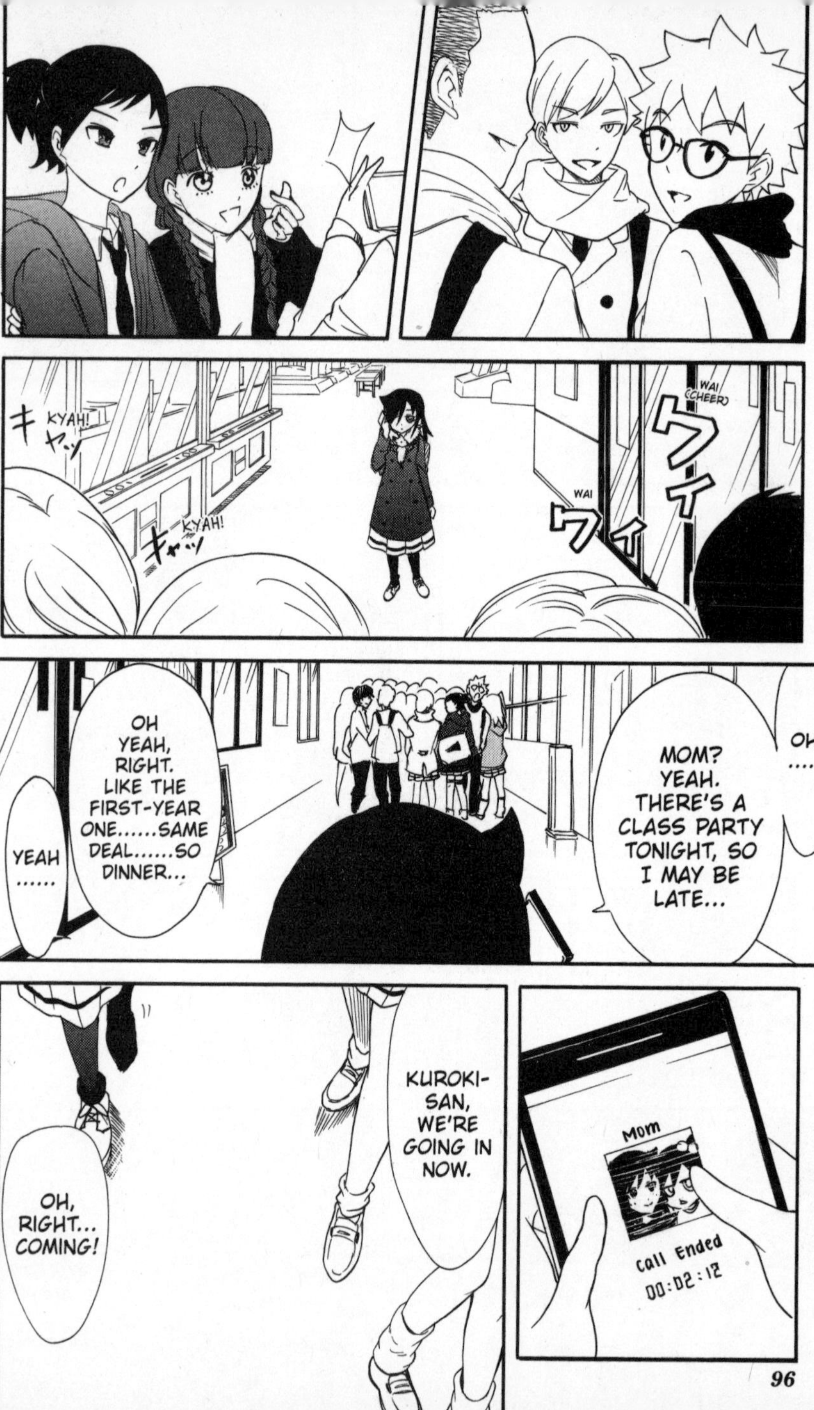
WAI (CHEER)
WAI
KYAH!
KYAH!
OH! ......
MOM? YEAH. THERE'S A CLASS PARTY TONIGHT, SO I MAY BE LATE...
OH YEAH, RIGHT. LIKE THE FIRST-YEAR ONE......SAME DEAL......SO DINNER...
YEAH ......
Mom
Call Ended
00:02:12
KUROKI-SAN, WE'RE GOING IN NOW.
OH, RIGHT... COMING!

No Matter How I Look at It, It's You Guys' Fault I'm Not Popular!

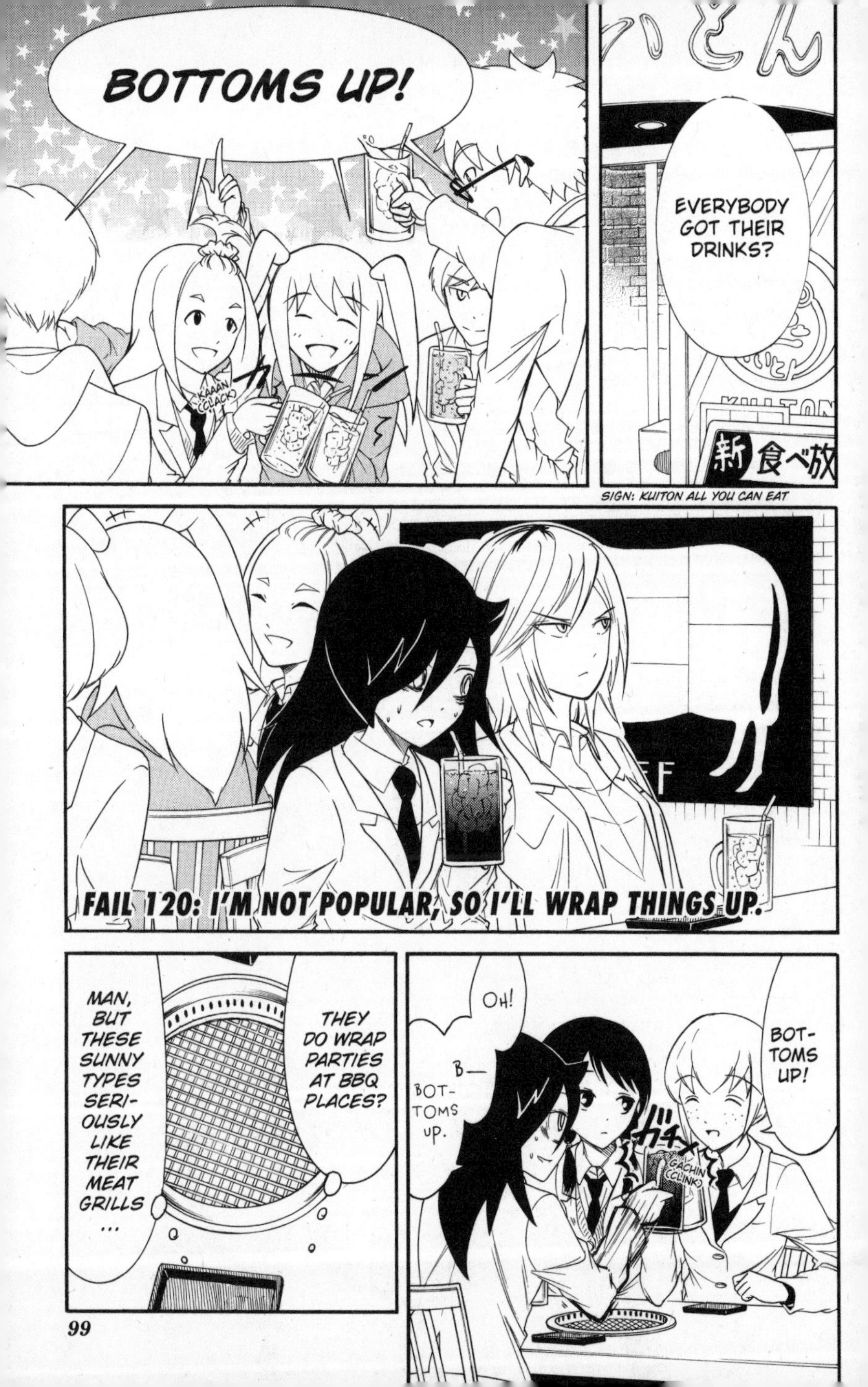
EVERYBODY GOT THEIR DRINKS?
新 食べ放
SIGN: KUITON ALL YOU CAN EAT
BOTTOMS UP!
KAAAN (CLACK)
FAIL 120: I'M NOT POPULAR, SO I'LL WRAP THINGS UP.
BOT-TOMS UP!
OH!
B— BOT-TOMS UP.
GACHIN (CLINK)
THEY DO WRAP PARTIES AT BBQ PLACES?
MAN, BUT THESE SUNNY TYPES SERI-OUSLY LIKE THEIR MEAT GRILLS ...

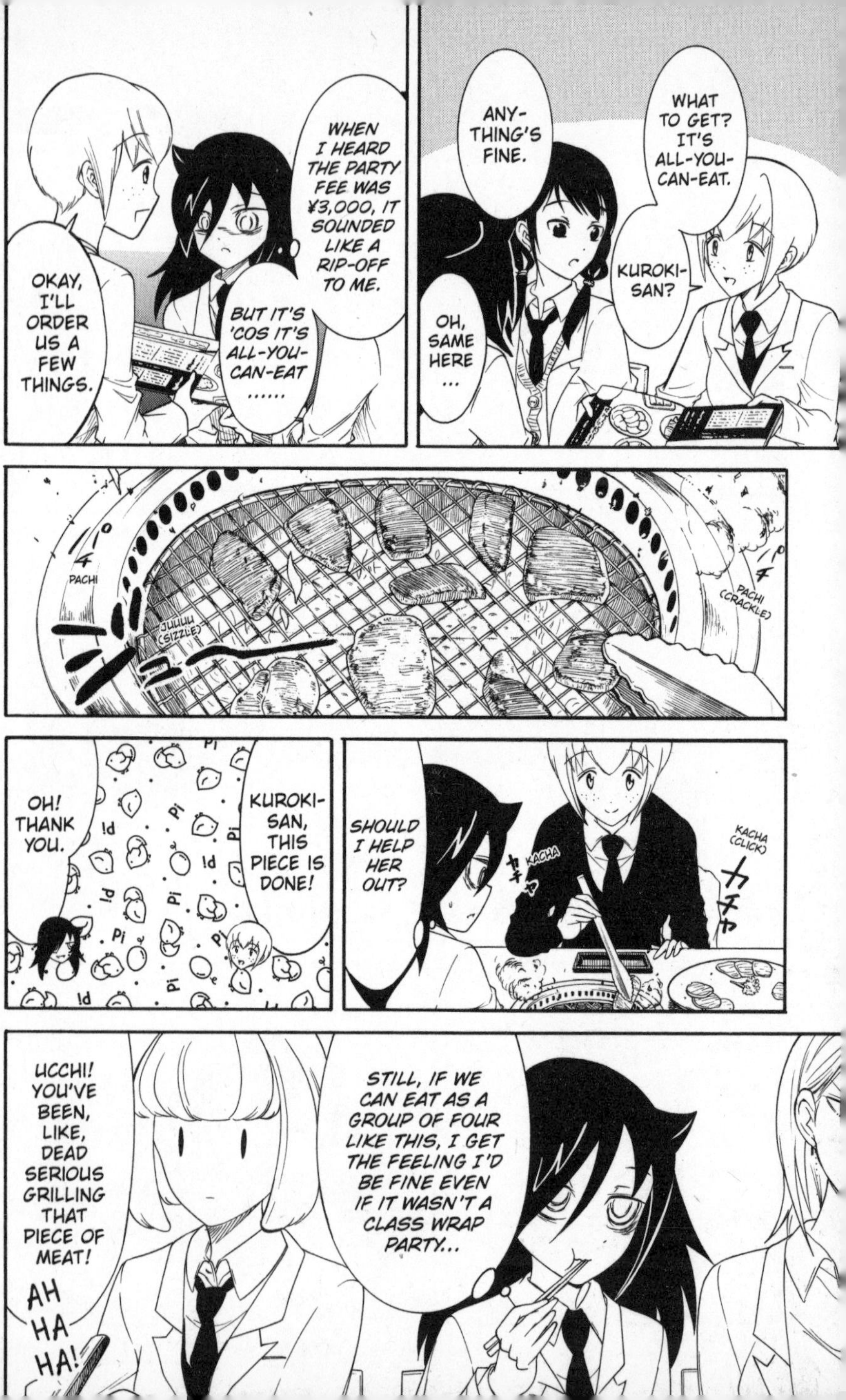
WHAT TO GET? IT'S ALL-YOU-CAN-EAT.
KUROKI-SAN?
ANY-THING'S FINE.
OH, SAME HERE ...
WHEN I HEARD THE PARTY FEE WAS ¥3,000, IT SOUNDED LIKE A RIP-OFF TO ME.
BUT IT'S 'COS IT'S ALL-YOU-CAN-EAT ......
OKAY, I'LL ORDER US A FEW THINGS.
PACHI (CRACKLE)
JUUUU (SIZZLE)
PACHI
KACHA (CLICK)
KACHA
SHOULD I HELP HER OUT?
KUROKI-SAN, THIS PIECE IS DONE!
OH! THANK YOU.
Pi
STILL, IF WE CAN EAT AS A GROUP OF FOUR LIKE THIS, I GET THE FEELING I'D BE FINE EVEN IF IT WASN'T A CLASS WRAP PARTY...
UCCHI! YOU'VE BEEN, LIKE, DEAD SERIOUS GRILLING THAT PIECE OF MEAT!
AH HA HA!

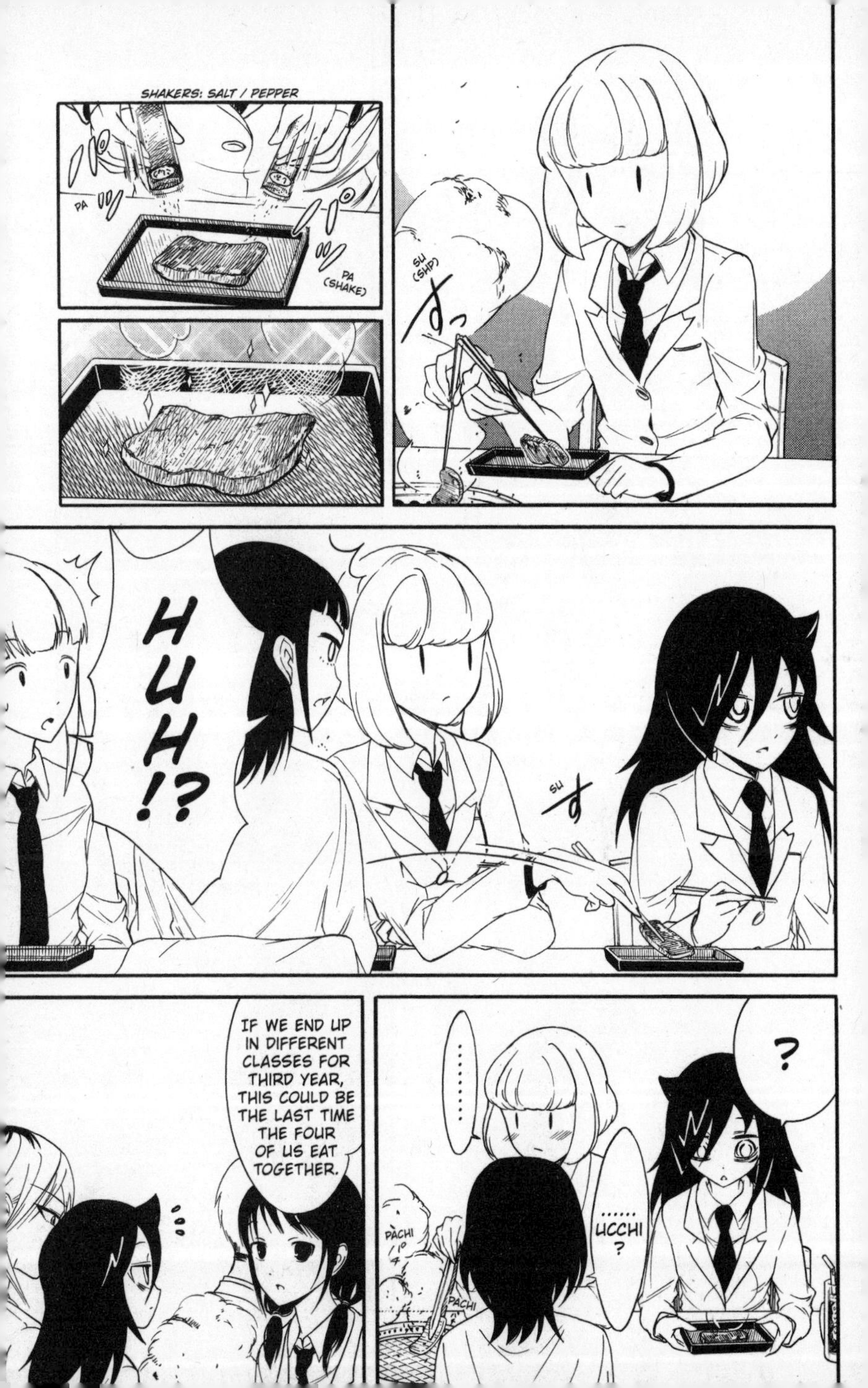
SU (SHP)
すっ
SHAKERS: SALT / PEPPER
PA
PA (SHAKE)
SU
す
HUH!?
?
......
......UCCHI?
PACHI
PACHI
IF WE END UP IN DIFFERENT CLASSES FOR THIRD YEAR, THIS COULD BE THE LAST TIME THE FOUR OF US EAT TOGETHER.

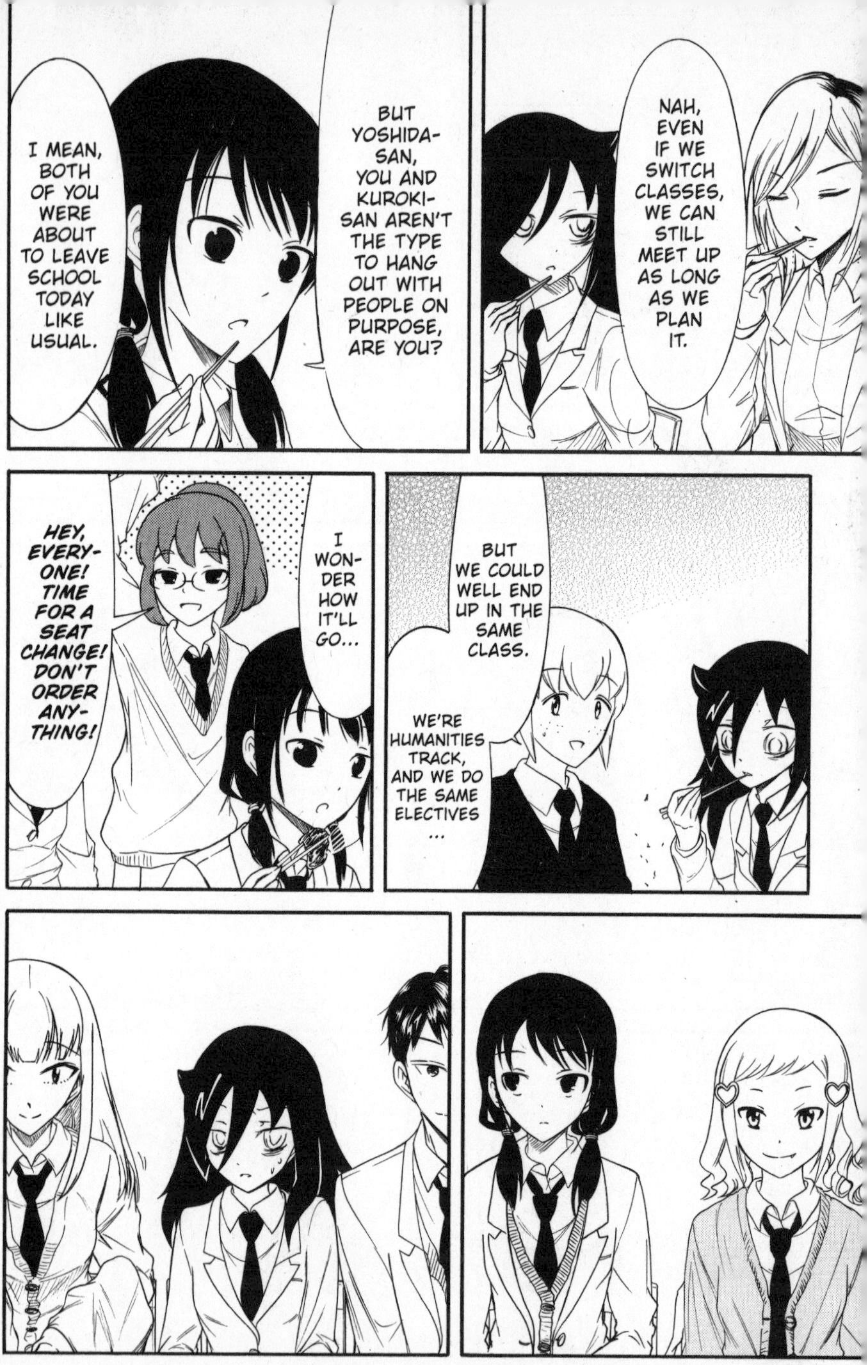
NAH, EVEN IF WE SWITCH CLASSES, WE CAN STILL MEET UP AS LONG AS WE PLAN IT.
BUT YOSHIDA-SAN, YOU AND KUROKI-SAN AREN'T THE TYPE TO HANG OUT WITH PEOPLE ON PURPOSE, ARE YOU?
I MEAN, BOTH OF YOU WERE ABOUT TO LEAVE SCHOOL TODAY LIKE USUAL.
BUT WE COULD WELL END UP IN THE SAME CLASS.
WE'RE HUMANITIES TRACK, AND WE DO THE SAME ELECTIVES ...
I WONDER HOW IT'LL GO...
HEY, EVERYONE! TIME FOR A SEAT CHANGE! DON'T ORDER ANYTHING!

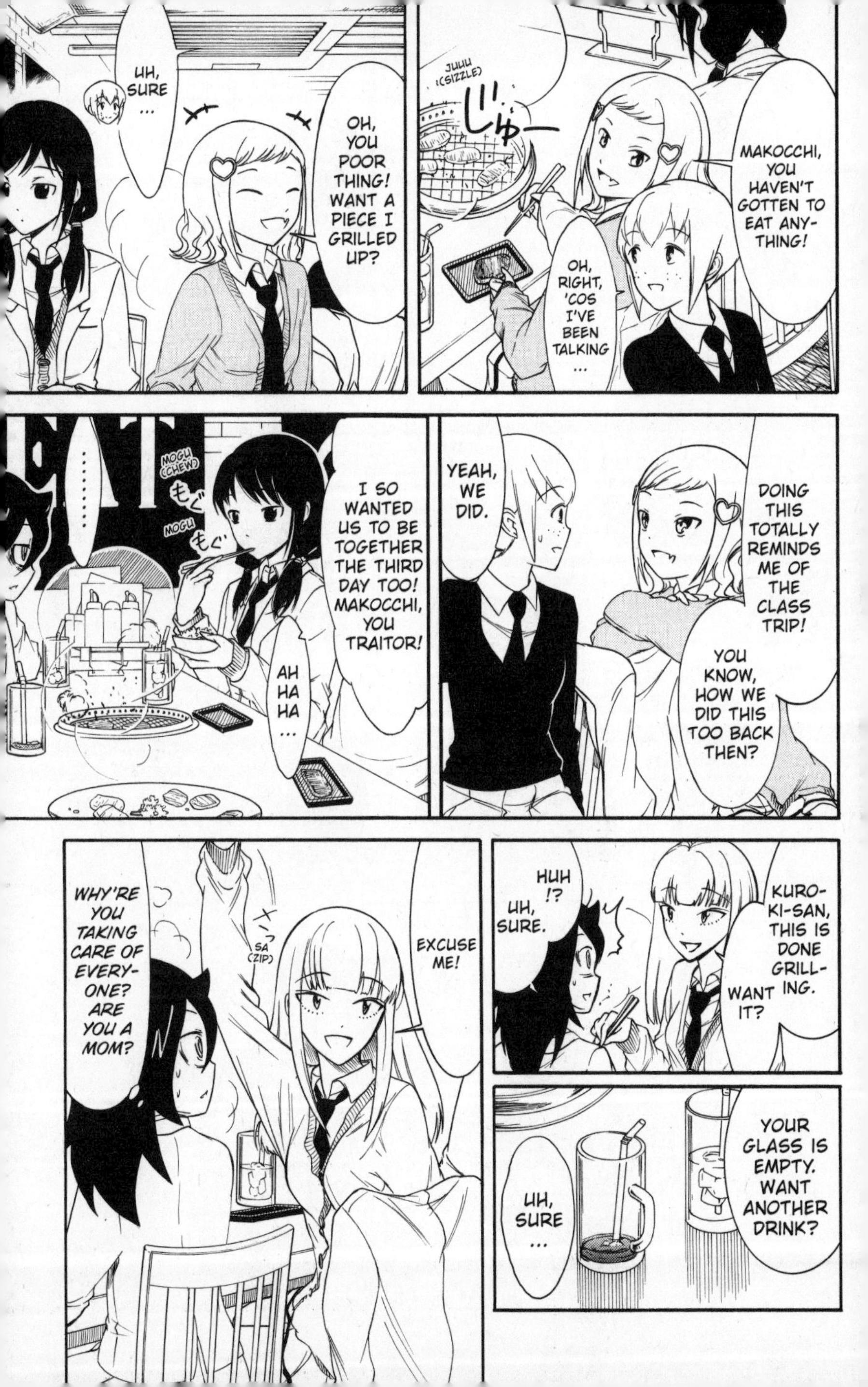
JUUU (SIZZLE)
じゅー
MAKOCCHI, YOU HAVEN'T GOTTEN TO EAT ANYTHING!
OH, RIGHT, 'COS I'VE BEEN TALKING ...
OH, YOU POOR THING! WANT A PIECE I GRILLED UP?
UH, SURE ...
DOING THIS TOTALLY REMINDS ME OF THE CLASS TRIP!
YOU KNOW, HOW WE DID THIS TOO BACK THEN?
YEAH, WE DID.
I SO WANTED US TO BE TOGETHER THE THIRD DAY TOO! MAKOCCHI, YOU TRAITOR!
AH HA HA ...
MOGU (CHEW)
もぐ
MOGU
もぐ
......
KURO-KI-SAN, THIS IS DONE GRILL-ING.
WANT IT?
HUH !?
UH, SURE.
YOUR GLASS IS EMPTY. WANT ANOTHER DRINK?
UH, SURE ...
EXCUSE ME!
SA (ZIP)
WHY'RE YOU TAKING CARE OF EVERYONE? ARE YOU A MOM?

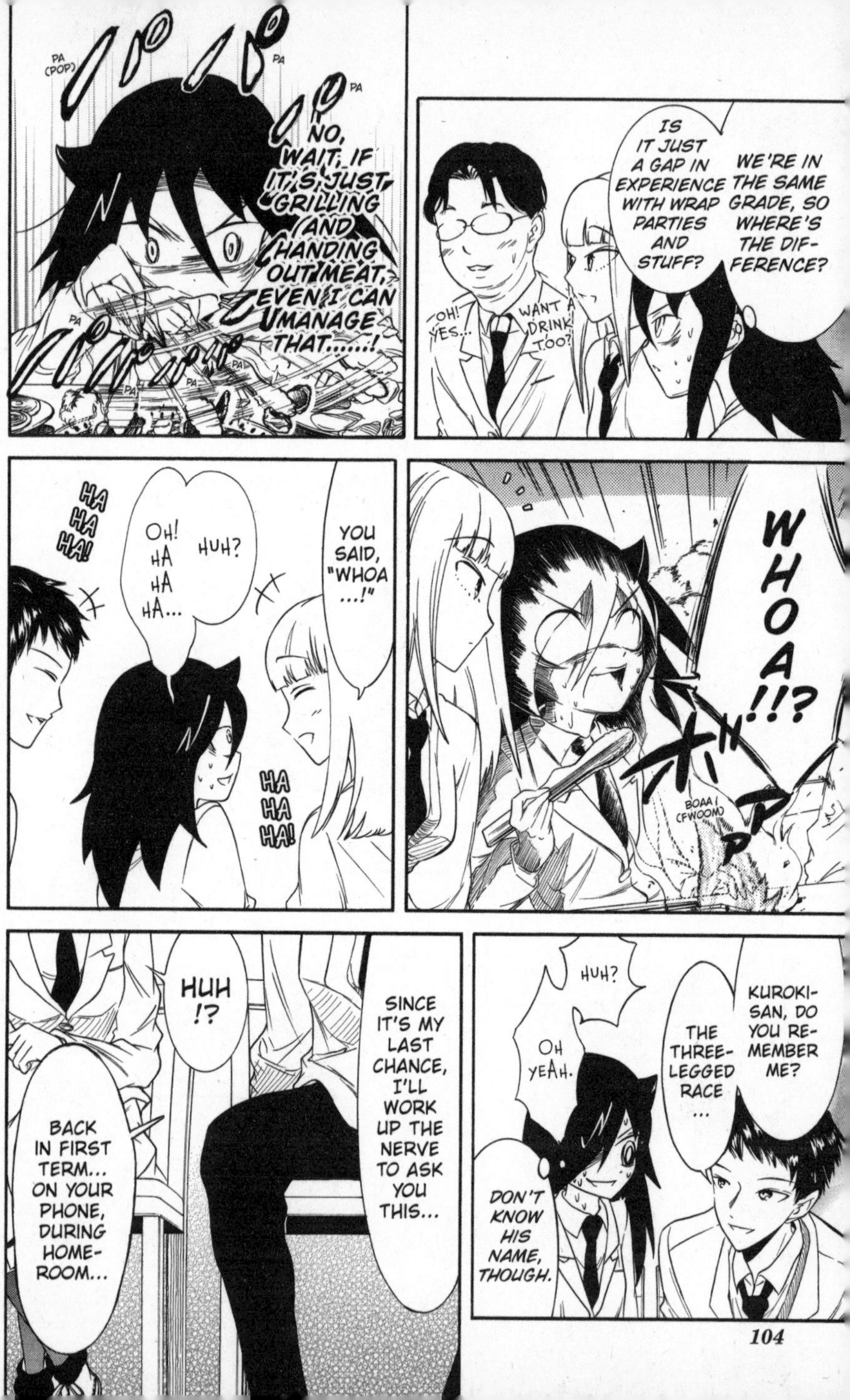
WE'RE IN THE SAME GRADE, SO WHERE'S THE DIF-FERENCE?
IS IT JUST A GAP IN EXPERIENCE WITH WRAP PARTIES AND STUFF?
WANT A DRINK TOO?
OH! YES...
PA PA
PA (POP)
NO, WAIT, IF IT'S JUST GRILLING AND HANDING OUT MEAT, EVEN I CAN MANAGE THAT......!
PA PA PA PA
WHOA!!?
BOAA! (FWOOM)
YOU SAID, "WHOA...!"
HUH?
OH! HA HA HA...
HA HA HA!
HA HA HA!
KUROKI-SAN, DO YOU RE-MEMBER ME?
THE THREE-LEGGED RACE...
HUH?
OH YEAH.
DON'T KNOW HIS NAME, THOUGH.
SINCE IT'S MY LAST CHANCE, I'LL WORK UP THE NERVE TO ASK YOU THIS...
HUH!?
BACK IN FIRST TERM... ON YOUR PHONE, DURING HOME-ROOM...

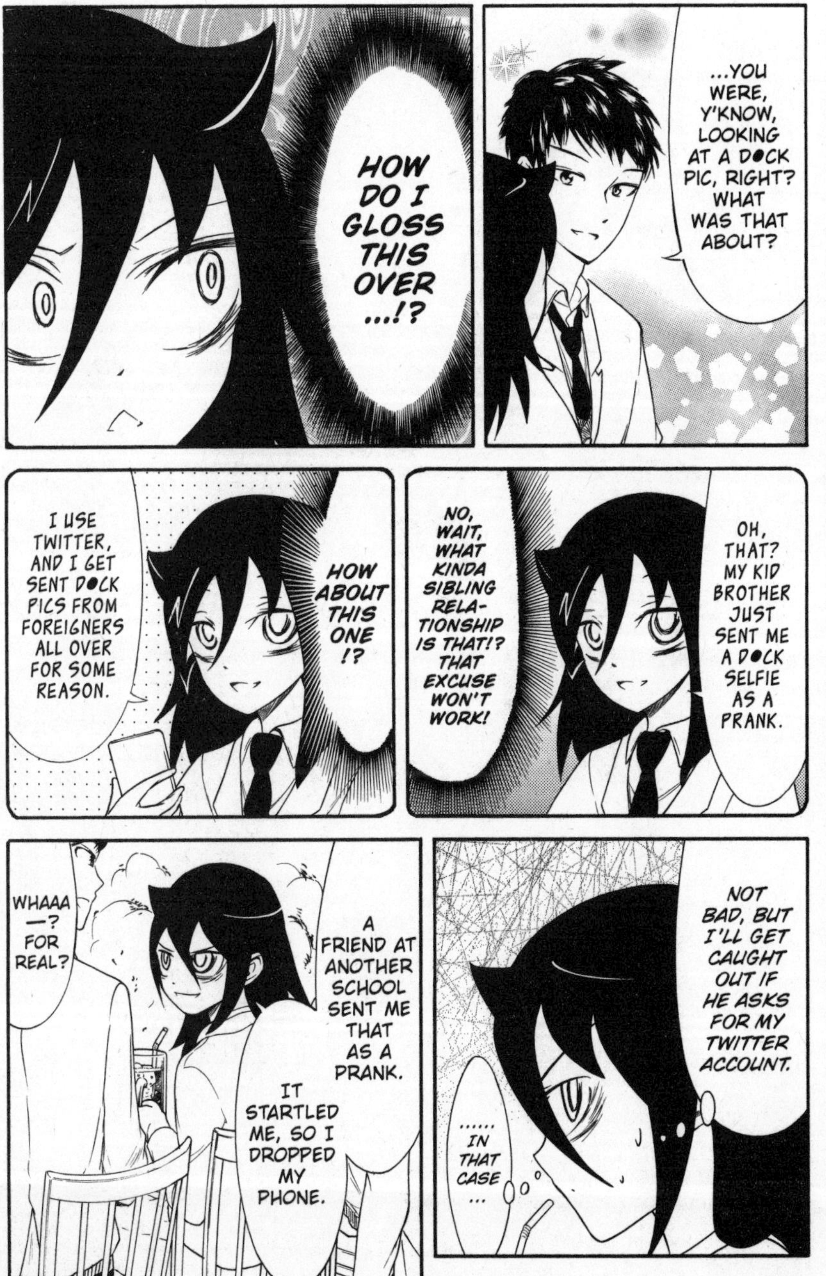
...YOU WERE, Y'KNOW, LOOKING AT A DOCK PIC, RIGHT? WHAT WAS THAT ABOUT?
HOW DO I GLOSS THIS OVER...!?
OH, THAT? MY KID BROTHER JUST SENT ME A DOCK SELFIE AS A PRANK.
NO, WAIT, WHAT KINDA SIBLING RELATIONSHIP IS THAT!? THAT EXCUSE WON'T WORK!
HOW ABOUT THIS ONE!?
I USE TWITTER, AND I GET SENT DOCK PICS FROM FOREIGNERS ALL OVER FOR SOME REASON.
NOT BAD, BUT I'LL GET CAUGHT OUT IF HE ASKS FOR MY TWITTER ACCOUNT.
......IN THAT CASE...
A FRIEND AT ANOTHER SCHOOL SENT ME THAT AS A PRANK.
IT STARTLED ME, SO I DROPPED MY PHONE.
WHAAA—? FOR REAL?

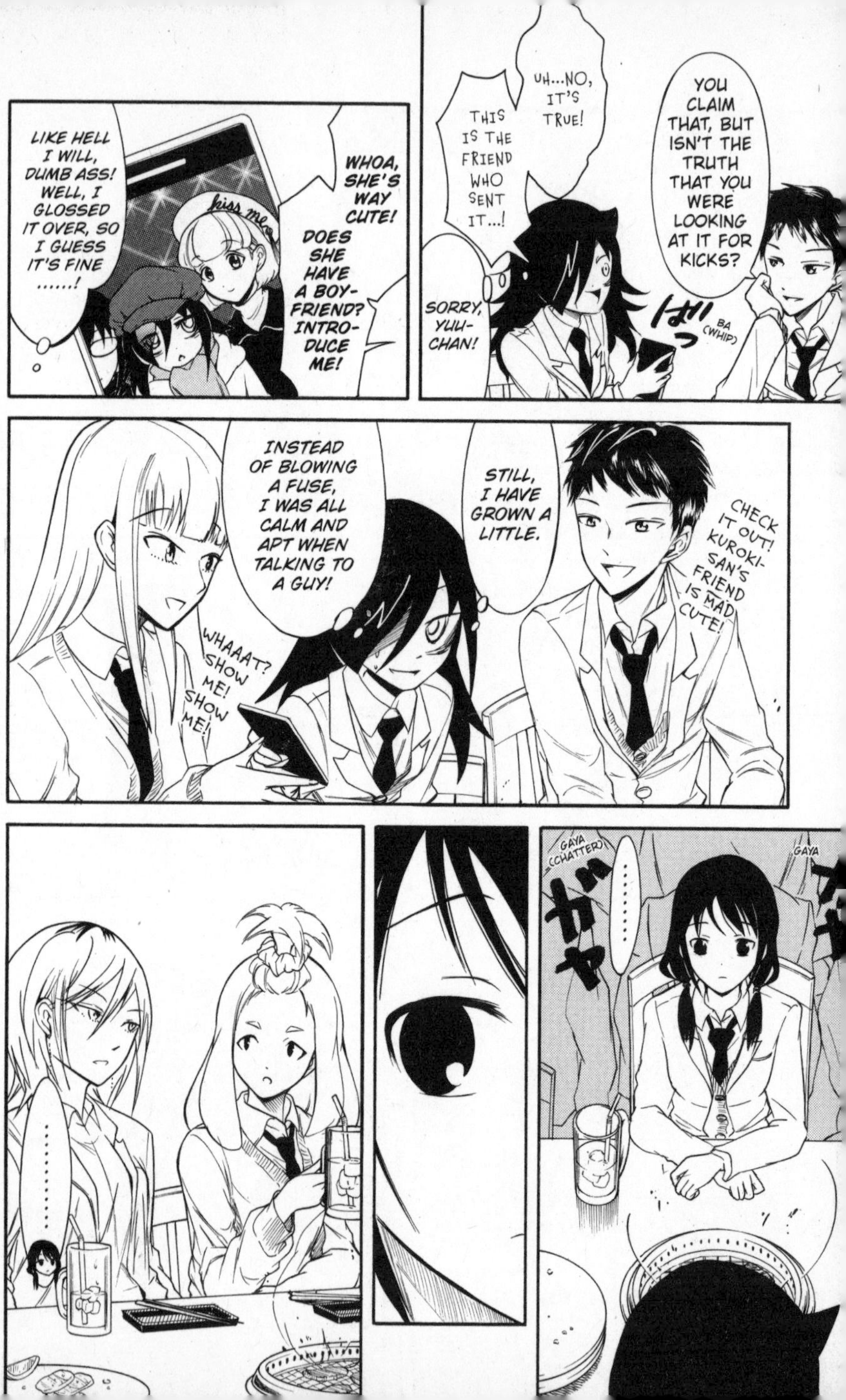

YOU CLAIM THAT, BUT ISN'T THE TRUTH THAT YOU WERE LOOKING AT IT FOR KICKS?
UH...NO, IT'S TRUE!
THIS IS THE FRIEND WHO SENT IT...!
BA (WHIP)
SORRY, YUU-CHAN!
WHOA, SHE'S WAY CUTE! DOES SHE HAVE A BOY-FRIEND? INTRO-DUCE ME!
LIKE HELL I WILL, DUMB ASS! WELL, I GLOSSED IT OVER, SO I GUESS IT'S FINE ......!
kiss me
CHECK IT OUT! KUROKI-SAN'S FRIEND IS MAD CUTE!
STILL, I HAVE GROWN A LITTLE.
INSTEAD OF BLOWING A FUSE, I WAS ALL CALM AND APT WHEN TALKING TO A GUY!
WHAAAT? SHOW ME! SHOW ME!
GAYA
GAYA (CHATTER)
......
......

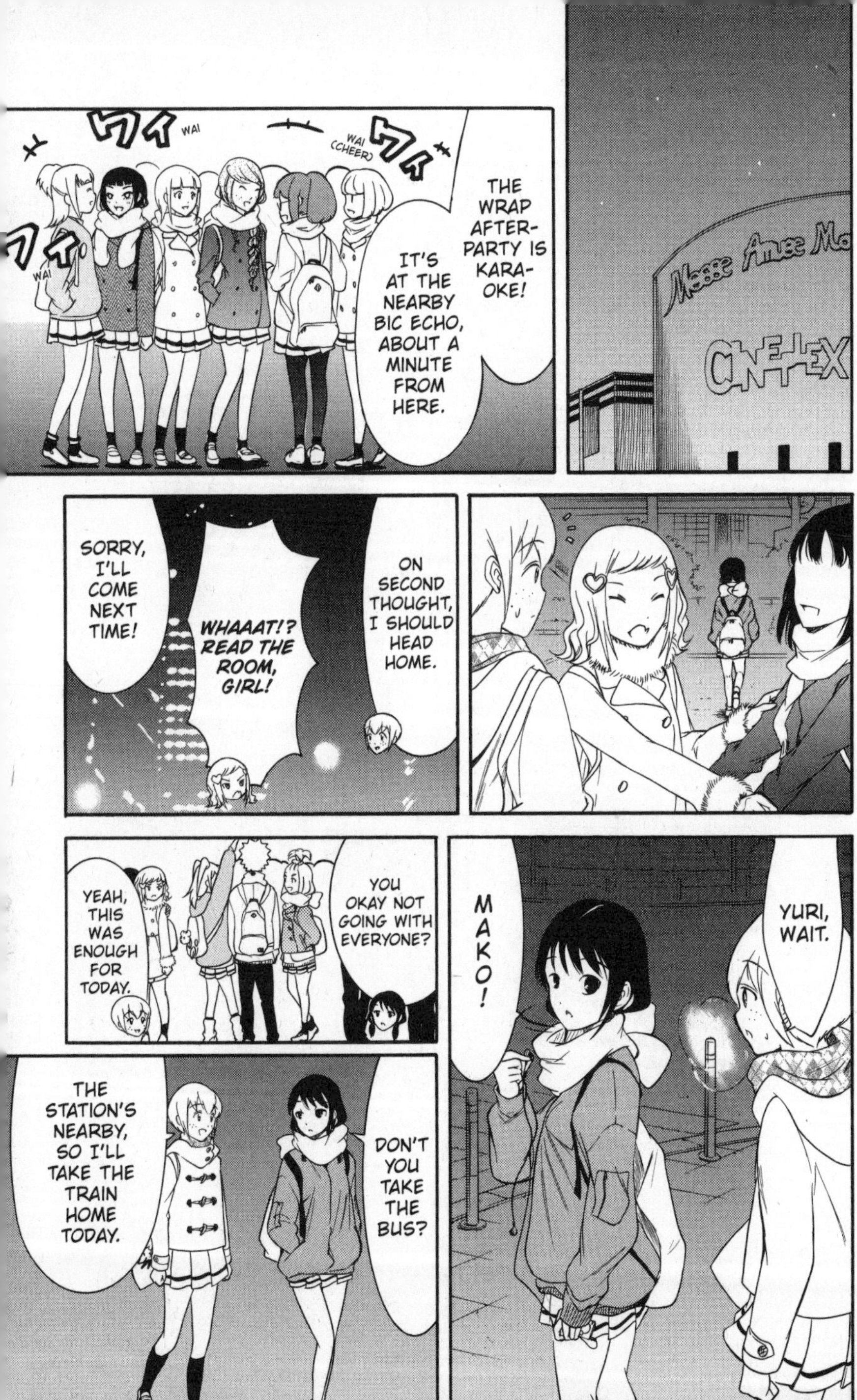
WAI
WAI (CHEER)
WAI
THE WRAP AFTER-PARTY IS KARAOKE!
IT'S AT THE NEARBY BIC ECHO, ABOUT A MINUTE FROM HERE.
ON SECOND THOUGHT, I SHOULD HEAD HOME.
WHAAAT!? READ THE ROOM, GIRL!
SORRY, I'LL COME NEXT TIME!
YURI, WAIT.
MAKO!
YOU OKAY NOT GOING WITH EVERYONE?
YEAH, THIS WAS ENOUGH FOR TODAY.
DON'T YOU TAKE THE BUS?
THE STATION'S NEARBY, SO I'LL TAKE THE TRAIN HOME TODAY.

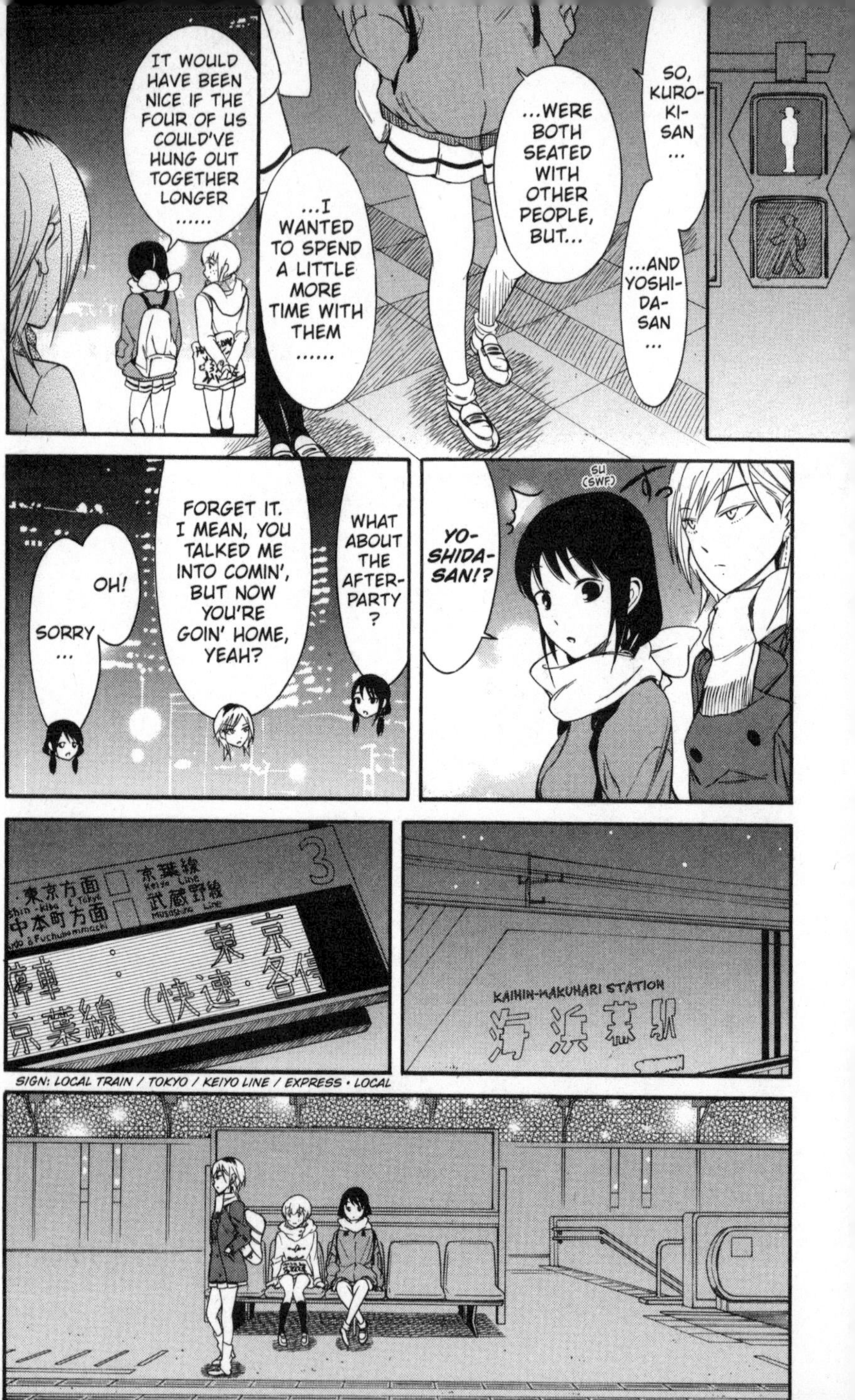
SO, KURO-KI-SAN...
...AND YOSHI-DA-SAN...
...WERE BOTH SEATED WITH OTHER PEOPLE, BUT...
...I WANTED TO SPEND A LITTLE MORE TIME WITH THEM......
IT WOULD HAVE BEEN NICE IF THE FOUR OF US COULD'VE HUNG OUT TOGETHER LONGER......
SU (SWF)
YO-SHIDA-SAN!?
WHAT ABOUT THE AFTER-PARTY?
FORGET IT. I MEAN, YOU TALKED ME INTO COMIN', BUT NOW YOU'RE GOIN' HOME, YEAH?
OH!
SORRY...
KAIHIN-MAKUHARI STATION
海浜幕張駅
3
京葉線
武蔵野線
東京
SIGN: LOCAL TRAIN / TOKYO / KEIYO LINE / EXPRESS • LOCAL

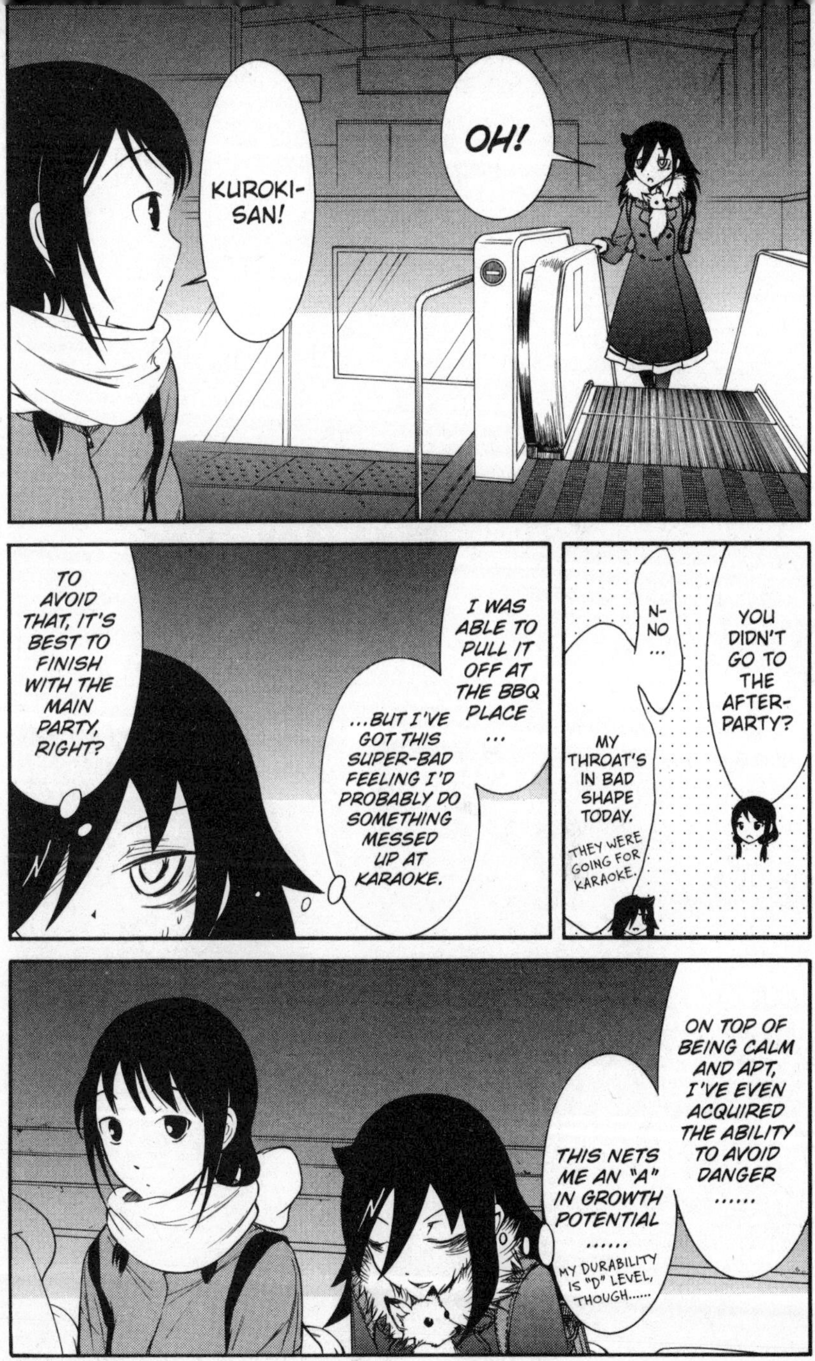
OH!
KUROKI-SAN!
YOU DIDN'T GO TO THE AFTER-PARTY?
N-NO ...
MY THROAT'S IN BAD SHAPE TODAY.
THEY WERE GOING FOR KARAOKE.
I WAS ABLE TO PULL IT OFF AT THE BBQ PLACE ...
...BUT I'VE GOT THIS SUPER-BAD FEELING I'D PROBABLY DO SOMETHING MESSED UP AT KARAOKE.
TO AVOID THAT, IT'S BEST TO FINISH WITH THE MAIN PARTY, RIGHT?
ON TOP OF BEING CALM AND APT, I'VE EVEN ACQUIRED THE ABILITY TO AVOID DANGER ......
THIS NETS ME AN "A" IN GROWTH POTENTIAL ......
MY DURABILITY IS "D" LEVEL, THOUGH......

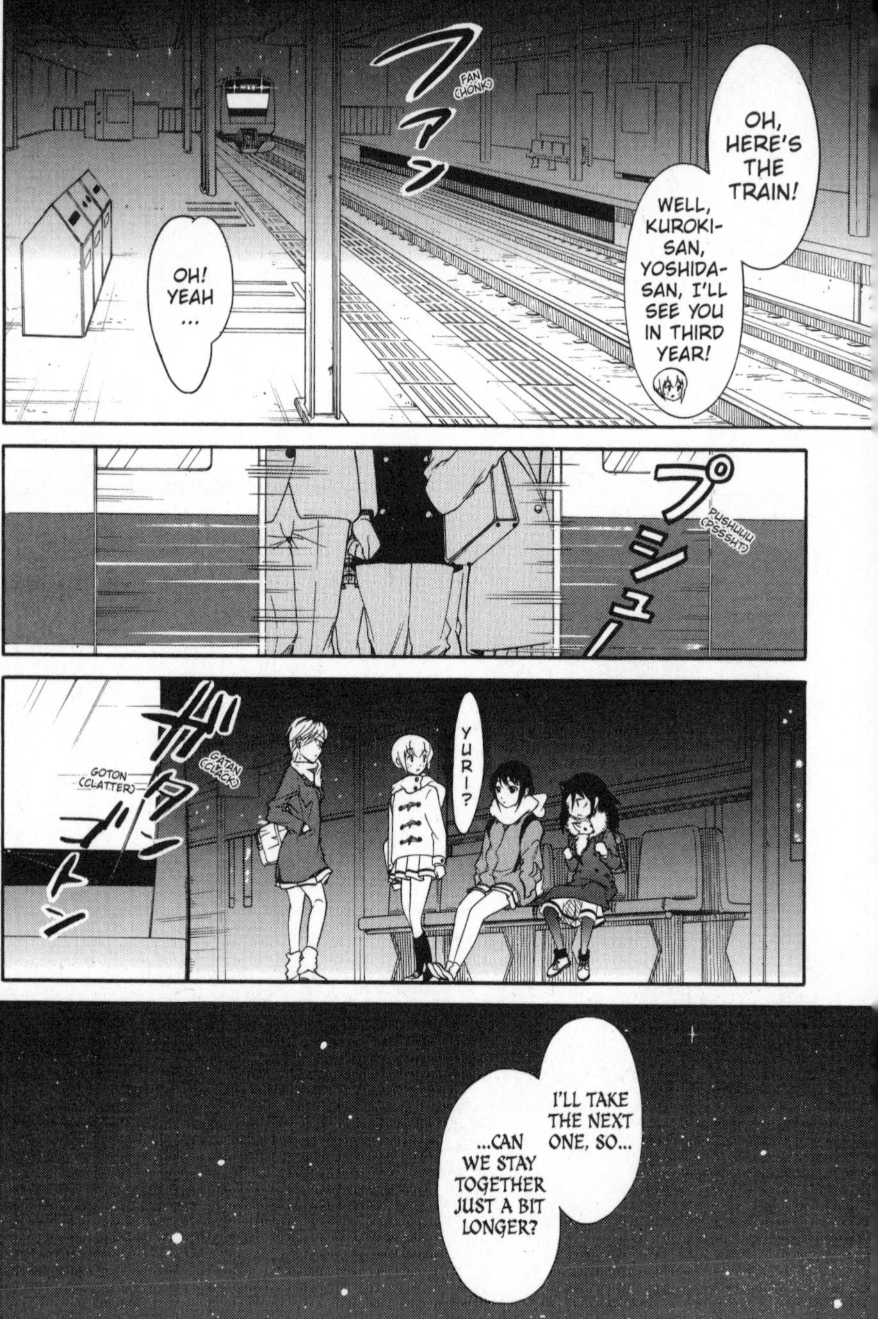
OH, HERE'S THE TRAIN!
WELL, KUROKI-SAN, YOSHIDA-SAN, I'LL SEE YOU IN THIRD YEAR!
FAN (HONK)
OH! YEAH ...
PUSHUUU (PSSSHT)
YURI?
GATAN (CLACK)
GOTON (CLATTER)
I'LL TAKE THE NEXT ONE, SO...
...CAN WE STAY TOGETHER JUST A BIT LONGER?

No Matter How I Look at It, It's You Guys' Fault I'm Not Popular!

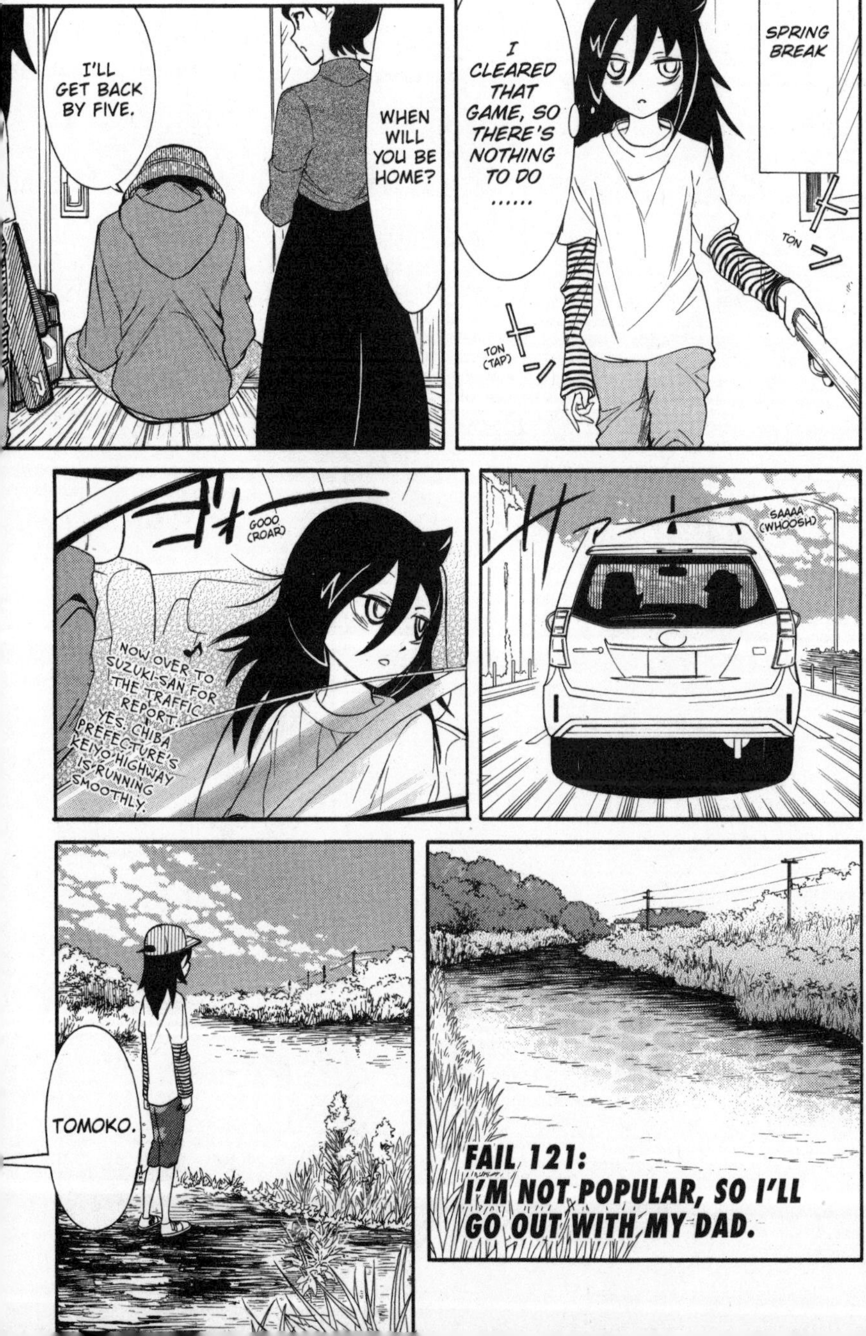
SPRING BREAK
I CLEARED THAT GAME, SO THERE'S NOTHING TO DO ......
TON
TON (TAP)
WHEN WILL YOU BE HOME?
I'LL GET BACK BY FIVE.
SAAAA (WHOOSH)
GOOO (ROAR)
NOW OVER TO SUZUKI-SAN FOR THE TRAFFIC REPORT. YES. CHIBA PREFECTURE'S KEIYO HIGHWAY IS RUNNING SMOOTHLY.
FAIL 121:
I'M NOT POPULAR, SO I'LL GO OUT WITH MY DAD.
TOMOKO.

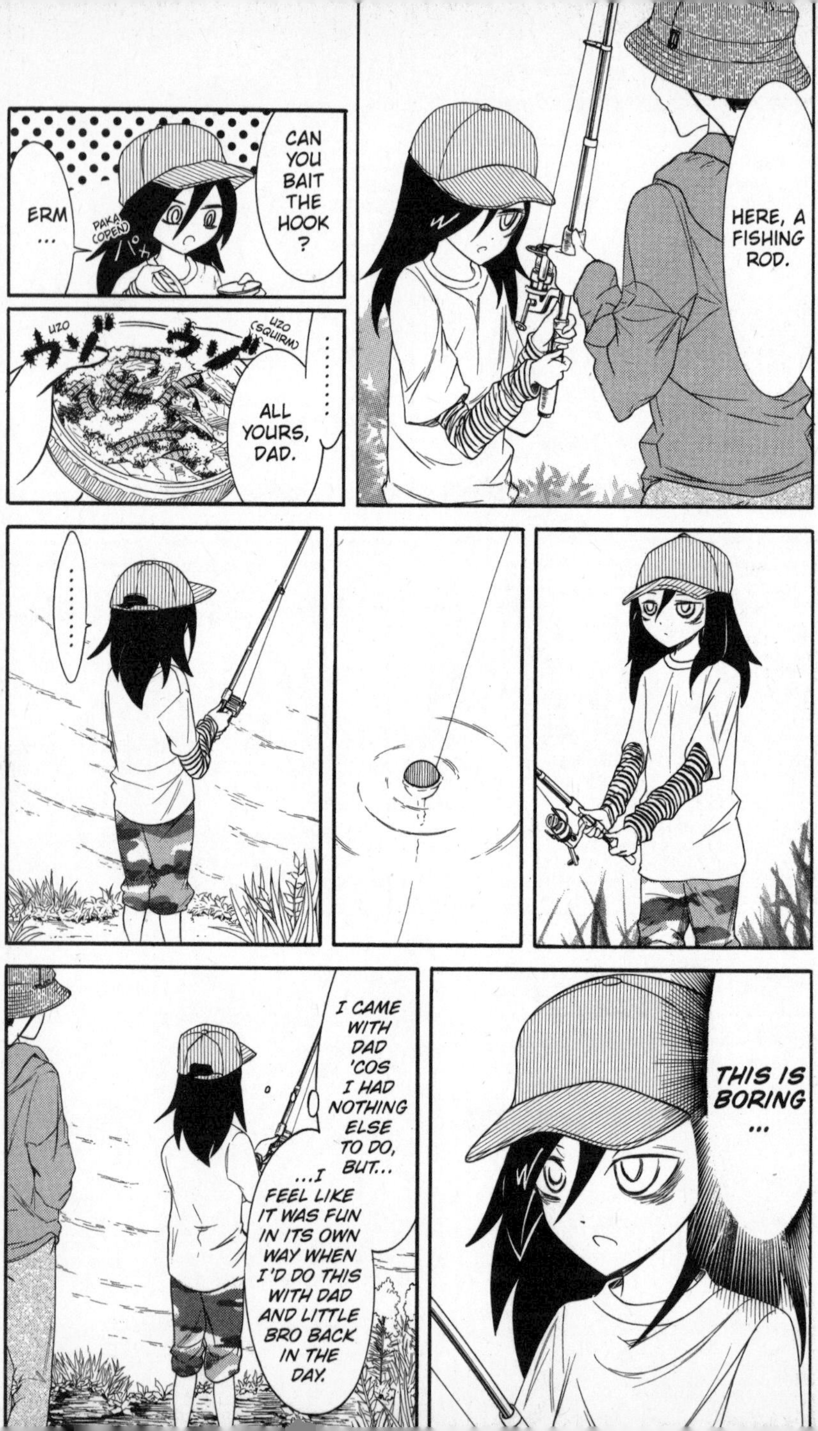
HERE, A FISHING ROD.
CAN YOU BAIT THE HOOK?
PAKA (OPEN)
ERM ...
UZO (SQUIRM)
UZO
......
ALL YOURS, DAD.
......
THIS IS BORING ...
I CAME WITH DAD 'COS I HAD NOTHING ELSE TO DO, BUT...
...I FEEL LIKE IT WAS FUN IN ITS OWN WAY WHEN I'D DO THIS WITH DAD AND LITTLE BRO BACK IN THE DAY.

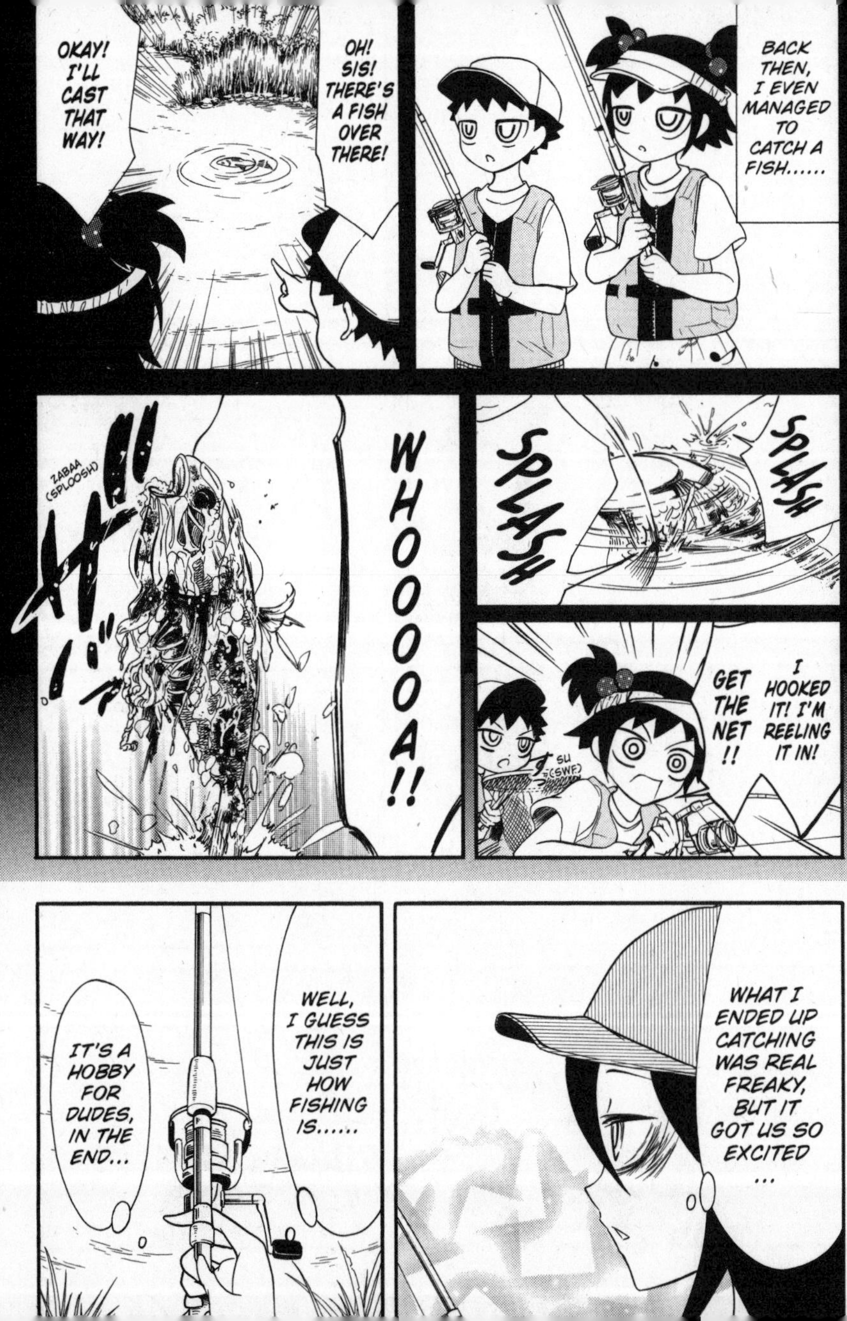
BACK THEN, I EVEN MANAGED TO CATCH A FISH......
OH! SIS! THERE'S A FISH OVER THERE!
OKAY! I'LL CAST THAT WAY!
SPLASH
SPLASH
I HOOKED IT! I'M REELING IT IN!
GET THE NET!!
SU (SWF)
WHOOOOOA!!
ZABAA (SPLOOSH)
WHAT I ENDED UP CATCHING WAS REAL FREAKY, BUT IT GOT US SO EXCITED...
WELL, I GUESS THIS IS JUST HOW FISHING IS......
IT'S A HOBBY FOR DUDES, IN THE END...

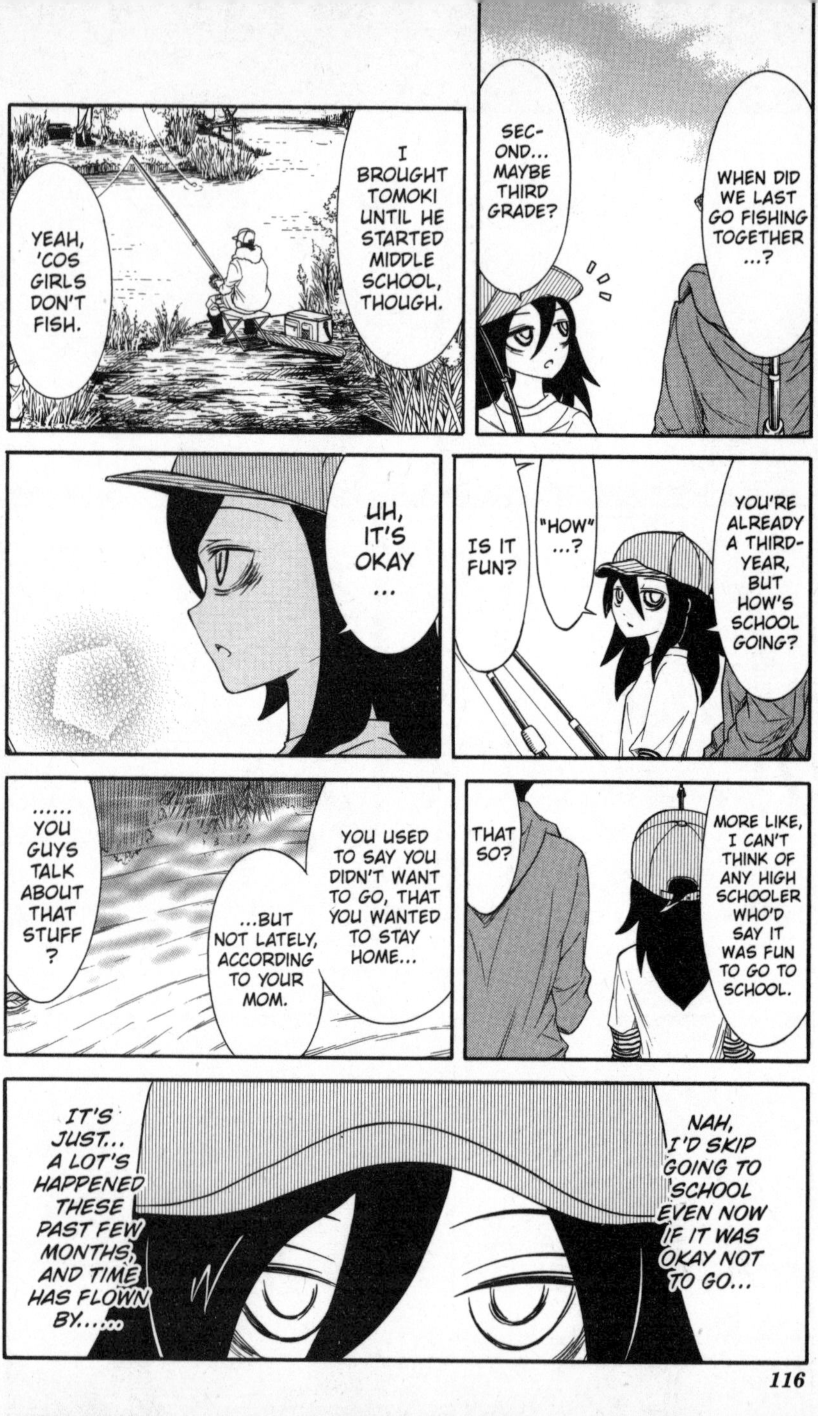
WHEN DID WE LAST GO FISHING TOGETHER ...?
SEC- OND... MAYBE THIRD GRADE?
I BROUGHT TOMOKI UNTIL HE STARTED MIDDLE SCHOOL, THOUGH.
YEAH, 'COS GIRLS DON'T FISH.
YOU'RE ALREADY A THIRD-YEAR, BUT HOW'S SCHOOL GOING?
"HOW" ...?
IS IT FUN?
UH, IT'S OKAY ...
MORE LIKE, I CAN'T THINK OF ANY HIGH SCHOOLER WHO'D SAY IT WAS FUN TO GO TO SCHOOL.
THAT SO?
YOU USED TO SAY YOU DIDN'T WANT TO GO, THAT YOU WANTED TO STAY HOME...
...BUT NOT LATELY, ACCORDING TO YOUR MOM.
...... YOU GUYS TALK ABOUT THAT STUFF?
NAH, I'D SKIP GOING TO SCHOOL EVEN NOW IF IT WAS OKAY NOT TO GO...
IT'S JUST... A LOT'S HAPPENED THESE PAST FEW MONTHS, AND TIME HAS FLOWN BY......

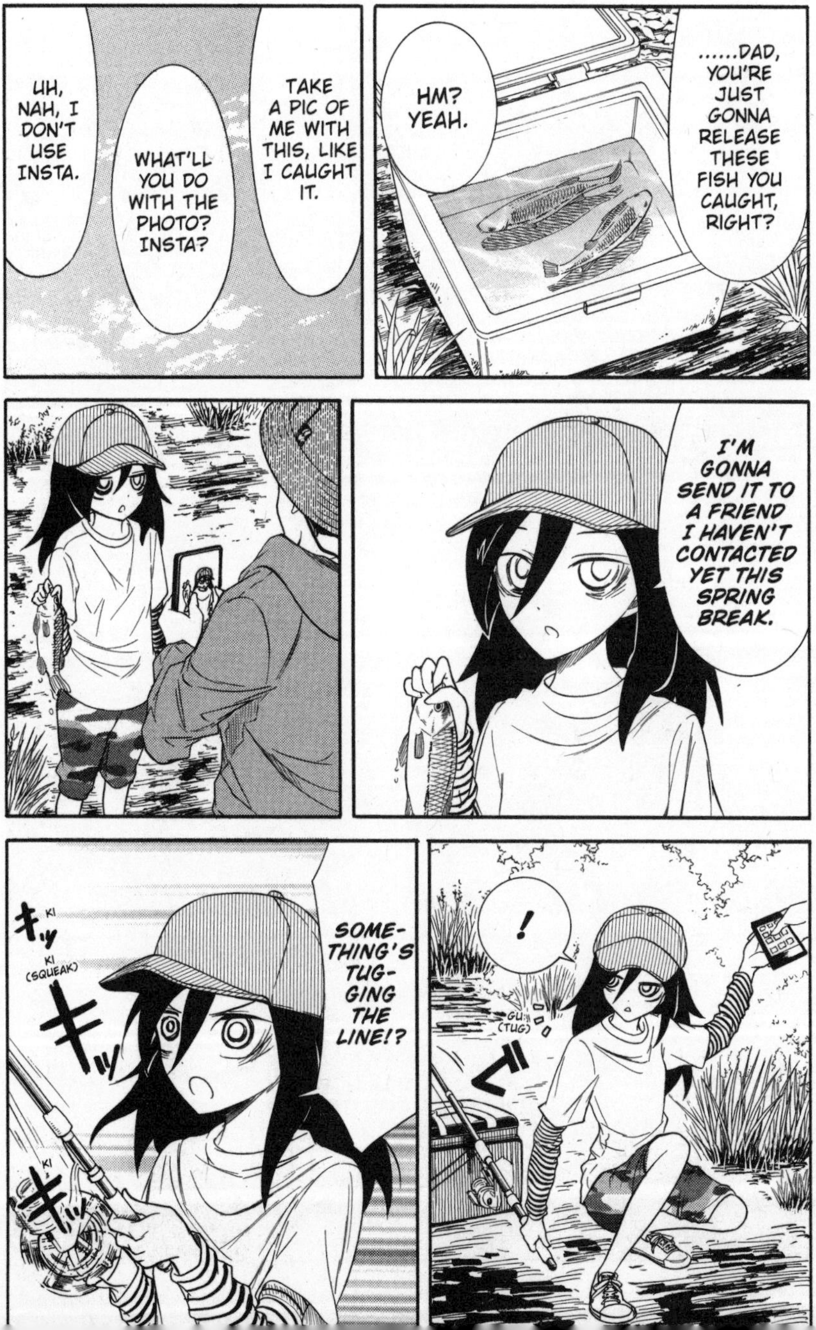
......DAD, YOU'RE JUST GONNA RELEASE THESE FISH YOU CAUGHT, RIGHT?
HM? YEAH.
TAKE A PIC OF ME WITH THIS, LIKE I CAUGHT IT.
WHAT'LL YOU DO WITH THE PHOTO? INSTA?
UH, NAH, I DON'T USE INSTA.
I'M GONNA SEND IT TO A FRIEND I HAVEN'T CONTACTED YET THIS SPRING BREAK.
!
GU (TUG)
SOME-THING'S TUG-GING THE LINE!?
KI
KI (SQUEAK)
KI

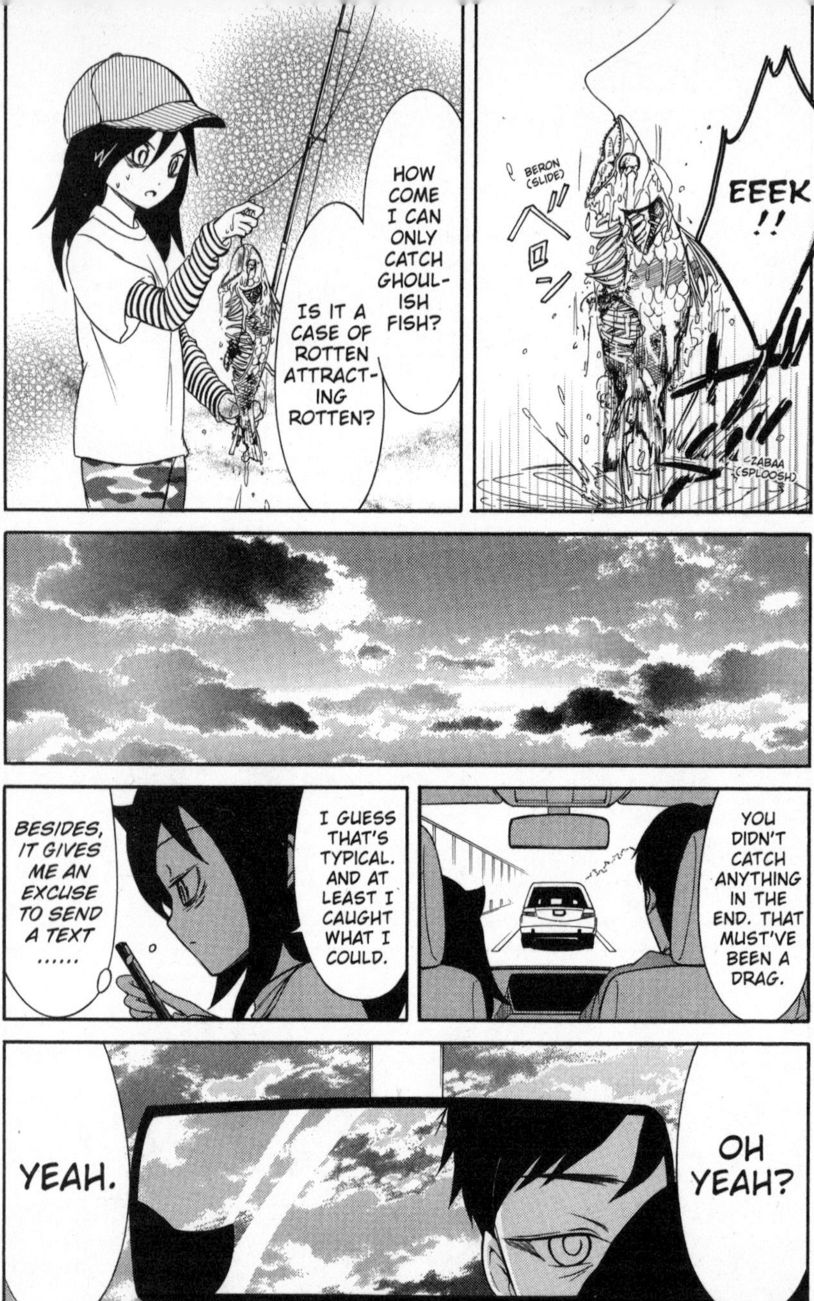
BERON (SLIDE)
EEEK !!
ZABAA (SPLOOSH)
HOW COME I CAN ONLY CATCH GHOUL-ISH FISH?
IS IT A CASE OF ROTTEN ATTRACT-ING ROTTEN?
YOU DIDN'T CATCH ANYTHING IN THE END. THAT MUST'VE BEEN A DRAG.
I GUESS THAT'S TYPICAL. AND AT LEAST I CAUGHT WHAT I COULD.
BESIDES, IT GIVES ME AN EXCUSE TO SEND A TEXT ......
OH YEAH?
YEAH.

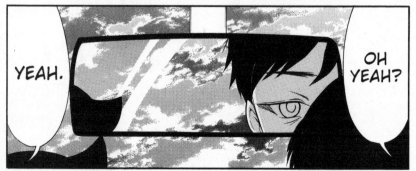

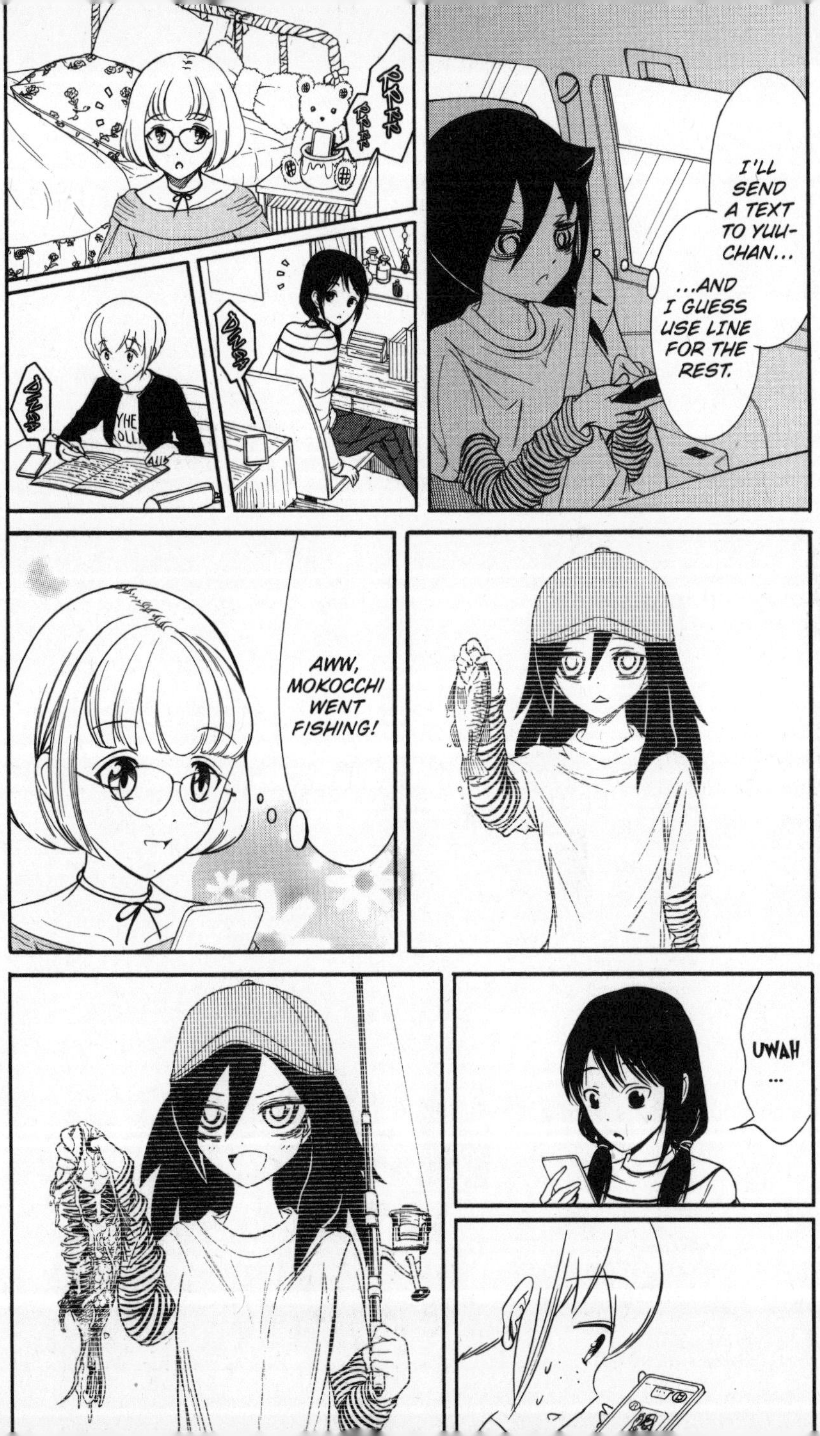
I'LL SEND A TEXT TO YUU-CHAN...
...AND I GUESS USE LINE FOR THE REST.
PRRR
PRRR
DINGA
DINGA
AWW, MOKOCCHI WENT FISHING!
UWAH ...

No Matter How I
Look at It, It's You
Guys' Fault I'm Not
Popular!

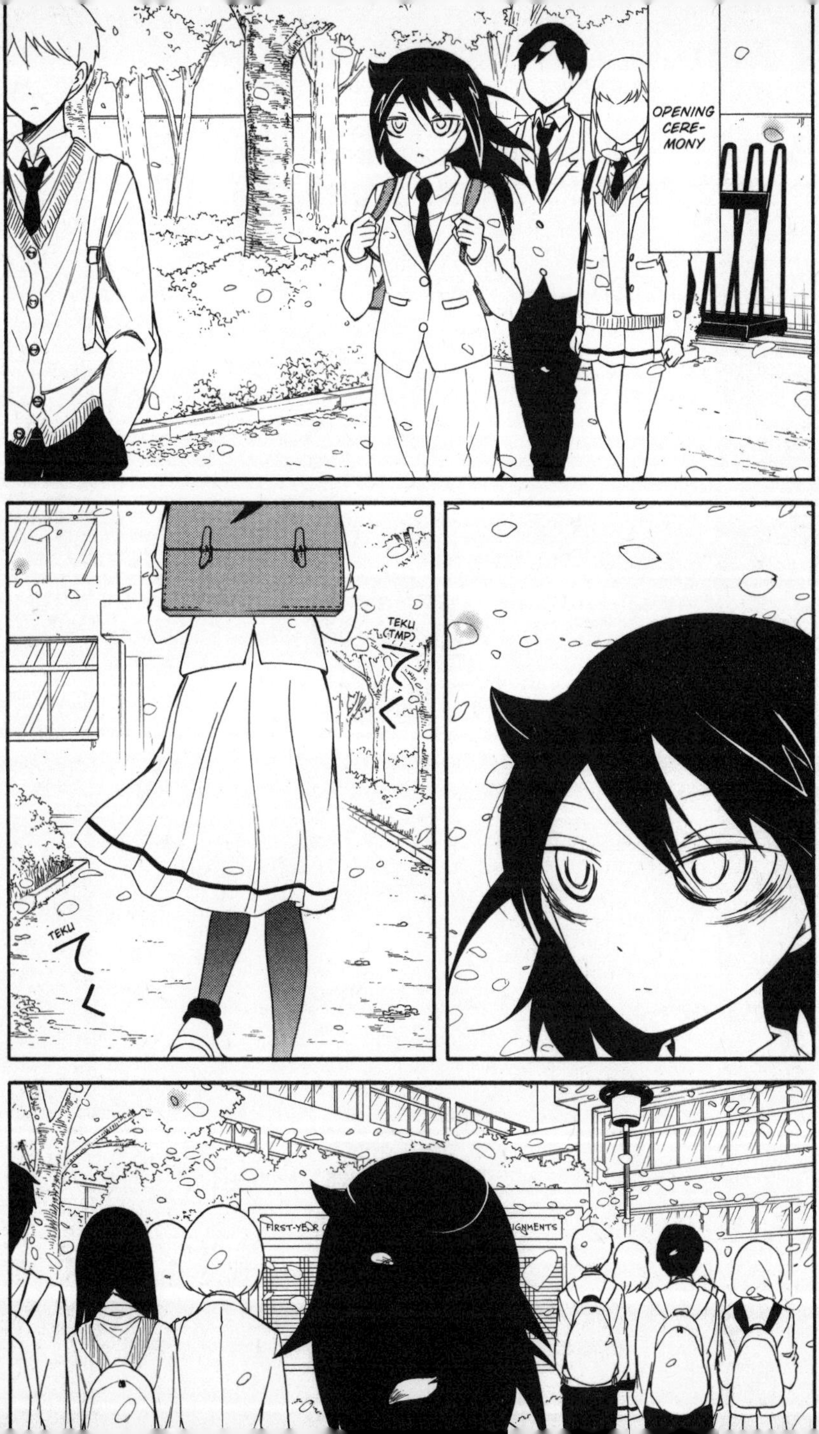
OPENING CERE-MONY
TEKU (TMP)
てく
TEKU
てく

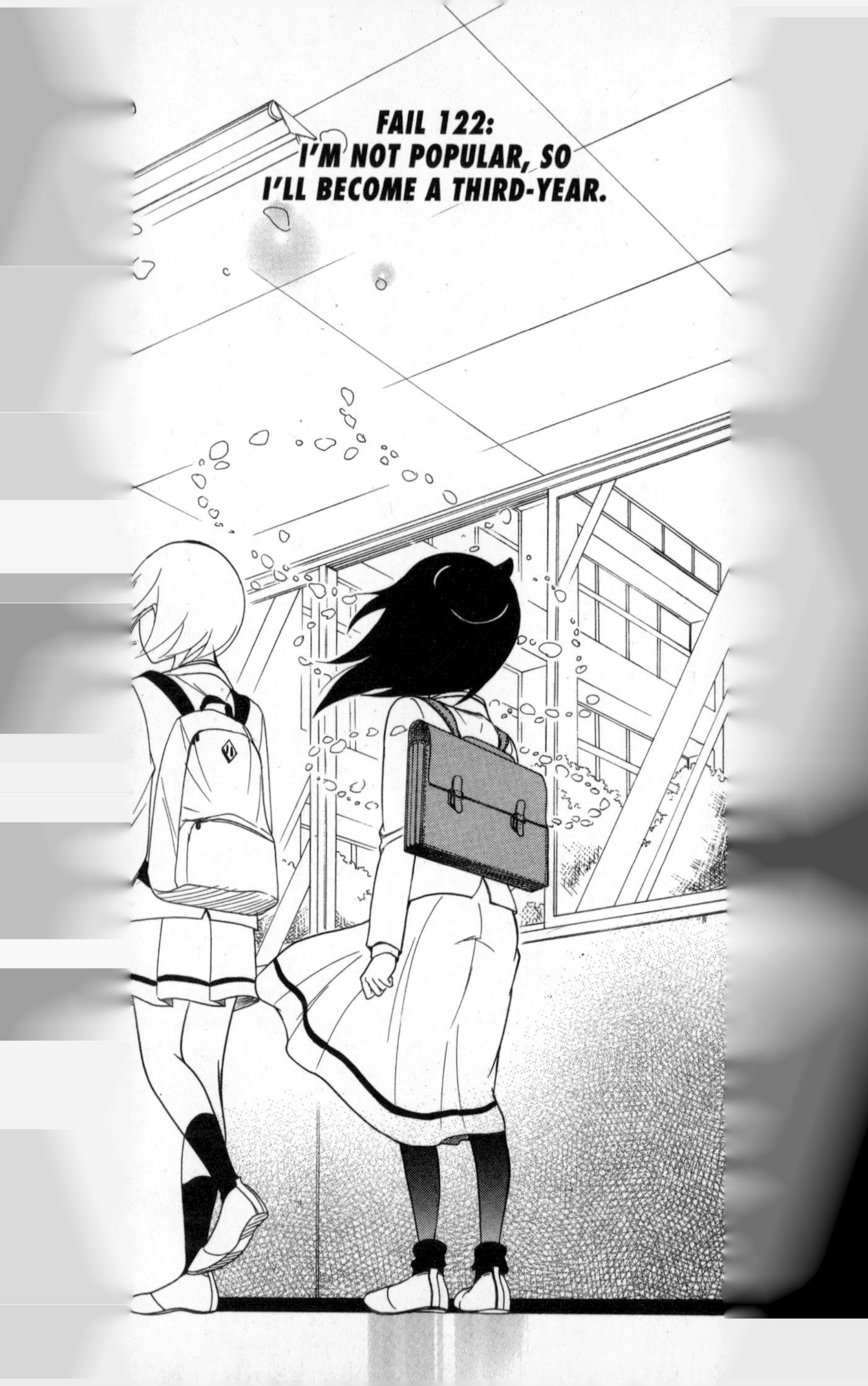
FAIL 122:
I'M NOT POPULAR, SO
I'LL BECOME A THIRD-YEAR.

CLASS 3-5

GAYA

ZAWA (MURMUR)

GAYA (CHATTER)

ZAWA

FOOO...

HAAAH...

| 26 | MAKO TANAKA | ! |
| 27 | YURI TAMURA | |

TOMOKO KUROKI !?

MASAKI YOSHIDA !!

WHEW...

......

SA (ZIP)

SU (SWF)

NOT REALLY, NAH...

UH, WELL, NOT LIKE IT'S A PROBLEM...

22	ASUKA KATOU	
23	TOMOKO KUR...	FOR REAL?
24	KOTOMI KOMIYAMA	

YEAH.

ALL THREE OF YOU—SACHI, NORI, MAKI—ARE IN 3-4!?

NO WAY!?

WELL, I'M WITH ITOU-SAN AGAIN, SO I GUESS IT'S FINE......

GAYA

GAYA (CHATTER)

YEP.

TO-GETHER AGAIN! LET'S HAVE A GOOD ONE.

NOT TO MENTION, MAKO-CCHI'S FRIENDS WITH HER...!

WON'T MAKOCCHI BE THERE?

SO I'LL BE ALL ALONE IN 3-5! ISN'T THAT MESSED UP!?

SO COME TO OUR CLASS FOR LUNCH.

ONLY MAKOCCHI WILL BE THERE, DUMMY!!

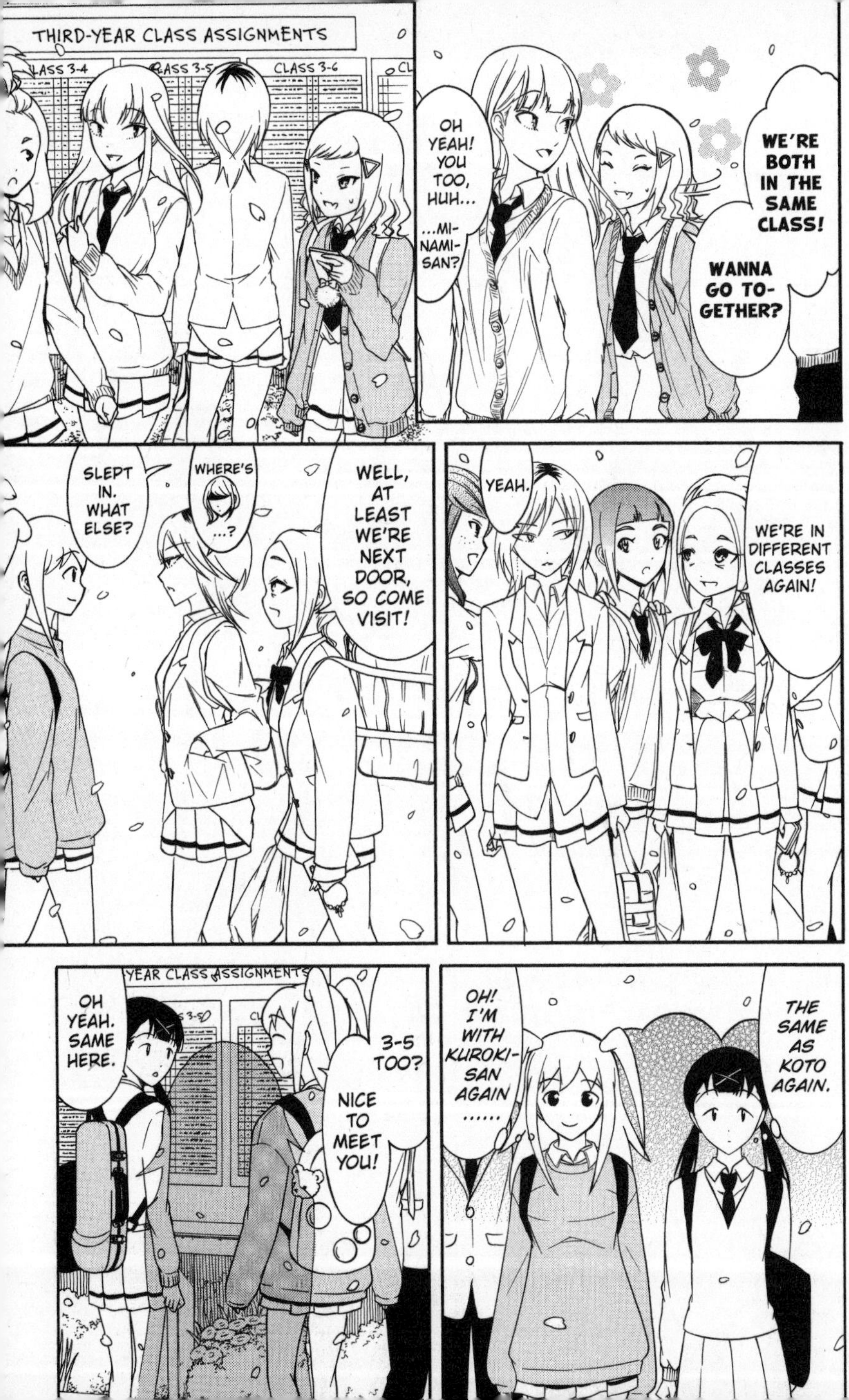
WE'RE BOTH IN THE SAME CLASS!
WANNA GO TOGETHER?
OH YEAH! YOU TOO, HUH... ...MINAMI-SAN?
THIRD-YEAR CLASS ASSIGNMENTS
CLASS 3-4
CLASS 3-5
CLASS 3-6
WE'RE IN DIFFERENT CLASSES AGAIN!
YEAH.
WELL, AT LEAST WE'RE NEXT DOOR, SO COME VISIT!
WHERE'S ...?
SLEPT IN. WHAT ELSE?
THE SAME AS KOTO AGAIN.
OH! I'M WITH KUROKI-SAN AGAIN ......
YEAR CLASS ASSIGNMENTS
3-5 TOO?
NICE TO MEET YOU!
OH YEAH. SAME HERE.

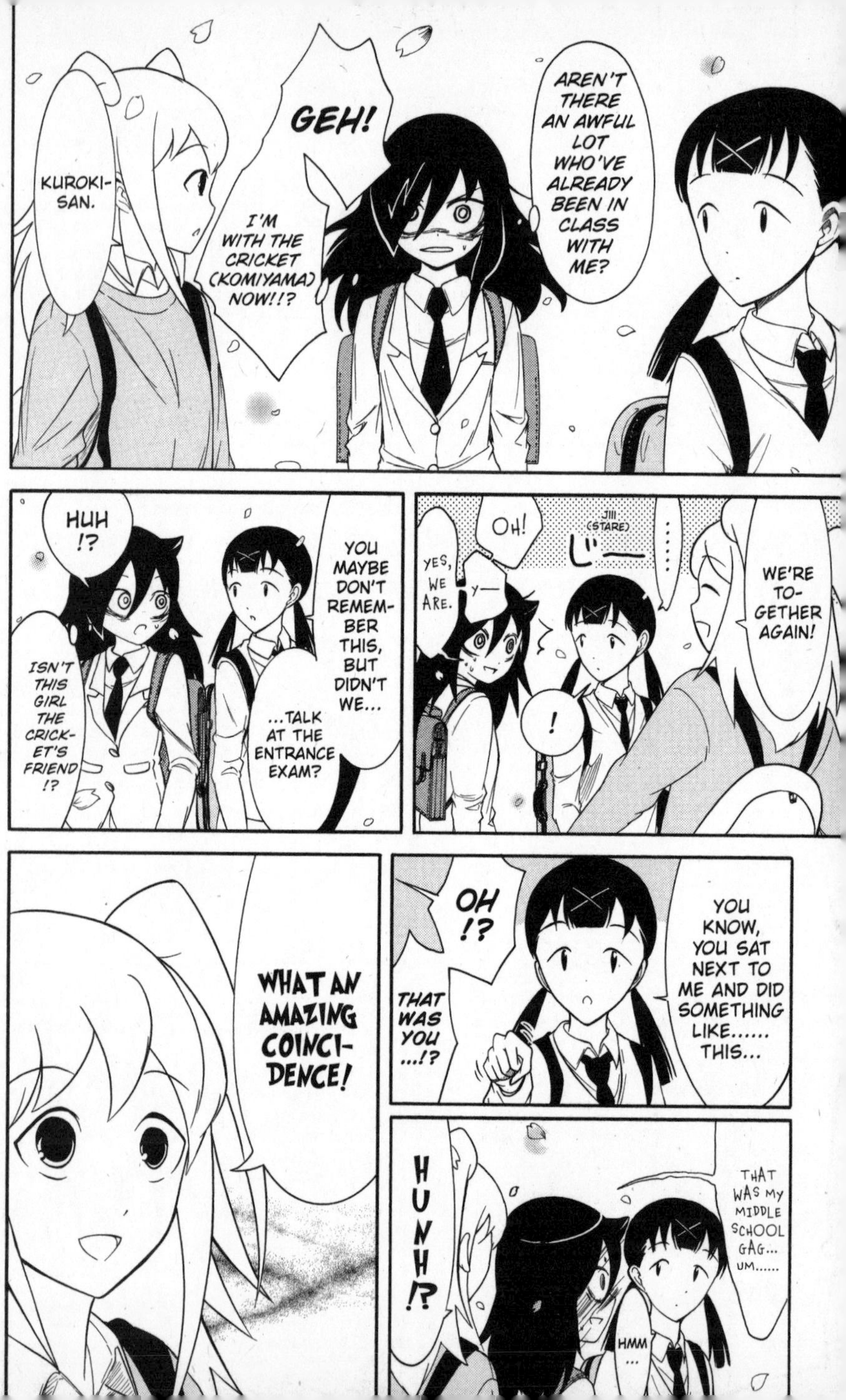
AREN'T THERE AN AWFUL LOT WHO'VE ALREADY BEEN IN CLASS WITH ME?
GEH!
I'M WITH THE CRICKET (KOMIYAMA) NOW!!?
KUROKI-SAN.
WE'RE TO-GETHER AGAIN!
......
ジー
JIII (STARE)
OH!
YES, WE ARE.
Y—
!
YOU MAYBE DON'T REMEM-BER THIS, BUT DIDN'T WE...
HUH!?
...TALK AT THE ENTRANCE EXAM?
ISN'T THIS GIRL THE CRICK-ET'S FRIEND!?
YOU KNOW, YOU SAT NEXT TO ME AND DID SOMETHING LIKE...... THIS...
OH!?
THAT WAS YOU...!?
THAT WAS MY MIDDLE SCHOOL GAG... UM......
HUNH!?
HMM...
WHAT AN AMAZING COINCI-DENCE!

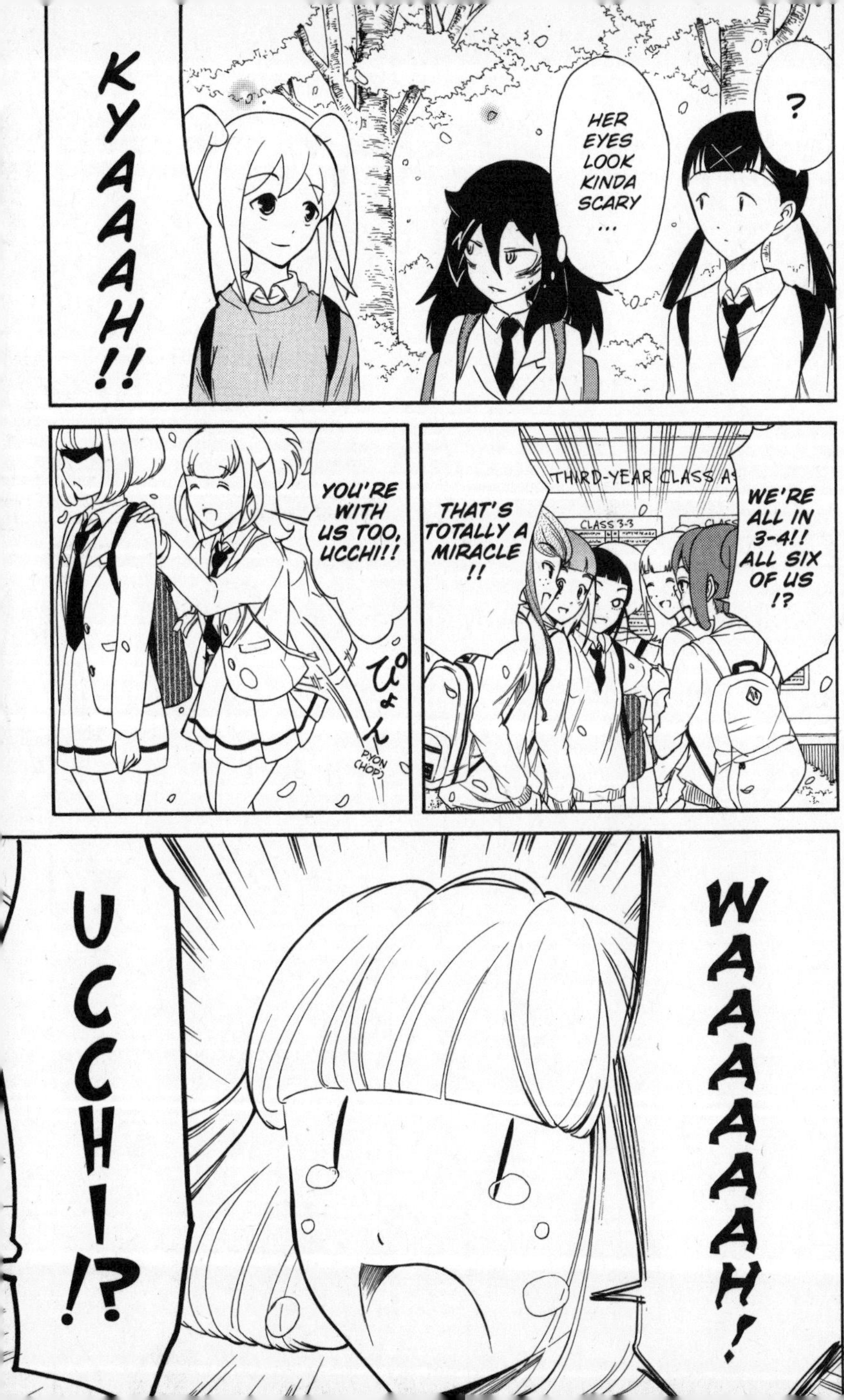
?
HER EYES LOOK KINDA SCARY ...
KYAAAH!!
WE'RE ALL IN 3-4!! ALL SIX OF US !?
THIRD-YEAR CLASS AS
CLASS 3-3
THAT'S TOTALLY A MIRACLE !!
YOU'RE WITH US TOO, UCCHI!!
ぴょん
P.YON (HOP)
WAAAAAAH!
UCCHI!?

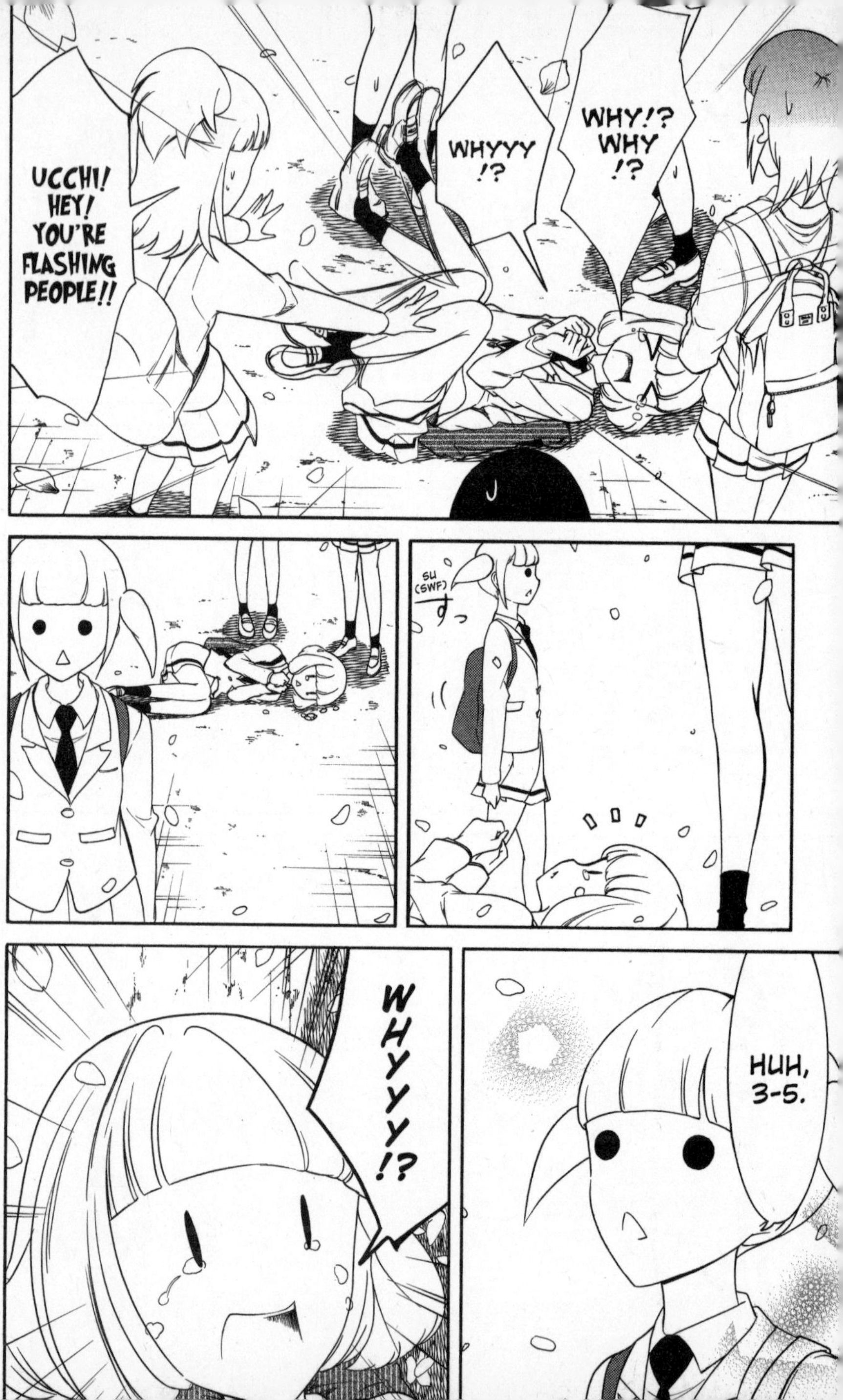
WHY!? WHY !?
WHYYY !?
UCCHI! HEY! YOU'RE FLASHING PEOPLE!!
SU (SWF)
すっ
HUH, 3-5.
WHYYY!?

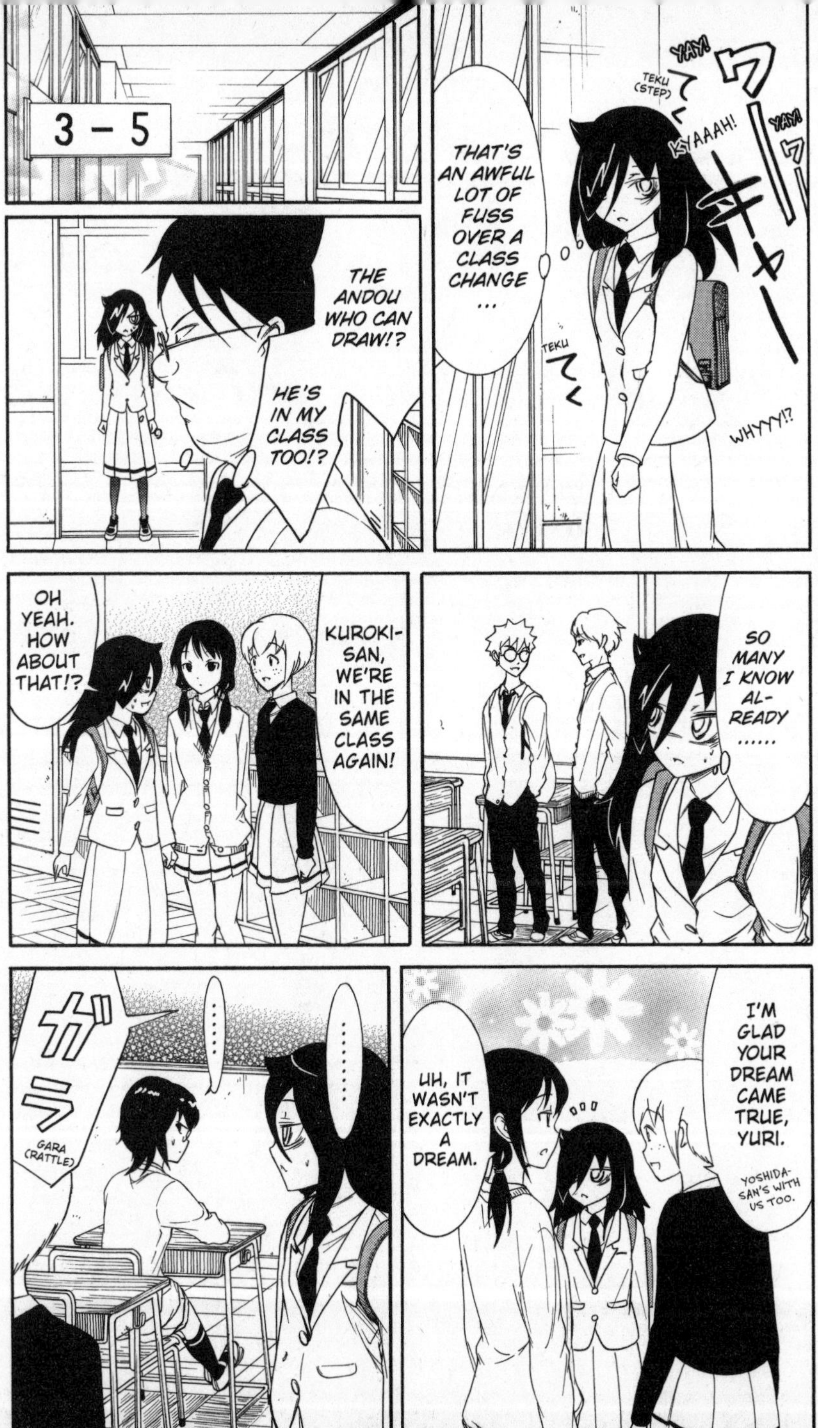
YAY!
TEKU (STEP)
YAY!
KYAAAH!
WHYYY!?
THAT'S AN AWFUL LOT OF FUSS OVER A CLASS CHANGE ...
TEKU
3 - 5
THE ANDOU WHO CAN DRAW!?
HE'S IN MY CLASS TOO!?
SO MANY I KNOW AL-READY ......
KUROKI-SAN, WE'RE IN THE SAME CLASS AGAIN!
OH YEAH. HOW ABOUT THAT!?
I'M GLAD YOUR DREAM CAME TRUE, YURI.
YOSHIDA-SAN'S WITH US TOO.
UH, IT WASN'T EXACTLY A DREAM.
......
......
GARA (RATTLE)

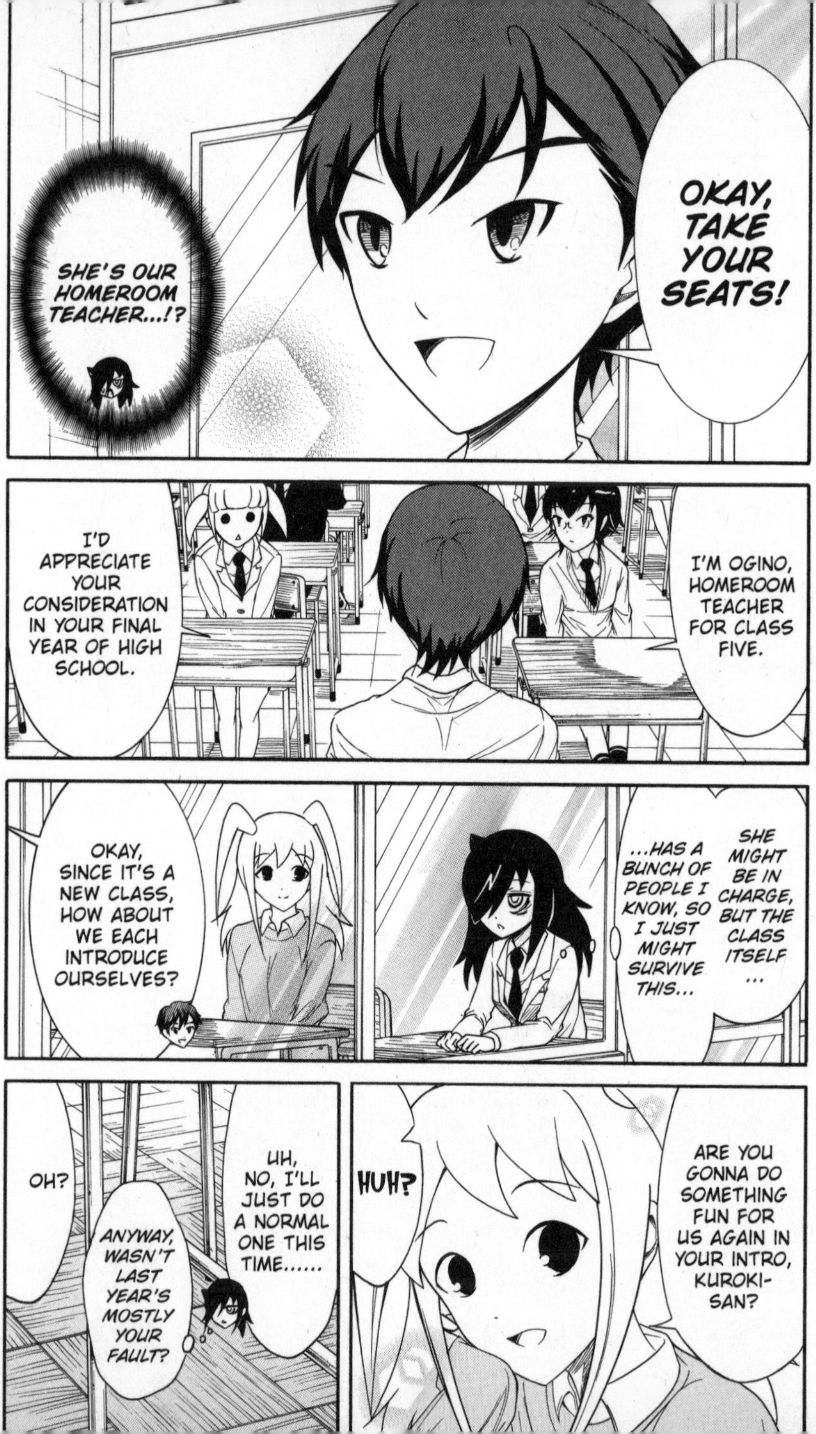
OKAY, TAKE YOUR SEATS!
SHE'S OUR HOMEROOM TEACHER...!?
I'M OGINO, HOMEROOM TEACHER FOR CLASS FIVE.
I'D APPRECIATE YOUR CONSIDERATION IN YOUR FINAL YEAR OF HIGH SCHOOL.
SHE MIGHT BE IN CHARGE, BUT THE CLASS ITSELF ...
...HAS A BUNCH OF PEOPLE I KNOW, SO I JUST MIGHT SURVIVE THIS...
OKAY, SINCE IT'S A NEW CLASS, HOW ABOUT WE EACH INTRODUCE OURSELVES?
ARE YOU GONNA DO SOMETHING FUN FOR US AGAIN IN YOUR INTRO, KUROKI-SAN?
HUH?
UH, NO, I'LL JUST DO A NORMAL ONE THIS TIME......
OH?
ANYWAY, WASN'T LAST YEAR'S MOSTLY YOUR FAULT?

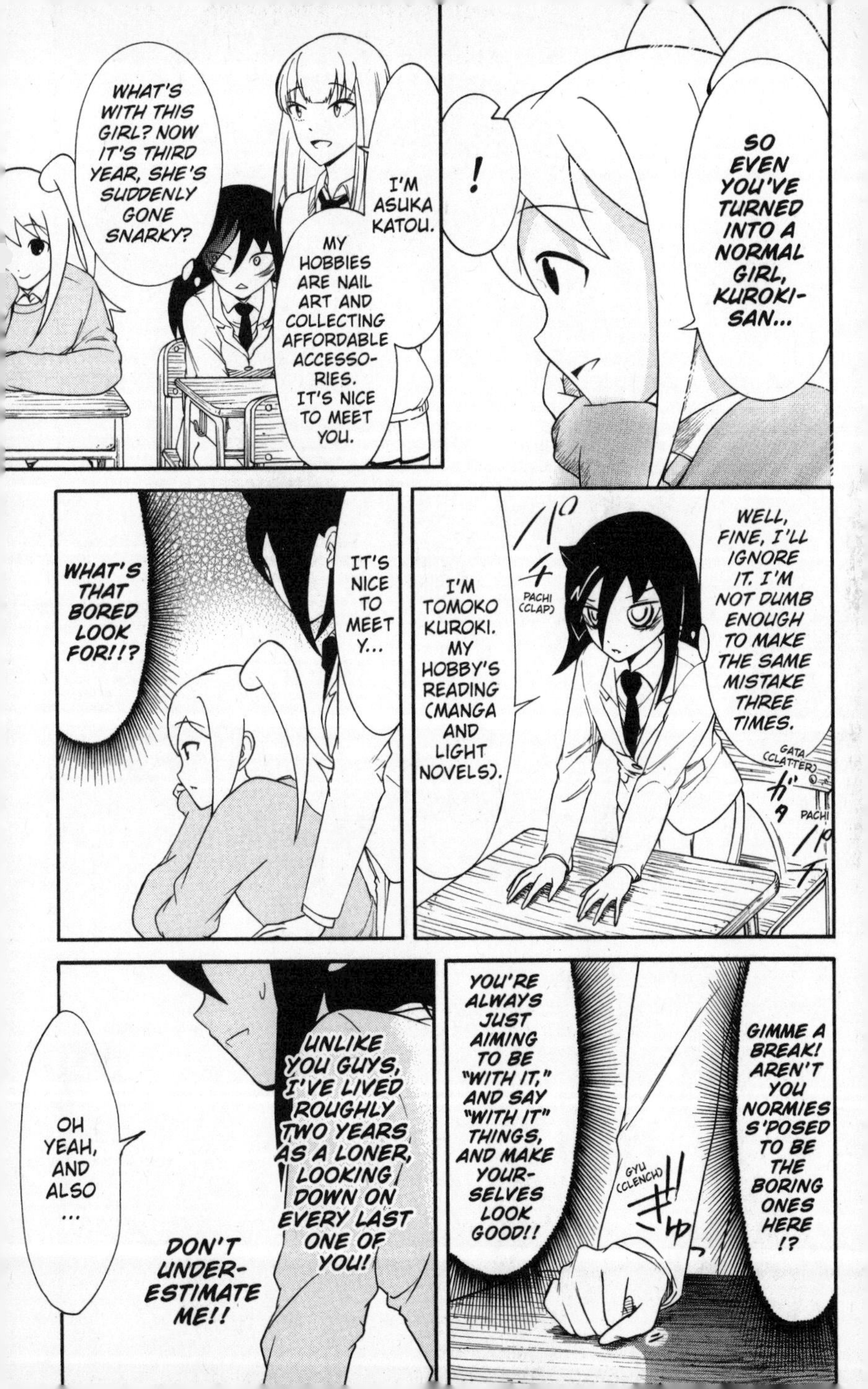
SO EVEN YOU'VE TURNED INTO A NORMAL GIRL, KUROKI-SAN...
!
I'M ASUKA KATOU.
MY HOBBIES ARE NAIL ART AND COLLECTING AFFORDABLE ACCESSO-RIES. IT'S NICE TO MEET YOU.
WHAT'S WITH THIS GIRL? NOW IT'S THIRD YEAR, SHE'S SUDDENLY GONE SNARKY?
WELL, FINE, I'LL IGNORE IT. I'M NOT DUMB ENOUGH TO MAKE THE SAME MISTAKE THREE TIMES.
GATA (CLATTER)
PACHI
I'M TOMOKO KUROKI. MY HOBBY'S READING (MANGA AND LIGHT NOVELS).
PACHI (CLAP)
IT'S NICE TO MEET Y...
WHAT'S THAT BORED LOOK FOR!!?
GIMME A BREAK! AREN'T YOU NORMIES S'POSED TO BE THE BORING ONES HERE !?
GYU (CLENCH)
YOU'RE ALWAYS JUST AIMING TO BE "WITH IT," AND SAY "WITH IT" THINGS, AND MAKE YOUR-SELVES LOOK GOOD!!
UNLIKE YOU GUYS, I'VE LIVED ROUGHLY TWO YEARS AS A LONER, LOOKING DOWN ON EVERY LAST ONE OF YOU!
OH YEAH, AND ALSO ...
DON'T UNDER-ESTIMATE ME!!

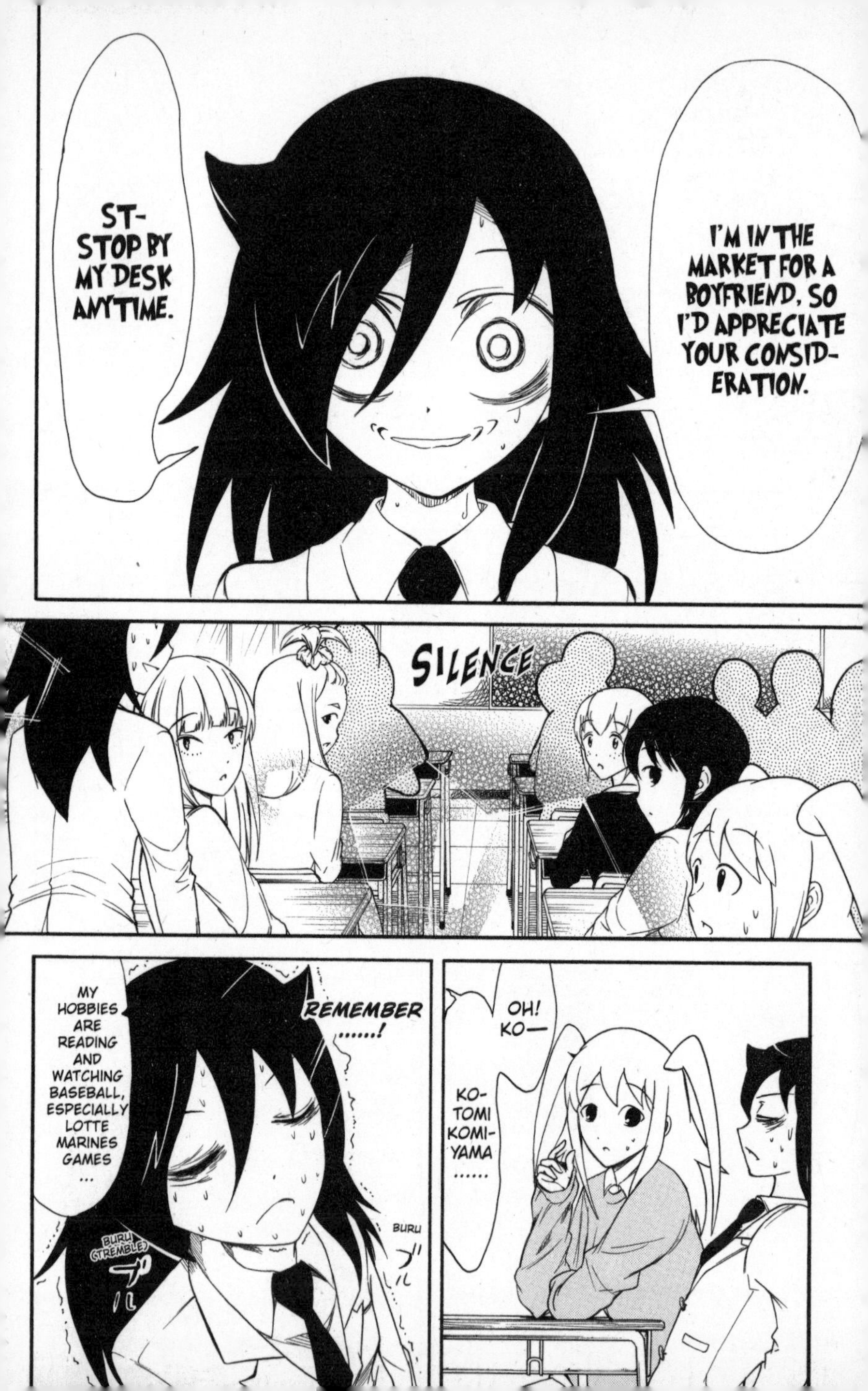
I'M IN THE MARKET FOR A BOYFRIEND, SO I'D APPRECIATE YOUR CONSID-ERATION.
ST- STOP BY MY DESK ANYTIME.
SILENCE
OH! KO—
KO-TOMI KOMI-YAMA ......
REMEMBER ......!
MY HOBBIES ARE READING AND WATCHING BASEBALL, ESPECIALLY LOTTE MARINES GAMES ...
BURU
BURU (TREMBLE)

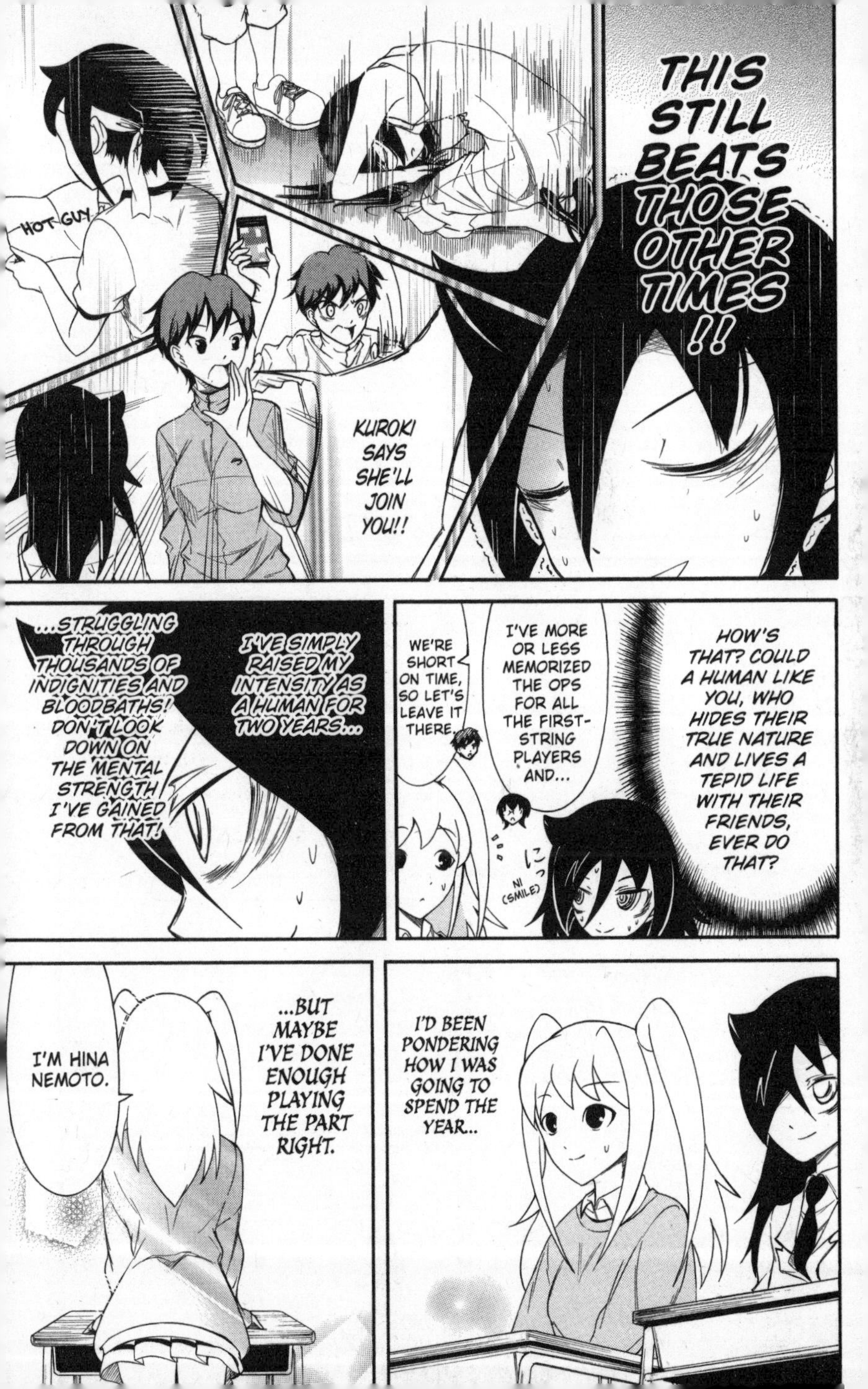
THIS STILL BEATS THOSE OTHER TIMES!!
HOT GUY
KUROKI SAYS SHE'LL JOIN YOU!!
HOW'S THAT? COULD A HUMAN LIKE YOU, WHO HIDES THEIR TRUE NATURE AND LIVES A TEPID LIFE WITH THEIR FRIENDS, EVER DO THAT?
I'VE MORE OR LESS MEMORIZED THE OPS FOR ALL THE FIRST-STRING PLAYERS AND...
WE'RE SHORT ON TIME, SO LET'S LEAVE IT THERE.
にっ
NI (SMILE)
I'VE SIMPLY RAISED MY INTENSITY AS A HUMAN FOR TWO YEARS...
...STRUGGLING THROUGH THOUSANDS OF INDIGNITIES AND BLOODBATHS! DON'T LOOK DOWN ON THE MENTAL STRENGTH I'VE GAINED FROM THAT!
I'D BEEN PONDERING HOW I WAS GOING TO SPEND THE YEAR...
...BUT MAYBE I'VE DONE ENOUGH PLAYING THE PART RIGHT.
I'M HINA NEMOTO.

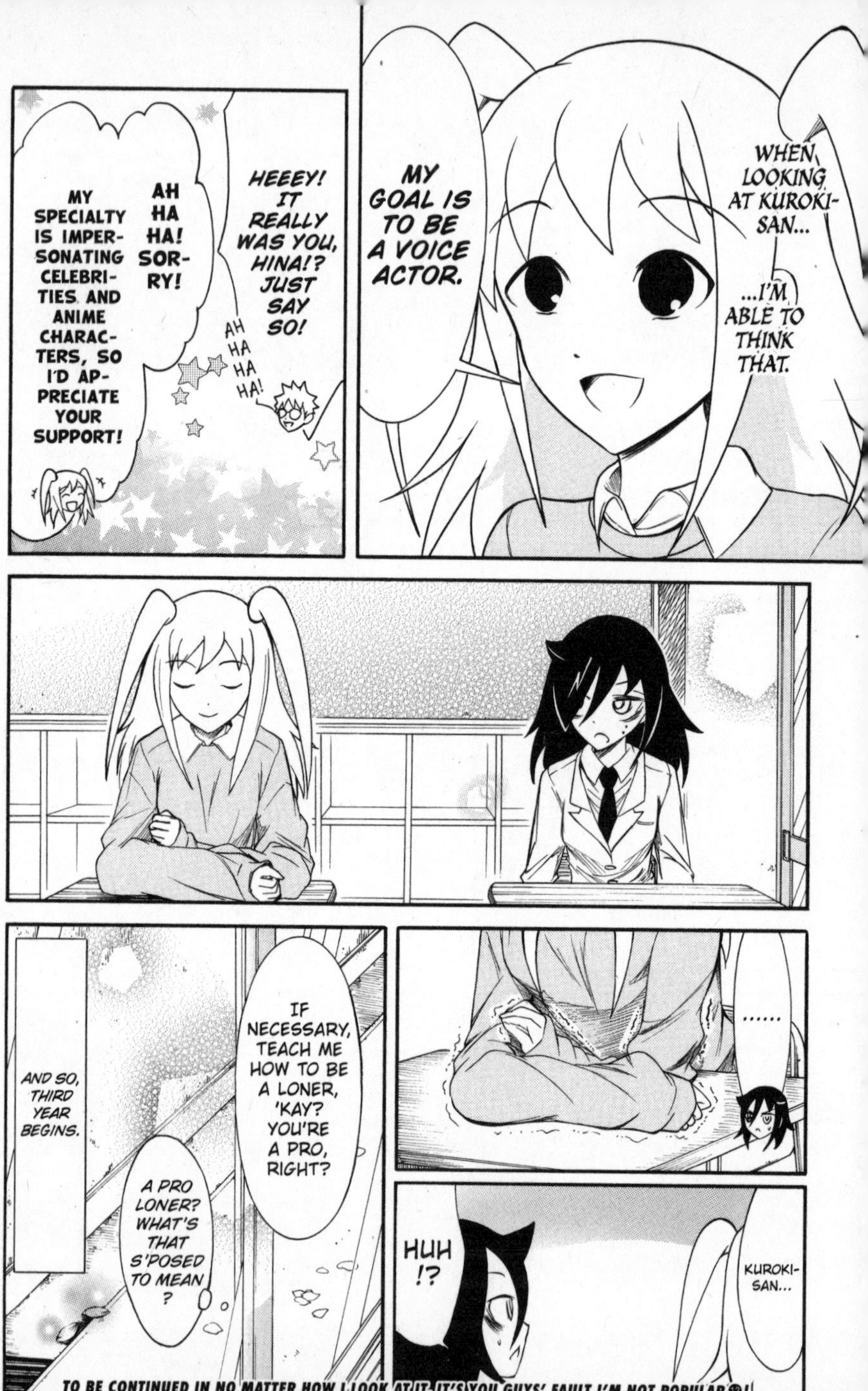
WHEN LOOKING AT KUROKI-SAN...
...I'M ABLE TO THINK THAT.
MY GOAL IS TO BE A VOICE ACTOR.
HEEEY! IT REALLY WAS YOU, HINA!? JUST SAY SO!
AH HA HA HA!
AH HA HA! SORRY!
MY SPECIALTY IS IMPERSONATING CELEBRITIES AND ANIME CHARACTERS, SO I'D APPRECIATE YOUR SUPPORT!
......
KUROKI-SAN...
HUH!?
IF NECESSARY, TEACH ME HOW TO BE A LONER, 'KAY? YOU'RE A PRO, RIGHT?
A PRO LONER? WHAT'S THAT S'POSED TO MEAN?
AND SO, THIRD YEAR BEGINS.

TO BE CONTINUED IN NO MATTER HOW I LOOK AT IT, IT'S YOU GUYS' FAULT I'M NOT POPULAR ⑬!

No Matter How I Look at It, It's You Guys' Fault I'm Not Popular!

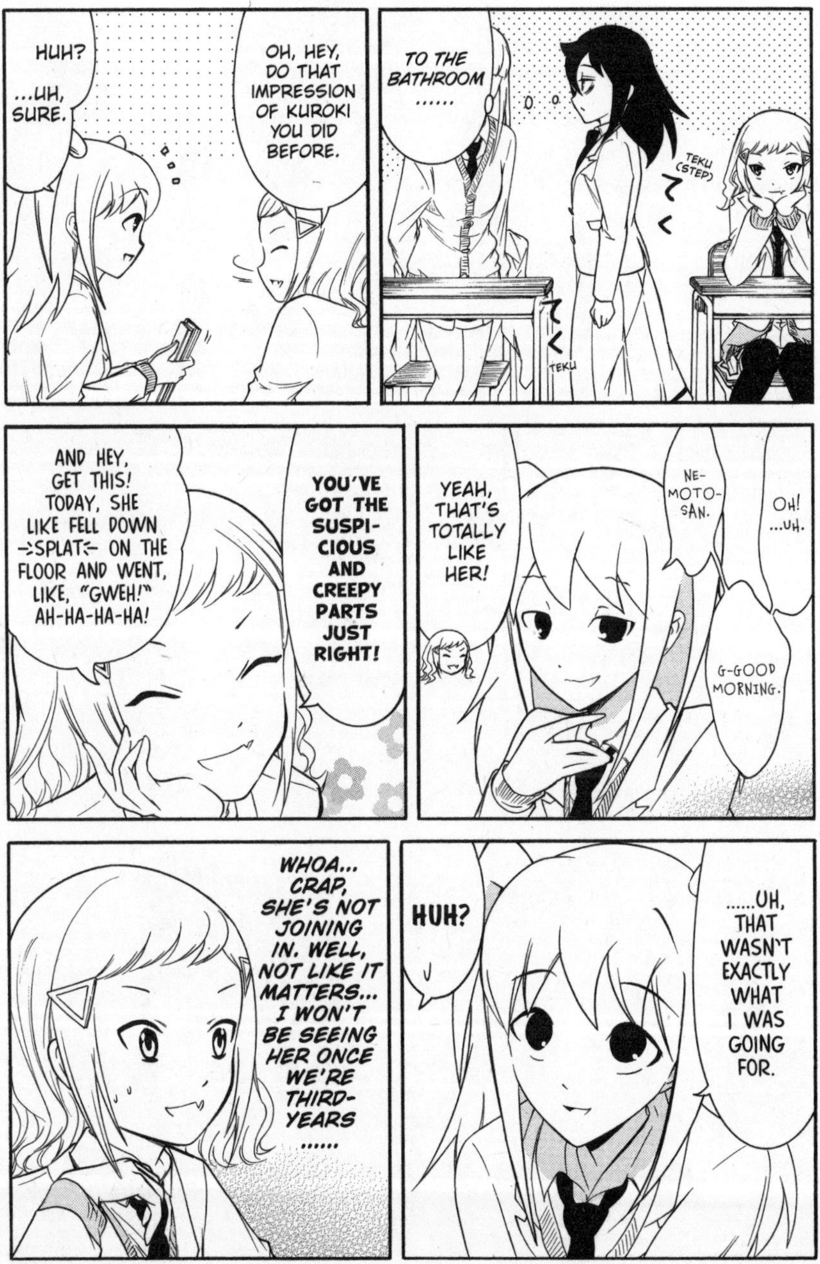
TO THE BATHROOM ......
TEKU (STEP)
TEKU
OH, HEY, DO THAT IMPRESSION OF KUROKI YOU DID BEFORE.
HUH?
...UH, SURE.
OH! ...UH.
NE-MOTO-SAN.
YEAH, THAT'S TOTALLY LIKE HER!
G-GOOD MORNING.
YOU'VE GOT THE SUSPICIOUS AND CREEPY PARTS JUST RIGHT!
AND HEY, GET THIS! TODAY, SHE LIKE FELL DOWN ⇒SPLAT⇐ ON THE FLOOR AND WENT, LIKE, "GWEH!" AH-HA-HA-HA!
......UH, THAT WASN'T EXACTLY WHAT I WAS GOING FOR.
HUH?
WHOA... CRAP, SHE'S NOT JOINING IN. WELL, NOT LIKE IT MATTERS... I WON'T BE SEEING HER ONCE WE'RE THIRD-YEARS ......

FAIL 119 FROM A DIFFERENT VIEWPOINT

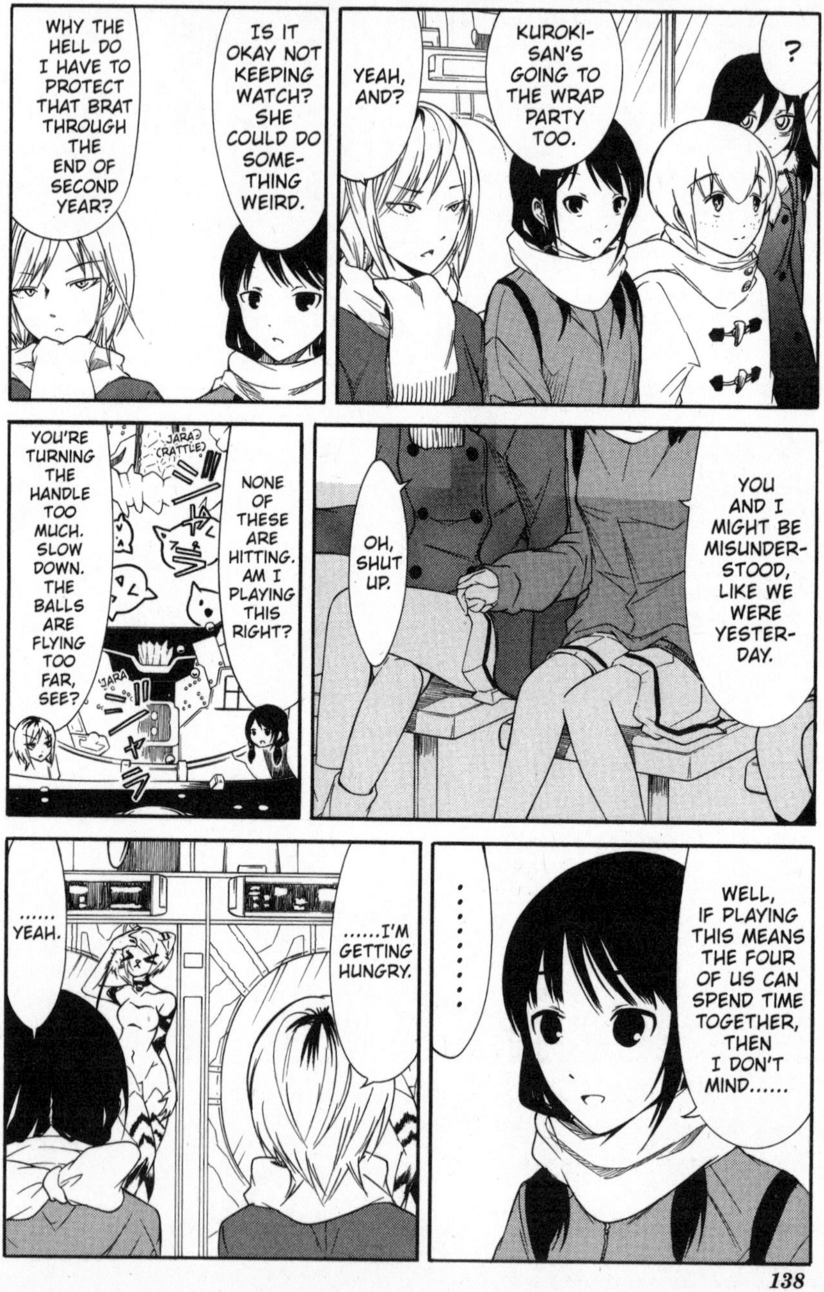

?
KUROKI-SAN'S GOING TO THE WRAP PARTY TOO.
YEAH, AND?
IS IT OKAY NOT KEEPING WATCH? SHE COULD DO SOMETHING WEIRD.
WHY THE HELL DO I HAVE TO PROTECT THAT BRAT THROUGH THE END OF SECOND YEAR?
YOU AND I MIGHT BE MISUNDERSTOOD, LIKE WE WERE YESTERDAY.
OH, SHUT UP.
NONE OF THESE ARE HITTING. AM I PLAYING THIS RIGHT?
JARA (RATTLE)
YOU'RE TURNING THE HANDLE TOO MUCH. SLOW DOWN. THE BALLS ARE FLYING TOO FAR, SEE?
JARA
WELL, IF PLAYING THIS MEANS THE FOUR OF US CAN SPEND TIME TOGETHER, THEN I DON'T MIND......
....
......I'M GETTING HUNGRY.
......YEAH.

TRANSLATION NOTES

PAGE 1
The eraser on this title page, **MATOMERU**, is a parody of the actual MATOMARU-KUN eraser. The verb *matomaru* means "to be in order."

PAGE 7
Tomoko's **"Yeah, dawg!"** in Japanese was "Ueeei!" which is a shout associated mainly with rowdy young guys and used as a greeting or while drinking. Fortunately we don't have to make sure Tomoko actually sounds cool.

PAGE 15
New Game+ is a feature unlocked after completing certain video games, which allows you to play again from the start of the story but with extra abilities or options, like carrying over your skills and inventory from your completed game. A **replay** is playing a video game from the start after finishing it once, in order to get achievements or for other reasons.

PAGE 17
Just like everyone else in the series, Tomoko's imagined rival, **Maki Sakai**, has the same last name as a Chiba Lotte Marines baseball player—Tomohito Sakai.

PAGE 18
Irregular is a reference to the light novel series *The Irregular at Magic High School*, a prime example of a series with a secretly overpowered protagonist that this chapter is parodying.

PAGE 21
OP is short for "overpowered," a term used in video gaming and related pop culture to refer to a player character or protagonist whose abilities are so high relative to the situation that they can win battles with hardly any effort. The original Japanese term she used was TUEE, a slangy romanized way of writing the adjective *tsuyoi* ("strong") that is used in a similar manner to OP in Japanese video gaming and pop culture.

PAGE 27
Translated as **cigar-shaped**, what Yuri actually thought when first seeing Tomoko's chocolates was *karinto*-shaped. *Karinto* is a traditional Japanese deep-fried snack flavored with brown sugar, and its dark-brown color and cylindrical shape give it a strong resemblance to, well, poo.

PAGE 76
"Neraiuchi" ("Sharpshooting") is a 1973 pop song by Linda Yamamoto, which has also been used as an "at-bat" cheer song by various baseball teams. **"Natsumatsuri"** ("Summer Festival") was originally released in 1990 by the band JITTERIN' JINN. The 2000 cover by the girl band Whiteberry was very popular and appeared in various TV shows, such as episode 12 of the anime ReLIFE in 2016, as well as in the *Taiko Drum Master* game series. Finally, *Romasaga* is short for the *Romancing Saga* video game series.

PAGE 81
"Nicole" is referring to Nicole Fujita, a Japanese model and TV personality. The line Nemoto used in her impersonation is an actual sentence Nicole said in one talk-show appearance (in Japanese, of course).

PAGE 85
The original chapter title was "*Ora-tsuku*," which works as a pun since the phrase means "act arrogant," but Tomoko also ends up with Yoshida yelling "ORAAA!" at her, which is an aggressive yell that some *JoJo's Bizarre Adventure* fans, among others, might be familiar with.

PAGE 85
Okada's drink, **Suhada Lemon**, is a joke variant of the actual drink Suppin Lemon. *Suhada* means "bare skin" and *suppin* means "face without makeup." It's a lemon drink with additives that are supposedly good for your skin, such as hyaluronic acid and collagen.

PAGE 91
An *uchiage*, or **wrap party**, is a party to celebrate the end of a project, usually a theatrical run, but here, it's their second year of high school. Also, fans of the *Gremlins* movies, check out Nemoto's Gizmo phone case on this page!

PAGE 93
Yoshida is playing the **CR Evangelion 8 pachinko** game but with goofy cat faces replacing the *Neon Genesis Evangelion* anime characters.

PAGE 99
KUITON is a parody of an actual restaurant. The *yakiniku* (Korean BBQ) place they're eating at is KUIDON (Messe Amuse Mall branch).

PAGE 104
Tomoko saying **"Whoa!"** is a bit of a reference to a scene in the manga series *Kodoku no Gourmet*, where the protagonist is at a *yakiniku* place grilling a bunch of little pieces of meat and thinks, *Whoa, I'm practically a human-fired power plant*.

PAGE 105
The bit about d●ck pics from foreigners worldwide being sent to their Twitter account is based on the manga artist's personal experience and has been referred to in a few of the afterwords.

PAGE 106
"Calm and apt" comes from the Japanese phrase "*reisei de tekikaku na*," which in turn is from an often-parodied panel in the *Kinnikuman* manga series by the duo Yudetamago. It shows the four Team Soldier characters thinking, *Nantoiu reisei de tekikaku na handanryoku da!!* ("What calm and apt judgment!!") in reaction to Kinnikuman dressing as a Catholic priest (with wrestling mask still on!) to rescue a child from a thief (an homage to *Seven Samurai*).

PAGE 107
Bic Echo is a parody of the actual karaoke chain Big Echo.

PAGE 109
"A" in Growth Potential and **"D" level Durability** are a reference to Stand parameters from the manga series *JoJo's Bizarre Adventure*, and the grade levels are how they're rated for each individual Stand, with "A" as the highest.

PAGE 129
Andou who can draw is a reference to the character in the manga/anime series *Kaiji* who betrayed the title character at a Restricted Rock-Paper-Scissors. In Volume 1, Tomoko had thought that this particular guy looks like someone who'd do that, namely Andou.

PAGE 133
OPS is a sabermetric baseball term that stands for "On-base Plus Slugging," while **"intensity as a human"** refers to the term *ningen kyoudo* from a line by protagonist Koyomi Araragi in the *Monogatari* series by NISIOISIN—"Making friends would lower my intensity as a human."

AFTERWORD

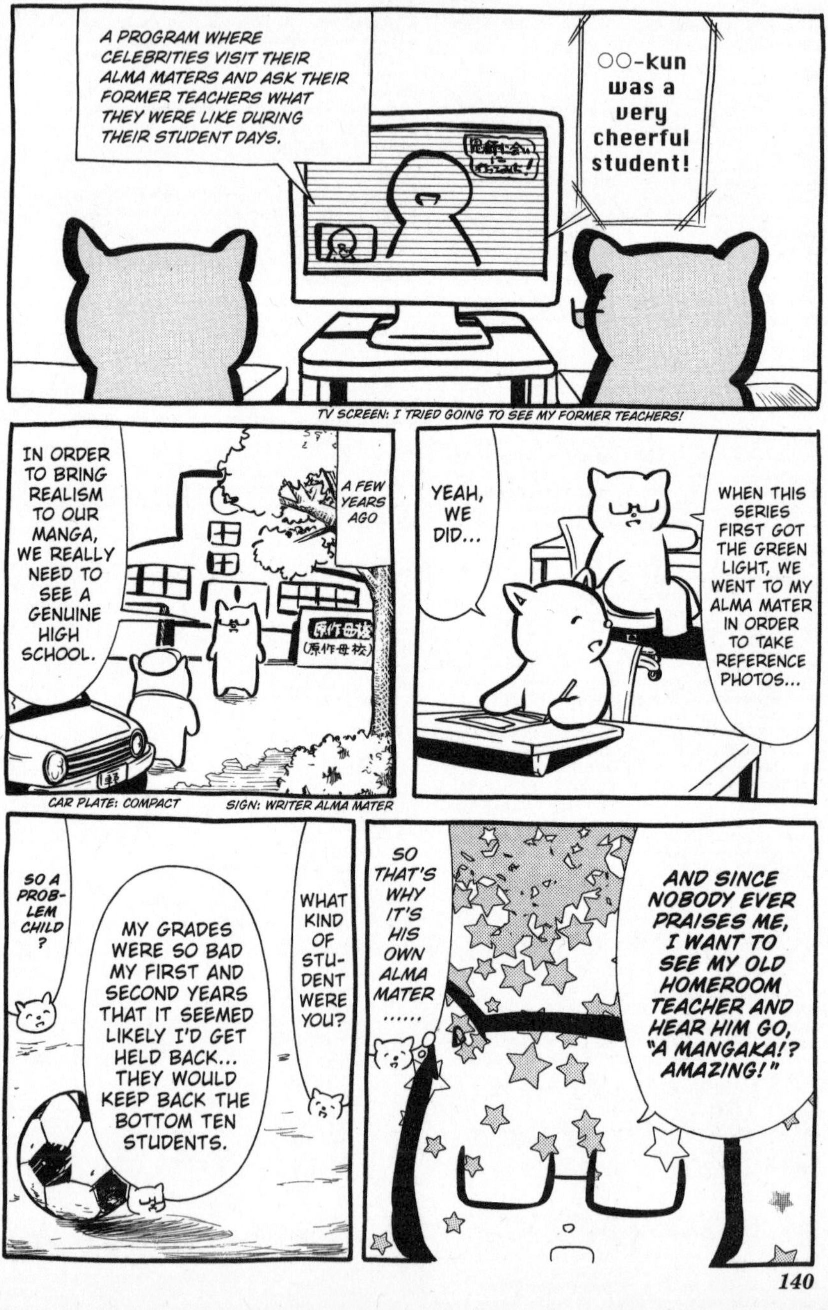
○○-kun was a very cheerful student!
A PROGRAM WHERE CELEBRITIES VISIT THEIR ALMA MATERS AND ASK THEIR FORMER TEACHERS WHAT THEY WERE LIKE DURING THEIR STUDENT DAYS.
TV SCREEN: I TRIED GOING TO SEE MY FORMER TEACHERS!
WHEN THIS SERIES FIRST GOT THE GREEN LIGHT, WE WENT TO MY ALMA MATER IN ORDER TO TAKE REFERENCE PHOTOS...
YEAH, WE DID...
A FEW YEARS AGO
IN ORDER TO BRING REALISM TO OUR MANGA, WE REALLY NEED TO SEE A GENUINE HIGH SCHOOL.
原作母校
(原作母校)
CAR PLATE: COMPACT
SIGN: WRITER ALMA MATER
AND SINCE NOBODY EVER PRAISES ME, I WANT TO SEE MY OLD HOMEROOM TEACHER AND HEAR HIM GO, "A MANGAKA!? AMAZING!"
SO THAT'S WHY IT'S HIS OWN ALMA MATER ......
WHAT KIND OF STUDENT WERE YOU?
MY GRADES WERE SO BAD MY FIRST AND SECOND YEARS THAT IT SEEMED LIKELY I'D GET HELD BACK... THEY WOULD KEEP BACK THE BOTTOM TEN STUDENTS.
SO A PROBLEM CHILD?

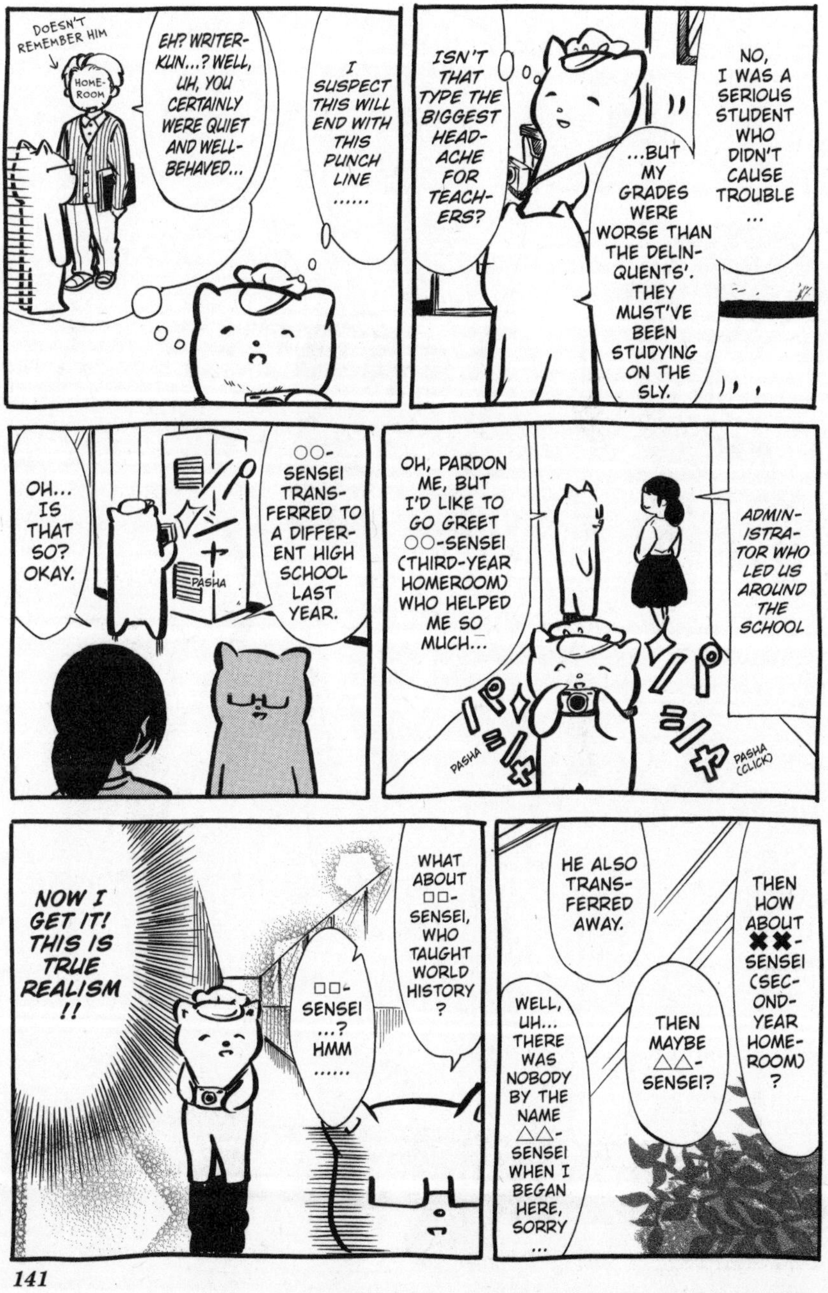
NO, I WAS A SERIOUS STUDENT WHO DIDN'T CAUSE TROUBLE...
...BUT MY GRADES WERE WORSE THAN THE DELINQUENTS'. THEY MUST'VE BEEN STUDYING ON THE SLY.
ISN'T THAT TYPE THE BIGGEST HEADACHE FOR TEACHERS?
I SUSPECT THIS WILL END WITH THIS PUNCH LINE......
EH? WRITER-KUN...? WELL, UH, YOU CERTAINLY WERE QUIET AND WELL-BEHAVED...
DOESN'T REMEMBER HIM
HOME-ROOM
ADMINISTRATOR WHO LED US AROUND THE SCHOOL
OH, PARDON ME, BUT I'D LIKE TO GO GREET ○○-SENSEI (THIRD-YEAR HOMEROOM) WHO HELPED ME SO MUCH...
PASHA (CLICK)
PASHA
○○-SENSEI TRANSFERRED TO A DIFFERENT HIGH SCHOOL LAST YEAR.
PASHA
OH... IS THAT SO? OKAY.
THEN HOW ABOUT ✖✖-SENSEI (SECOND-YEAR HOMEROOM)?
HE ALSO TRANSFERRED AWAY.
THEN MAYBE △△-SENSEI?
WELL, UH... THERE WAS NOBODY BY THE NAME △△-SENSEI WHEN I BEGAN HERE, SORRY...
WHAT ABOUT □□-SENSEI, WHO TAUGHT WORLD HISTORY?
□□-SENSEI...? HMM......
NOW I GET IT! THIS IS TRUE REALISM!!

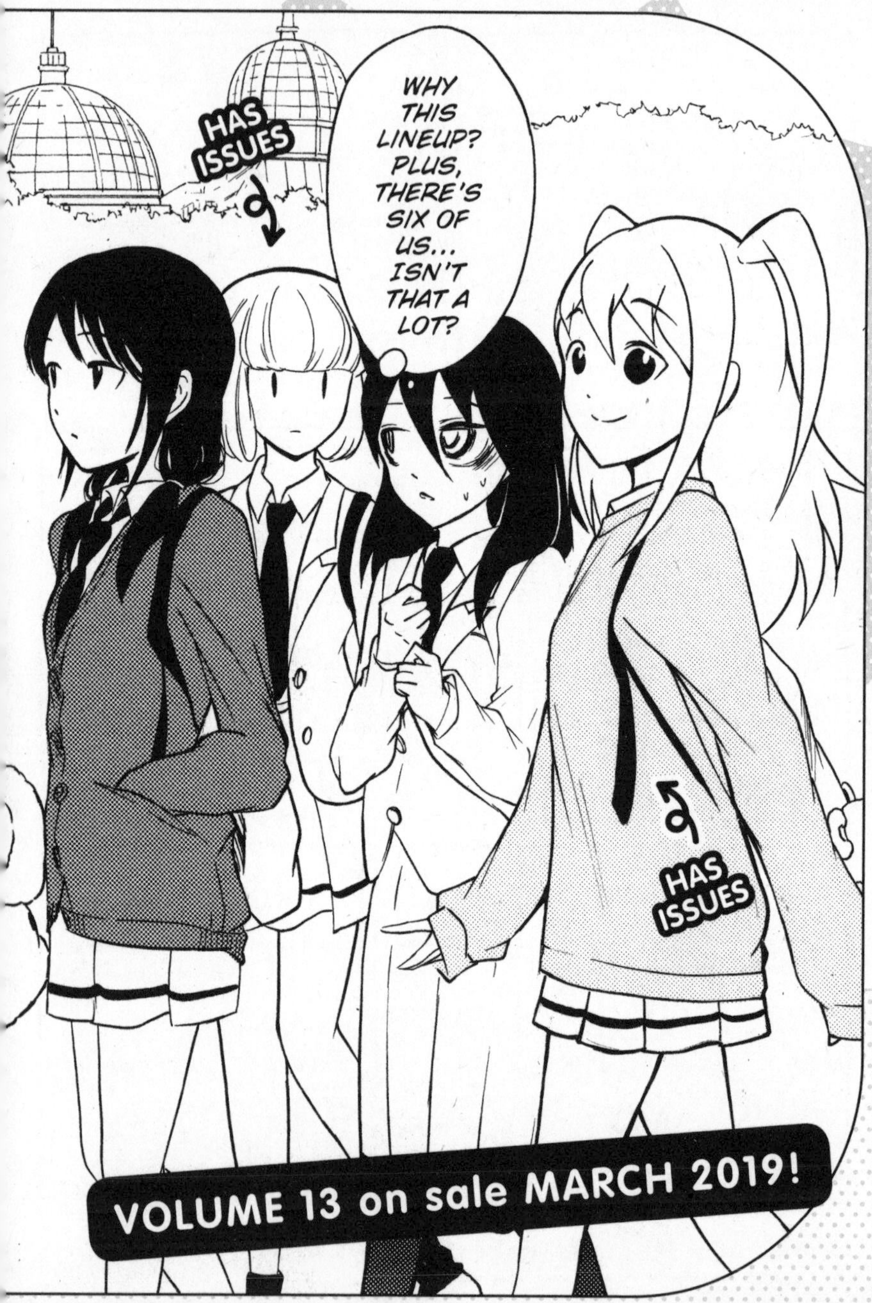
WHY THIS LINEUP? PLUS, THERE'S SIX OF US... ISN'T THAT A LOT?
HAS ISSUES
HAS ISSUES
VOLUME 13 on sale MARCH 2019!

A BEVY OF GIRLS AND THEIR ISSUES CONVERGE!!

THE ANGST-FILLED FIELD TRIP ARC BEGINS!!

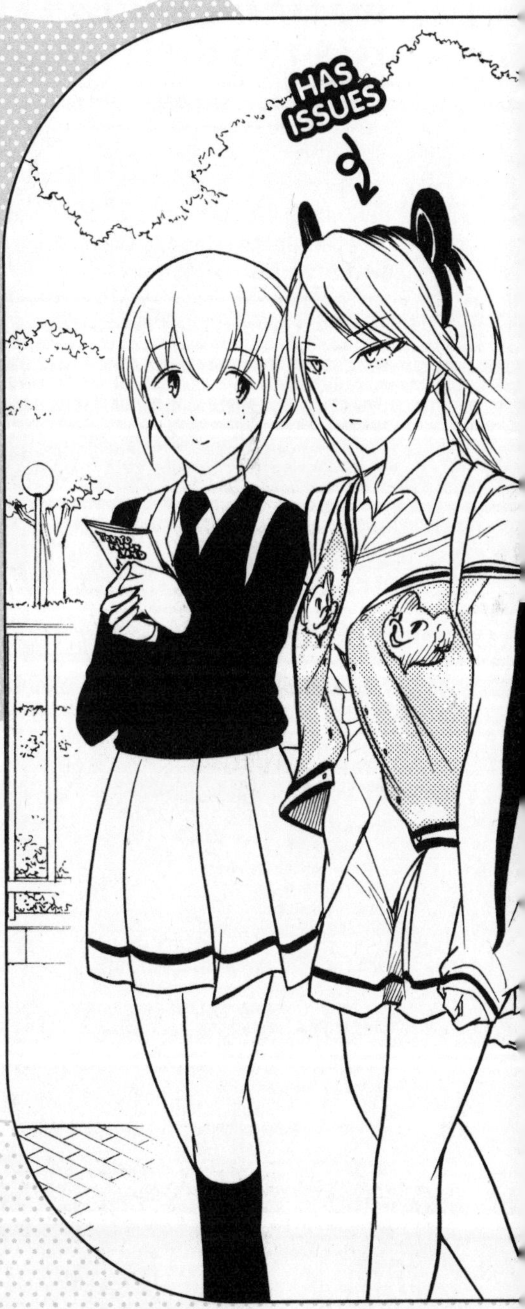
HAS ISSUES

NO MATTER HOW I LOOK AT IT, IT'S YOU GUYS' FAULT I'M NOT POPULAR! ⑫

WITHDRAWN

Nico Tanigawa

Translation/Adaptation: Krista Shipley, Karie Shipley
Lettering: Bianca Pistillo

WATASHI GA MOTENAI NOWA DOU KANGAETEMO OMAERA GA WARUI! Volume 12 © 2018 Nico Tanigawa / SQUARE ENIX CO., LTD. First published in Japan in 2018 by SQUARE ENIX CO., LTD. English translation rights arranged with SQUARE ENIX CO., LTD. and Yen Press, LLC through Tuttle-Mori Agency, Inc., Tokyo.

English translation ©2018 by SQUARE ENIX CO., LTD.

Yen Press
1290 Avenue of the Americas
New York, NY 10104

Visit us!
⚞ yenpress.com
⚞ facebook.com/yenpress
⚞ twitter.com/yenpress
⚞ yenpress.tumblr.com
⚞ instagram.com/yenpress

First Yen Press Edition: November 2018

Yen Press is an imprint of Yen Press, LLC.
The Yen Press name and logo are trademarks of Yen Press, LLC.

The publisher is not responsible for websites (or their content) that are not owned by the publisher.

Library of Congress Control Number: 2013498929

ISBNs: 978-1-9753-2817-7 (paperback)
        978-1-9753-2832-0 (ebook)

10 9 8 7 6 5 4 3 2

WOR

Printed in the United States of America